D1756080

University of Law

Identity Orchestration

Identity Orchestration

Black Lives, Balance, and the Psychology of Self Stories

Edited by

David Wall Rice
Foreward by Edmund W. Gordon
Afterword by Biko Harris Rice

LEXINGTON BOOKS
Lanham • Boulder • New York • London

Published by Lexington Books
An imprint of The Rowman & Littlefield Publishing Group, Inc.
4501 Forbes Boulevard, Suite 200, Lanham, Maryland 20706
www.rowman.com

86-90 Paul Street, London EC2A 4NE

British Library Cataloguing in Publication Information Available

Library of Congress Cataloging-in-Publication Data

Names: Rice, David Wall, editor.
  Title: Identity orchestration : Black lives, balance, and the psychology of
    self stories / edited by David Wall Rice ; afterword by Biko Harris
    Rice.
  Description: Lanham : Lexington Books, [2022] | Includes bibliographical
    references and index. | Summary: "David Wall Rice is professor in the
    Department of Psychology at Morehouse College and principal investigator
    of the Identity, Art & Democracy Lab"-- Provided by publisher.
  Identifiers: LCCN 2022004090 (print) | LCCN 2022004091 (ebook) | ISBN
    9781793644022 (cloth) | ISBN 9781793644039 (epub)   Subjects: LCSH:
  African Americans--Race identity. | Black people--Race
    identity--United States. | Group identity--United States. | Identity
    (Psychology) | Citizenship--United States. | Democracy--United States.
  Classification: LCC E185.625 .I34 2022 (print) | LCC E185.625 (ebook) |
    DDC 305.896/073--dc23/eng/20220310
  LC record available at https://lccn.loc.gov/2022004090
  LC ebook record available at https://lccn.loc.gov/2022004091

For Stokely

Contents

Acknowledgments

I am grateful for the opportunity and for the space to think and write. And I am especially appreciative of the student scholars who have chosen to make the Identity, Art, and Democracy Lab a place that is worthy of their genius. Thank you to those who contributed here and to those lab members who have been a part of this project in spirit, word, and good thought from the beginning to now; you are loved and appreciated. Thank you to dear Provost Garikai Campbell. Your belief in my thinking and pushing me to do has meant so much. This book is inspired in large part by your trust in me and your challenges for me to get out of my head and beyond my introversion. I thank the Morehouse College Department of Psychology for allowing me to grow from a boy to a man in their hallways. A special thanks to Jann Adams and Sinead Younge for trusting me as a colleague and as a friend, and for always holding me accountable. I am forever grateful to Howard University's Department of Psychology for their support of me while I was a student and since. Camara Jules P. Harrell, A. Wade Boykin, and Cynthia Winston-Proctor, you are such brilliant thinkers and good people. I am fortunate to have you as role models. Kimberley E. Freeman and Rashunda L. Stitt Richardson, thank you for allowing us to be more than just a research center. Thank you to Otis Moss III, who for years encouraged me, asking when the next book was dropping after seeing me share some ideas on C-SPAN some time ago. Thank you to Cedric Hughes for making the campus bookstore such a special place for me. Thank you to Troy, Art, Kim, DY, Usama and C. Baab. I am compelled to write again, as I did in *Balance*, thank you to the towering intellects who cared enough to give a kind word in my stepping toward their tremendous works: W. Curtis Banks, Reginald L. Jones, Asa G. Hilliard, William Cross III, Margaret Beale Spencer, Anderson J. Franklin, Howard Stevenson, James Jones, Lucius T. Outlaw, Robert M. Franklin, Walter E. Fluker, Michael Eric Dyson, Eddie S. Glaude Jr., Robert Sellers, Carol Camp Yeakey, Michelle Fine, and Freeman Hrabowski. And, above all, thank you to Professor Edmund W. Gordon for being such a tremendous spirit and for inspiring me to be better still. Thank you and love to my brother P. Kevin Smith; you and Nadra mean the world to me. To Kristopher Chrishon, Darnel Emir Barnes, Mossi Tull, John Jason Lamont Cecil, Jerry, Cara, Cayden-Rose, Grayer, Jenny Hop, Daria, Mr. and Mrs. Grayer, CAC and The Whew; I love you all so much. Thank you for being there when it matters. Thank you and super love to my God family: Beverly, Everod, Erin, Cord, Carrie, and Cordie. Jean René, Harrison, Shannon, Cassie, Chip, and J.P.; thank you for your consistent support and love. Thank you, Billy, Jeanie, and Clyde; Little Arthur, you are the best first cousin on the planet; Randall, Hazel, Khalea, Jabari, and Anike, I love you all very much. Aunt Molly and Uncle Elroy, thank you, you mean so much to our family. Thank you and love to Rahima, Alexis, Shebbie, and Dad. Mom, thank you for being a relentless and unflappable support no matter what, when, where, how, or why—I love you. Mikki, I love you above and through everything. Thank you for committing your best to us and for the grace you afford with your love—you are beauty personified. Biko, you are a blessing like no other. Thank you for defining our family with so much good and loving kindness. And Stokely, thank you for being such a light for us, for showing us how to love radically with strength and without compromise. For all these wonderful people and for the brilliant life I have been blessed to live, I thank God.

FOREWORD

A Commentary on the Orchestration of Identity

The orchestration of one's identity is, perhaps, the quintessentially critical task of human development. It is a task made more challenging for developing non-whites in multi-cultural and multi-racial societies where cultures, alien to that of one's own, have gained hegemony. This is the norm for Black people in North and South America, and in much of the Caribbean, where European colonialism defined political economic development, shaped the dominant forms of culture, and defined the prevailing conceptions of race that have mirrored conceptions that gained hegemony in Europe and that privilege white people in the technologically advanced world. Not alone do white conceptions of beauty and privilege prevail, the standards of democratic practice which are cast in the concrete of democratic manifestos and constitutions dictate practice. It is not alone the custom, it is the law!

If I identify as a person of color, my identity is less valued than that of whites because that self-identity is an *other than* and/or *less than* white model. For human beings, one's identity is largely determined by one's lived experiences. It is to our advantage that the attributions that the reacting person assigns to those experiences prevail.

Du Bois wrote so poignantly:

After the Egyptian and Indian, the Greek and Roman, the Teuton and Mongolian, the Negro is a sort of seventh son, born with a veil, and gifted with second-sight in this American world,—a world which yields him no self-consciousness, but only lets him see himself through the revelation of the other world. It is a peculiar sensation, this double-consciousness, this sense of always looking at one's self through the eyes of others, of measuring one's soul by the tape of a world that looks on in amused contempt and pity. One feels his two-ness,—an American, a Negro; two souls, two thoughts, two unreconciled strivings; two warring ideals in one dark body, whose dogged strength alone keeps it from being torn asunder (August, 1897).

Professor David Wall Rice has collected an interestingly provocative group of essays in which scholars of human development document and examine the lived experiences of people of color as they adapt and attribute meanings as they establish—orchestrate—their identities. This is a perspective on psychology to which we are not exposed in typical texts. These authors refer to exercises in the self-construction of a sense of one's self, one's identity, "against the odds." And yet they prevail to defy these odds. In another context, I have referred to these unique human beings as "Defiers!"

How are the conceptual and reality problems of identity in human developmental psychology to be understood if they are not studied differentially, to reflect the full range of human variance? We are indebted to these scholars for expanding our understanding of the discipline.

Edmund W. Gordon
John M. Musser Professor of Psychology, Emeritus - Yale University
Richard March Hoe Professor of Psychology and Education,
Emeritus - Teachers College, Columbia University

Preface

Beyond Balance

In 2008, *Balance: Advancing Identity Theory by Engaging the Black Male Adolescent* was published, making the case for approaching Black men and boys from a set of assumptions that figures the best of us by looking at psychological strengths in the everyday.

In the time since, popular culture and the body politic have shifted in ways that further complicate the tenets of hegemony and white supremacy that *Balance* worked to explain as socially embraced pathologies necessary to figure in understanding Black people.

The United States' forty-fifth president, emboldened by a fearful and mean legislature, ushered to the forefront of our democracy punishing laws, appointments, and an overall approach that was against the everyperson and racist at its base. This way of doing was accented by the coronavirus pandemic, which disproportionately struck the marginalized, and an enduring spectacle of police killings of too many Black people to count.

The murder of George Floyd by police in Minneapolis, Minnesota, was a sobering Black death that sparked global protests for racial justice and equity that made rhetorical if not practical changes to mainstream white supremacist norms. Monuments to historical racists that littered the country were challenged; money was poured into diversity, equity, and inclusion programming; and "black lives matter" was a sensibility embraced by even the more strident "all lives matter" devotees.

Still, the nation remains thick with the tar of racism, sexism, homophobia, and xenophobia. This is the moment within which we meditate on identity as a pathway toward pragmatic dealing and paradigm shifting.

In *Identity Orchestration* the asset-based construct of identity orchestration, which has the goal and process of effectively managing many parts of the self based on circumstance, is considered imaginatively. The book riffs beyond Balance, using its framework to reach further than just Black men and boys.

There is a nod to "typical" theory writing about identity and the self that is given even more resonance by being grouped with pop-culture spins and reflexive essays on identity, context, and adaptation. Collectively, the writings tap in to lived experiences that demonstrate the understanding of identity balance as of special consequence in understanding behavioral health.

The collection of writers included here are laboratory members and transdisciplinary thinkers within the orbit of the Identity, Art, and Democracy Lab, an incubator for fresh thinking on identity that began as the Identity Stasis Research Lab, then the Identity Orchestration Research Lab, before arriving at its present iteration.

The thinkers here deeply engage identity and psychological strength by examining race, gender, class, and context through stories. Centering stories is based on the idea that identity is a life story (McAdams 2001), "resonat[ing] with a number of important themes in developmental, cognitive, personality and cultural psychology."

Identity orchestration at once formalizes and renders accessible the psychology of life stories. This is done with the improvisation and radical storytelling of hip-hop that serve as a beginning of identity orchestration as a theoretical construct. Mapping this is an important start to the book because it sets the tone for an axiological freedom in finding identity and self in the writing that follows. This along with a critical participatory action research sensibility reveals important meaning making in how a person knows themselves and others.

Identity Orchestration shows dynamic ways that we are enough despite static categorizations and explanations that attempt to reduce us to less.

David Wall Rice, PhD
Atlanta, 2022

Introduction

Buddy

David Wall Rice

The earliest memory I have is of my grandfather, Arthur Albert Wall, my mother's father. His nickname was Buddy. It was 1975 Portsmouth, Virginia. I remember Granddaddy coming to get me as I awoke one morning and being comforted by his big smile and the smell of bacon and eggs coming from the kitchen.

It was part of a visit my parents made, driving down from our home in Washington, DC, to visit Grandma, Granddaddy, an assortment of aunts, and my great-grandfather Nathan Jones—my mom's family. But this scene was just Granddaddy and me; no telling where the rest of the crew was.

I remember him carrying me as he answered the front door, greeting a non-descript caller, and saying something terrific to them about me—something like, "Ah yes, this is my big boy here," in a booming prideful voice. And then Granddaddy closes the front door, hustles me to the kitchen, and sits me on his knee, allowing me to lean heavy into his stomach as he reads the morning paper. In remembering, I can smell the newsprint and squint a bit from the bright sunlight beaming through the window just above the kitchen sink.

I love my granddaddy. And this narrative—my framing of it—anchors much of how I engage the world. It is simple. It is regular. In it there are affirmations and assets. The story is the nucleus of how I construct my identity with those around me. No doubt, there is a romantic and perhaps a naïve spin on this memory with Granddaddy. The notion of it seems fantastical, like one of those dope Charles White pieces I ponder on that hangs in Professor Gordon's home.

But the world *is* fantastical and romantic. It is other things too.

Buddy, by all accounts the nicest man I ever met, would pass soon after that recollection of him. I was between one and two years old. I wish I'd known him and that he'd known me. I often want to hear him say that I've made him proud; that I'm raising my sons the right way; that I've done right by my mother, his youngest, as I've grown; and that I am a great professor like he was . . . but that wasn't to be. I feel an absence because of it—but not empty.

My storied truth of Granddaddy grounds my worldview. Certainly, other people and a lifetime of experiences complicate this lens, adding to a base good, enriching the responsibilities and the faithfulness I bring to it.

I can appreciate alternatives that push against this norm of mine. It is a part of my experience as a Black man to understand that what is placed at center for me to ascribe to is pathology and deficit. These are the suns around which hegemony[1] has set Black folk to revolve.

Of course, the multiverse is so much bigger than what is normally offered to us.

Western thinking is typically reductionistic. It is categorical and rigid in its placement of things and is irresponsible in fitting persons into the category of object. People of color are easily understood this way. We are engaged as objects because of how popular culture conditions us to understand our contributions to society. Black people's contributions are reduced to being chattel—whether as the enslaved, athletes, entertainers, or inmates. Contemporary thrall is found in the perfunctory exercise of wondering around the edges of racism. Media hypes the tragedy of separateness between people. The sensational somehow becomes commoditized through programming, and we are left to fill our voids with whatever materialism is being peddled.

This mad, peculiar cycle of radicalized commerce and its actors are different than sincere efforts toward social justice that work to hold accountable America's original sin of physicalized white supremacy and its twenty-first-century collateral. The distinction between the ill-fitting, but socially affirming, dramatization of race and the axing away at the disease of white supremacy can be found in the assumptions and narratives that govern behavior. The shifting of master narratives from stale and violent tropes of exclusivity to constructivist stories of normed inclusion and humanity is the difficult work to be done. In school—first at Morehouse and Howard, then as mentored by Professor Edmund W. Gordon—this Sisyphean feat of paradigm shifting is what we were charged to do.

Certainly, changing the patterned ways we are conditioned to understand our relationships to one another is daunting. We are trained as much. The impossibility of it is embedded in the pattern. In looking at the rules of race, class, gender, and standards of superiority, there is an acceptance that things will remain as they are.

But as elaborate, as elegant, and as thorough as hegemony is, it is small in that it reduces people to the oppressor and the would-be oppressed. The fuller scope of the person is pushed down deep to fit assumptions and related actions that are simply wrong. Though perversely broad, hegemony and its enactor, racism, is a narrow and weak performance of power.

So then, the work of paradigm shifting does not have to be done with the foregone expectation of failure. It can be done knowing that the whole person is largely untapped. And that untapped part is full with the possibility of healthy change and good stuff that can be found in our stories of love and soul security. These are undeniable narratives that if privileged and positioned just so, can anchor us in the genuine,[2] even in the midst of racialized terrorism.

Not *knowing* Granddaddy could present as innocuous when matched to the stereotypic Black drama of Pops being a stranger because he's in jail or Moms being an addict. These and other conflated narratives of pathology and Black identity, where the two become errantly indistinguishable, are the dystopian images of self and society that are acceptable starting points when thinking on Black people. The forty-fifth president and his confused understanding of people and how to relate to them beyond the prison of white privilege is an example—better, the model—for how Black people, or persons of color, or anyone who sits about the altar of whiteness is to be engaged.

Assumptions might square with a very real Black experience that is buckshot with pain and punishment because of our Blackness. The experiences are not our identities, however. They might inform our identities, but they are contexts that are constructed in large part by legacies and impacts of slavery, Jim Crow segregation, and imperialism in US institutions. They are contexts to which we adapt by implementing narratives that provide cohesion and connectedness to the larger society.

The assumption here is that "Buddy" narratives are common threads that deserve attending to at least as much as our extrajudicial killings, socioeconomic marginalization, disproportionate incarceration rates, and judicial inequalities. This is not to suggest that we turn a blind eye to social injustice, rather that we incorporate assets and affirmation in dealing with all the trash that is pumped as a singular reality for colored folk.

Granddaddy—Buddy—is my start. That first memory with him is one that grounds a healthy first step in mapping to other, important complications of my identity.

Buddy was super positive—at least that's what I get from my quilting together of him from family and the vibe I get from those 1970s-colored photos I have tucked in books throughout the crib. He was also giving. I take pride in my son Biko's name meaning "a person for other people" in Bantu. It is a connection to Granddaddy that I think is important.

As chair of the Chemistry Department at Norfolk State University, Grandaddy was, by example and deed, the gateway for many in our family to a college education. He allowed a number of relatives to post up at the house and provided advice and good counsel to a number more.

This goodness extended to my mother, who, as a clinical psychologist, has always situated her gift of good counsel so that she could get at those who were often denied services. She has always connected with community in meaningful ways that are an extension of her southern roots, of Buddy. We tease a lot in talking about how broke we are fiscally but how rich we are in human touch. I'm certain that if we added it up, Mom would have seen more clients for free than she saw who paid.

Of course, there is the very real need for money and providing for family. That never slipped. But that elitist glow of being the son of a Vassar graduate and a Yalie was never a part of who I was allowed to be. Degrees and access to privilege fall flat in our family if those tools are not in service to community more than they are in service to you. They are things matched to the genius of you that are supposed to help free people.

No doubt, this is an echo of Buddy's father, Arthur Allen Wall. Born in 1881, Great-Granddaddy Wall was a doctor in Rankin, Pennsylvania. He was beloved. He accepted chickens as payment a time or ten. And it is said that he got up out of his deathbed to treat patients. If so, it would make sense given that his way through Leonard Medical School (Shaw University) was paid by his sisters, who had been enslaved. Great-Granddaddy owed because of his privilege. My cousin Arthur A. Wall III, an emergency physician in Cincinnati, is the modern twist of both Granddaddy and Great-Granddaddy, as his kindness and medical chops are far beyond ordinary yet are a norm.

Evelyn Jones Wall, Grandma, must also be pulled to front in grounding Buddy. She is as heroic as Great-Granddaddy Wall's sisters. Grandma assumed the price of the ticket for her family in their very specific type of freedom work. Her example demands credit, though she, like many Black women, was forgiving of gendered slights. The ironic privilege of Black masculinity is that the hegemonic flavor of patriarchy celebrates us in ways that loosen our embrace of Black women by negating their unconditional sacrifice on behalf of Black men, children, and other Black women.

I still process the interesting distance I had with Grandma for much of my young adult life. In thinking about it, I imagine she might have been waiting for me to earn the life she helped make possible. She is my true-to-life Captain Miller.[3]

Sitting with Grandma often through her passing in 2002, I learned that she and Buddy found the best in people and magnified it like a science. They were practical and methodical. As teachers—Grandma was a celebrated, albeit hardcore, high school English teacher for thirty-two years—they were not uncommon in how they lifted people. Nor were they uncommon if stretched beyond their professions. Black people are good in exceptional ways on the regular. It has a lot to do with the exceptional violence affixed to our cultural and historical DNA and to our biopsychological oxygen. This coping is often invisible, however, because of the desire for us to assume the profit of cool American material without the rough work of accountability.

This is obvious in a forest-for-the-trees sort of way. I began exploring it intently between heavy CD spins of *Lord Willin'* and *Room for Squares* on my drives to and from visits with Grandma in the 2000s. Clipse and John Mayer offered an interesting relief from courses just before the weight of my dissertation. Their dramatized everyday provided familiar sketches that I could fill in or riff on by matching theory, coursework, and familial sensibilities. This is where I began to *really* appreciate the work of Buddy and Grandma Wall.

The Buddy narrative of being exceptionally regular plays well for me. It is a science I respect. It defines me in many ways, not the least of which in how I approach research, lectures, teaching Sunday school, and setting life tones for Biko and his brother Stokely. Their life of family cohesion is different from mine, though it is exceptionally regular because of the good I got from the rough and the smooth, and because of their mother, Mikki, of course.

The Buddy narrative is a lens that some might suggest as having rose-colored glass. I understand it as a perspective that is based in asset and agency, irrespective of context or prescribed condition.

When dominant culture assumes health and wholeness as default, it is normal, a natural starting point. I figure the same ontological fit and proceed accordingly.

NOTES

1. Simply, hegemony is privileging one culture over all others. The term is used frequently throughout this writing as a synonym for white supremacy. It is less prickly and gets the point across.

2. "There is something in every one of you that waits, listens for the sound of the genuine in yourself and if you cannot hear it, you will never find whatever it is for which you are searching and if you hear it and then do not follow it, it was better that you had never been born" (Howard Thurman, 1980 Spelman College commencement address).

3. In the 1998 film *Saving Private Ryan*, protagonist Captain John H. Miller—played by actor Tom Hanks—was a thirty-year-old American serving in the Second Rangers Battalion of the United States Army during World War II. Miller was fatally wounded, and his last words to Ryan, the soldier he and his men were charged to save, were, "James, earn this. Earn it."

PART I

The Lab and Storied Identity

Chapter 1

Hip-Hop Narratives
as a Natural Start

David Wall Rice

The exposure I was allowed while a summer intern at TransAfrica from age twelve through my junior year in college is a significant part of how I've come to know the strength of strategic activism and the value of pushing the great experiment that is American democracy. The lobbyist group best known for its antiapartheid work marshalled the whole of community to help free South Africa and to positively influence US foreign policy concerning the African diaspora. Helmed by Randall Robinson, there were knife-sharp young attorneys putting in work alongside the likes of Arthur Ashe, Stevie Wonder, Dorothy Height, Iman and David Bowie, Walter Mosely, Tony Randall, Ron Dellums, KRS-One, Danny Glover, and so on.

This exposure in combination with my growing up as the son of a statistics professor and a clinical psychologist has defined my perspective relative to summarizing behaviors, their interconnectedness to democracy, and how it can be realized in artful expression, particularly as performed and represented by those who experience the margins.

The Identity, Art, and Democracy Laboratory is my scaffolding for this thinking. It was put together to help me better understand "the self" by being in conversation with artists, activists, athletes, and those who center their performance of identity. The figuring is that with these accessible personalities, there is an opportunity to push beyond stereotypes with fuller stories of and relating to the person.

This means the lab's research scientists and visiting collaborators are its greatest assets. The student scholars, all brilliant, have cycled in and out of the lab, giving thought and purpose to developing theory and programming, never *really* leaving the lab, as this volume attests.

As for the visiting collaborators, some come to the Nabrit Mapp McBay science building at Morehouse College to spend time, others to the classroom. Some share time on stage, and still others rock one-on-one, saying that we're spot on, or telling us to try again, critiquing emerging ideas and suppositions. They share their stories, allowing a vulnerability that is often taken advantage of and used as brick and mortar to build against people who are like them. Their trust and investment in the process are invaluable.

Themes from those who have thought with us through the lab place significance on family, community, citizenship, the politics of being Black, and attachment to the self-defining and affirming experiences related to these parts of life. The psychology of their representative narratives are standards that provide direction in terms of inquiry and solution.

People who have contributed to the lab range from civil rights icon John Lewis to activist Patrice Cullors to scholar Eddie S. Glaude Jr. to neuroscientist Carl Hart. And the narrative, their self stories, are through lines that extend back to when I was a kid at the bus stop cranking Public Enemy, Beastie Boys, and MC Lyte, thinking about the day ahead and what it all means.

Full circle, I place stories with hip-hop artists as a foundation for the writing ahead. This is an intellectually honest start and gives the reader and the writer permission to be bold and innovative in how we share stories and ascribe meaning. It broadens the conversation and potential for understanding the self by substantively positioning these important narratives as a battery in the back for the essays that follow.

BRAD

Brad Jordan returned to the holding area just ahead of my slipping in. Brad, also known as Scarface or Face, the iconic rapper from Houston, Texas, who first gained notoriety as a member of the hardcore reality hip-hop group Geto Boys, was easy. We were introduced, then walked out to a main room in the hotel's conference area.

We were there to do a sit-down as part of Atlanta's All Three Coasts Hip-Hop Festival. It was the tenth year of a conclave that has matured into a twenty-first-century Jack the Rapper of sorts. Face didn't smile at me when introduced, but he was polite. As we went from the super small room to the bigger one, there were a number of admirers motioning for the emcee's attention. He smiled and nodded respectfully to each one as I explained to him the setup for the hour or so that we would spend together. "Whatever is cool," he said.

The title of the talk was "In Conversation: Scarface, Self, and Storytelling as Balm." Face offered off the top, "I had a teacher named Ms. McCluskey. In [her] class we had to write our feelings and read them, in front of the class. The stuff I wrote made her call the house." Those collected to listen to the discussion laughed a bit as Face gave a hard chuckle himself. He continued, "I was like, 'Yes, Grandmama, I wrote that.' She passed it around to all her friends and was like, 'Damn, how does this come out a little kid, why is he thinking like *this*.'"

Brad explained his lyricism as a strong part of his being: "A musician first, okay, I can play every instrument that you can name." He pridefully said that he got his "funk" from his uncle Eddie, a bass player who gave him his first real guitar at about eight.

The storytelling, though, shows a special kind of catharsis: "Make no mistake about it, growing up, it was different for me. I dealt with a lot of elements of a mental issue that I found out was deep rooted in my genes for years, that's schizophrenia, depression, manic depression. It's important for me to talk about [depression and suicide] because that's how I feel." Brad's sincerity was felt as those in the auditorium were struck silent by the sharing. He finished, "I speak [and] write my heart."

The family and the insight that Brad's pathology offers explains the value he places on the block where he grew up: "I've never changed. I'm always here. I'mma always be tied to these people one way or another. I'm not gonna never ever change. I can't face that woman that raised me with five hundred security guards around me, around her house, like I need some kind of protection because," he mockingly asserted. "I made something out of myself. I'm not gonna do her like that. I'm going in that house, gonna kick them shoes off, park in the driveway, gonna eat and stretch myself on that couch like I been doing all my life. I'm gonna walk up and down that same street until the day that I die."

Brad's fidelity, awareness, and responsibility extends with, "I have to share that with y'all. I know what we up against. I already know what they finn'do to us."

He fashions his "deep rootedness" as a protection against the state of things: "I'm cool. I'm just everyday folk. I'd rather just tell the truth," Brad says, declaring further,

The people that's in charge of what America does really gives less than a fuck about me. And it's evident by the way they laying our kids out, putting bullets in the back of they head, *that's* American justice. They still hanging people in the judicial system. They may not be hanging by the rope, but they hangin' 'em by putting them away for the rest of they life. It's crazy. I don't want nobody to go out there and just start beating people up and shit, but you gotta stand your ground too. Stand your ground. Stand your ground, man. I love the idea of civil unrest. Let's stand up for each other, for each other's children. [When] shit is wrong, act accordingly.

COREY AND VINCE

Vince hadn't come to Morehouse College to be impressed by the renowned Glee Club or the bow ties and dress shoes zipping across campus. He did not come for Graves Hall or to see the statue of Martin Luther King Jr. that pointed toward the Mercedes-Benz Stadium, home to the Falcons and the United, and a clumsy ornament of aggressive gentrification in the SWATS neighborhood. Simply, Vince came to attend chapel.

On Thursdays at eleven o'clock, Morehouse hosts speakers in an updated version of weekday church. Crown Forum is a space where politicos, artists, preacher folk, academics, and others share time with about one thousand Morehouse College students and talk about life. A tag for the experience is, "Where students are connected to and develop their dynamic humanity."

On this particular day, the speaker was a man who stepped out of the college twenty-plus years prior. Corey Smyth did so to manage the progressive, Native Tongues stalwart musical trio De La Soul. And an accomplished career in the arts was sprung from there. But Corey hadn't come back to the school since leaving that many years ago, his self stymied a bit, feeling he'd left a commitment unfulfilled. Corey was so cautious in his return that it took a year and a half for him to agree to speak at Crown Forum.

In the discussions leading up to his comeback, Corey modestly explained successes that punctuated modern culture with social consciousness and critique. A product of this work was a family bond he'd developed with Dave Chappelle while working on projects with the comedic thinker for over a decade. In fact, a glimpse of Corey on an episode of *Inside the Actors Studio* featuring Chappelle led to calls for him to return to Morehouse to share his experiences and creative contributions to social justice.

Talks were extensive and committed. Corey spoke a lot about purpose and cultural responsibility. A new project that he was assuming was consistently referenced in those conversations. But, as in his discussing work with Chappelle, it was less project and more an added layer of his community attachment to and love for people who were likeminded. It had Corey mentioning a Sprite campaign, a concert here and a movie feature there, all in service to a "kid" he understood as his little brother of sorts—Vince.

Vince was a step back into a world of hip-hop management that Corey could easily have relegated as a place he'd outgrown. Vince's talent, his wisdom, his circumstance, and an idiosyncratic naïveté pulled Corey into working with the Long Beach, California, native.

And there they were—Vince, his friend and DJ Westside Ty, and Corey—rolling up to the side of King Chapel, prepped for the talk, no one having returned calls dealing with flights, honorarium, or a hotel stay for several weeks. Corey was having none of it. The talk was his homecoming. There was no price to be paid for him finally returning to a place that he maintained as being very important in how he developed himself and how he took on the world.

Corey gave a good talk. It was heartfelt. Vince was there, quiet and thoughtful. Students made a respectful crush around the two at the end of the hour, then the team made its way to a psychology class, where they challenged one another and those enrolled on concepts of identity and ways of being a Black man in twenty-first-century America.

There were no pyrotechnics, shiny suits, or exposés detailing the protagonists narrowly escaping fill-in-the-blank to become hip-hop heroes. The guests *were* eating chicken sandwiches during the classroom session, but the drama was in the process of being, and in being embraced as, regular.

A few months later, Vince Staples visited Harvard. Roles were flipped; he was on stage explaining self, and Corey was in the front row, quiet and reserved.

As delighted as the Ivy was to host him, the *Harvard Crimson* by way of their blog *flyby* missed the point of his talk. Their peg was, "Vince Staples is better than you, and us." Of course, Vince is no better, no worse than any of us—he would tell you as much. In fact, *that* was a fundamental peg of Vince's talk at the school. Though the article was attempting to be complimentary, explaining him as "better than" placed him apart, as object, as other. He is painted as the magical Negro, exceptional because of the celebrity and "smarts" set atop him, so that we don't have to do the work of matching his exceptional regularity.

At Harvard, perhaps because of a not-so-subconscious pang to present as erudite, I began talking with Vince about his references to James Joyce, the Irish novelist renowned as a modernist avant-garde writer who made a significant impact on the twentieth century. The two—Vince and Joyce—are not dissimilar, and Vince's knowing and telling as much was dope.

In his recording "Loco," Vince explains, "I rap the James Joyce. Don't need the Rolls-Royce," distinguishing himself from a hip-hop playbook he could easily be assumed to play by. The lyric suggests that he is an intellectual who is not consumed by materialism. It reads as surprising to those who sidestep self-complexity. This is where *flyby* got struck in its characterization of Vince's time spent on campus. Never mind that sociologist and Harvard graduate W. E. B. Du Bois explained double-consciousness and the tension between Black culture and American culture in 1903.[1]

So then, by comparison, Vince's declaration, "I'm a gangsta Crip. F**k Gangsta rap," in "Norf Norf"—a song that Staples reluctantly released on his major label debut, *Summertime 06*—can be appreciated as an adaptive identity contained within a double self. Though not easily seen as such, gang membership at the individual level is an identity employed to functionally temper cultural and institutional racism. It's part of an agenda to be understood, if not received, as "regular," albeit within a particular context.

The peculiar allows for a square pivot to James Joyce: "For myself, I always write about Dublin, because if I can get to the heart of Dublin I can get to the heart of all the cities of the world. In the particular is contained the universal."

Joyce's first novel, *A Portrait of the Artist as a Young Man*, is an exploration not only of the self but of what the self *is* and how it comes *to be*. The tome is widely understood as autobiographical and as such proves particularly particular—the inner narrative of Stephen Dedalus mirroring at once a universal and specific embrace of Vince Staples, for both his Joycean epiphanies and his poetic and practical illustration of a portrait of the artist as a young man.

Culture, race, language, and narratives are significant constructs by which the self is cobbled together and through which identities explain the self. They are huge themes at play in understanding and anticipating behavior because they are common denominators, accessible pieces of the everyday.

Culture, race, language, and narratives are spun here as how people figure themselves by default (dispositional traits), how they make their default ways fit situations (characteristic adaptation), and how they explain who they are (life story tellings) given culture and social context (McAdams and Pals 2006). This is the academic grounding of a "Buddy narrative" pragmatism, Corey and Vince's common good, and a formal mapping of how folk work to be regular. It is the paper on which the agenda for being regular is sketched. If drawn together, they magnify with even greater clarity the significance of storied selves. It is the practiced and practical application of theory. It is identity orchestration 360.

Corey Smyth, accomplished in his professional life as a manager and businessman, is regular in his everyday life. In fact, his professional accomplishments pale relative to how he impresses upon his personal. Vince is an example of this, and the same can be said for him, showing up for his friend Corey—regular-type stuff that is profound because of how it is regularly ignored with respect to Black folk.

WILLIAM

I asked William L. Roberts II to come to Morehouse College to be in conversation with students about agency and social learning as described by Albert Bandura. Roberts, better known as Rick Ross, came to the Theories of Personality class on a Thursday at one o'clock. Though he announced his visit via Snapchat while in the car leading up to his classroom visit, the scheduled time was a quasisecret because of the celebrity that Ross enjoys. We didn't want the frenzy that we got with the J. Cole visit a few months prior.

In sitting down in front of the psychology majors, Ross kept his sunglasses on, allowing for a bit of distance between himself and the young men who were just ten feet or so in front of him. The plan was to have Ross engage the students around how he understood his democratic space, an amplified platform of a popular hip-hop artist, as conditioning context for those who listened to his music. Instead, Ross eventually gave an even more penetrating explanation of how he was socialized and how he assumed responsibility on the other side of a difficult childhood.

Except in answering the first question put to him, Rick Ross was Rick Ross for the first thirty minutes and William Roberts for the last twenty. The lesson was in that last twenty minutes. This is where authentic engagement was fomented; each of us in the class became participants to one another, not objects. Bridging his own precocious boyhood to the present, as the class was almost over, the scholars having taken flicks with Rick Ross to show off to folks on social media, William Roberts said plainly, "Now, what the fuck are you going to do?"

The room was still.

"I never thought I'd be in a college classroom, much less at Morehouse, when I was growing up. And now I'm here, with all of the limitations and the obstacles put in front of me, I'm doing the best that I know how." William continued, "You have so much more than I had. You are at the best time of your life right now. Enjoy it, but how are you going to get our people free?"

That was the tipping point, where William was at once reflexive and defalsifying, allowing himself to be seen and the persona of Rick to fade from the present. The question for Rick up top was, "What is the difference between Rick Ross and William Roberts?" Without skipping a beat, William said, "Rick Ross is for sale and William isn't."

This is a brilliance of the Black experience, an acute awareness of—not preoccupation with—the strength of our visibility and an adroit adaptation to the fundamental duality of the American context: "One ever feels his two-ness—an American, a Negro; two souls, two thoughts, two unreconciled strivings; two warring ideals in one dark body, whose dogged strength alone keeps it from being torn asunder. The history of the American Negro is the history of this strife" (Du Bois 1903).

In cross-fading the Rick Ross allusion to freedom in declaring his absent price point and Du Bois's defining double-consciousness, there is laid bare the construct of psychic balance. Ross has struck it in some respect, and Du Bois has outlined the dilemma.

The great American education and behavior intellect Edmund W. Gordon offers the very rich term *orchestration* to explain relationships across behaviors, teaching, and learning. His vocabulary cleanly describes a perpetual measuring of circumstance and the consequent application of agency. In building out the Ross-and-Du Bois-touched construct of psychic balance, identity orchestration fits well.

Du Bois articulates freedom work with the tough process of striking a psychological balance between oppositional Western cultural norms and Black cultural norms. And then William, in asking the young men in that classroom, "How are you going to get your people free?" and declaring that "Rick Ross is for sale and William isn't," places emphasis on the everyday work of "beingness."

Frederick Douglass and Stokely Carmichael help to punctuate this iteration of identity orchestration—identity dilemma articulation. Douglass declaring that "freedom is a road seldom traveled by the multitude" is not quite right. The spirit of the prose is reasonable, but it assumes a posture of exceptionalism that strains an ability to authentically engage and, if bought into, compromises agency relative to our reality of freedom.

To be clear, I use *agency* here as offered by *Human Agency, Freedom, and Determinism*: "Freedom is not conceived negatively as the absence of external coercion or constraints. Rather, it is defined positively in terms of the exercise of self-influence. . . . Self-generated influences operate deterministically on behavior the same way as external sources of influence do. . . . It is because self-influence operates deterministically on action that some measure of self-directedness and freedom is possible" (Bandura 1989). "To be an agent is to influence intentionally one's functioning and life circumstances. In this view, personal influence is part of the causal structure. People are self-organizing, proactive, self-regulating, and self-reflecting. They are not simply onlookers of their behavior. They are contributors to their life circumstances, not just products of them" (Bandura 2006). There are four core properties of human agency: intentionality, forethought, self-reactiveness, and self-reflectiveness.

Identity orchestration has everything to do with *the core truth of beingness*. It is a figuring of goodness of fit (Chess and Thomas 1977; 1999), matching the individual's adaptability to the environment and its expectations. The theoretical construct is birthed from the preconsciousness found in Black boys that is frequently a result of demands put on them to act older than they are because of a threat that their physicality presents to a white, patriarchal, supremacist structure.

The freedom road *is* traveled by the multitude. However, the destination of freedom is a process that plays as more elusive. This is because a process dynamic is placed atop the philosophical absolute of freedom. Stokely Carmichael pushes the freedom absolute further in his 1966 Berkeley Black Power speech with the simple declaration that "no man can give anybody his freedom. A man is born free." The process dynamic of freedom is argued here as a psychological process that is not a destination, rather a continuum that is context-riddled and adapted to.

Identity orchestration is an expression of that freedom process.

NOTES

1. Vince adds even more here with, "I'm on a new level. I am too cultured and too ghetto. . . . Please do not treat me like I'm not a genius. I'm runnin' on empty the new River Phoenix." This note from *Homage* off Vince's second major LP, *Big Fish Theory* portends the deep self-disclosure in Vince's 2021 self-titled LP and the 2022 *Ramona Park Broke My Heart*.

Chapter 2

Rakim, Ice Cube, then
Watch the Throne

David Wall Rice

Stereotypes are elastic. They stretch to context and time in ways that position stale tropes as new. The portrait of Black men in America painted by mainstream devices is an example. The terms *criminal*, *athlete*, and *entertainer* too often provide a type of cultural-historical shorthand that has defined Black men in popular spaces for decades. These are accessible identities that intimate "other," positioning Black men away from normalcy and full consideration within larger society.

This fits a comfortable master narrative of race[1] for the Black family in the United States. It is a narrative extended by the misinterpretation and narrow understanding of Black masculinity in general[2] and in the positioning of voices of Black men and boys as invisible. This invisibility,[3] however, is misfit considering the diversity of narratives from Black men and boys available within present mass culture—specifically a popular culture heavily influenced by hip-hop.

The present thinking considers the multiple and varied life stories found in the language of hip-hop such that Black men and boys are understood relative to their identity form and function—beyond pathology. To most effectively do this, there is need for ontological and axiological contextualizing that allows for access to the visibility that hip-hop recording artists offer. James Baldwin (1985, 650) helps with instruction that "language is also a political instrument, means and proof of power. It is the most vivid and crucial key to identity: It reveals the private identity, and connects one with, or divorces one from, the larger public, or communal identity." Here we stand up the idea that the language of hip-hop is afforded an important inlet into alternative worldviews through lyricists Rakim, Ice Cube, Jay-Z, and Kanye West.

HIP-HOP NARRATIVES AS A LANGUAGE OF
ENGAGEMENT FOR BLACK MEN AND BLACK BOYS

Certainly, caution should be exercised in summarizing Black men through any singular lens, hip-hop or other. A global perspective of Black men necessitates multiple arteries toward understanding, chief among them engagement. The language of hip-hop narratives has the capacity to facilitate this engagement and understanding when looked at beyond stereotype. There is visibility in the lyrics when the lives outlined are privileged as valuable knowledge.

Rakim and Ice Cube help in illustrating this potential for knowing Black men differently with definitive personal self-disclosure and revelation, and the Jay-Z/Kanye West long play *Watch the Throne* similarly demonstrates important lived experiences but from a more public-primed perspective. This group of four men and their work was selected for review because of a popular appreciation of their music and personas and a critical appreciation of their storytelling through rhyme. The adolescent marker that Rakim and Cube represent with their lyricism as demonstrated in the current piece is matured but remains as salient as the adult lyrics of Jay-Z and Kanye West that are selected for deconstruction. This illustrates a consistency in the vitality of narratives offered by the artists across a developmental arc—boy to man—that is rarely examined.

With their catalogues and positioning within hip-hop, Rakim, Ice Cube, Jay-Z, and Kanye West show a push toward psychological balance that lends fullness to the consideration of who and how Black men are. The developing theory of identity orchestration (Rice 2009; Rice et al. 2010) dynamically responds to the work of each lyricist in his reconciling person to context. The construct provides scaffolding for their expressions of self through raced and gendered identity construction, and Winston's (2010; 2011) theory of race self-complexity helps to bridge these lyricists' storied lives and popular representations to psychological significance.

RAKIM AND ICE CUBE PORTEND
THE THRONE, A PRIMER

In the summer of 1987, the DJ/MC duo Eric B. & Rakim released *Paid in Full*. The straight-ahead set of ten songs contributed to a redefinition of contemporary hip-hop. While the genre certainly existed before them, Eric B. & Rakim advanced the musical form with innovative production and with Rakim's mature, stylized, and thoughtful rhymes. Acknowledged as helping to leverage a significant cultural shift forward for hip-hop in the late 1980s, Rakim is understood along with Chuck D. and KRS-One as "[a] serious Black [man] with something important to say" (Charnas 2010, 182).

Often referred to as The God MC because of a consistent emphasis on knowledge of self gained through his belief in the Nation of Gods and Earths—a religious offshoot of Islam (Knight 2007)—and because of a deep respect afforded him by his peers, Rakim's conversational flow imprint can be found throughout modern rap music. Eminem and other mainstream artists have integrated classic Rakim into their songs, and "progressives" like Talib Kweli have done the same.

Though Rakim's 2019 autobiography, *Sweat the Technique*, and subsequent touring into the 2020s helped to remind us of his importance to the culture, he is not referenced by mainstream to scale given his impact.[4] This is unfortunate. Notable for meticulously thoughtful lyrics with spiritual through lines, his framing of self is more in line with a whole story of Black American men than with pervasive associations with the drug trade and a celebration of intoxicants, material gains, and sexual exploits.

Ice Cube was the voice of golden age[5] West Coast hip-hop as the lyrical architect of notorious rap collective N.W.A and then with his solo discs *AmeriKKKa's Most Wanted* and *Death Certificate*. Cube was most easily identified as that rapper with *the* explicit "reality rap" lyrics, a super wet Jheri curl, and an ever-furrowed brow, who never smiled. His content and identity constructions were, and remain, part rough-edged social critique, sometimes misogynist jingles, and unapologetically "g-a-n-g-s-t-a."

Ice Cube's prevailing place within current popular culture is in stark contrast to his recordings, having established himself as a strong earner as a movie and television writer, producer, and star, and as a founder of the Big3 basketball league. The content of Cube's rhymes across albums, however, has remained consistently resistant despite his occasionally fuzzy persona in films. It was in "F—k tha Police" in 1988 with N.W.A and "Arrest the President" in 2018, where Cube rails against the forty-fifth president of the United States of America.

The masculinities that Rakim and Cube occupy through their identities across their recorded works are complex. For those who give more than a passing consideration to hip-hop lyricism, this is not particularly novel from artist to artist. Stories of self relative to love, war, friendship, death, race, culture, and faith are common themes presented in an effort to negotiate emerging adolescence toward adulthood. Fact and fiction, the stories told are psychological efforts to reconcile identity. Rakim and Cube perform this task in distinctive and overlapping ways.

The two lyricists tell complex stories of self and context across three decades, and they anticipate the verve of collected, contradictory stories of orchestrated selves like those that comprise *Watch the Throne*. The connection of Rakim and Cube to Jay-Z and West, then, provides an expanse of topic, time, and context that allows for an approach to the consideration of Black men and their visibility beyond the developing years of adolescence into the developed years of adulthood. This is new to hip-hop insomuch as the genre and the artists are relatively young. Just now are lyricists coming of age and beginning to mark their development in their music. Rakim and Ice Cube establish a beginning because of their longevity and position within the broad narrative of hip-hop, and Jay-Z and Kanye West emphasize the established visibility in current language—*Watch the Throne*—that helps to join this narrative of visibility from recent past to the present. The life stories offered demonstrate psychological demands and accommodations inherent in human behavior and have the capacity to yield insight into the construct of identity orchestration.

BALANCE THEORY AND RACE SELF-COMPLEXITY

Identity orchestration is a personality process theory that describes the motives of the self system as an ego-balancing mechanism. The theory explores how achieving psychological equilibrium is accomplished in discursive acts of Black males. As such, these motives of the self become an overlapping part of the process of Black males' identity construction. Identity orchestration is the activity and goal of negotiated identity balance (Rice et al. 2010). It is psychological work done by the individual where the self is situated as a complex system that provides a container for many identities, or self-aspects (Linville 1985; Rafaeli-Mor and Steinberg 2002). These identities are naturally driven toward a state of equilibrium and avail themselves to a self-stability that is person and situation driven. The person makes sense of the world by fitting their identity to it, and identity orchestration is the process by which this is done.

This adaptation is represented in four forms: identity dilemma articulation, burden of proof, unadulterated presentation of self, and acute identity expression. These building blocks of identity orchestration are exemplars of identity constructions that represent the awareness of identities to be negotiated (identity dilemma articulation), defiance in the face of negotiation (unadulterated presentation of self), responsibility of identity assumption and the relationship to stereotype (burden of proof), and hyperarticulated self-affirmation through an outline of strengths or weaknesses that allow for recognition (acute identity expression). These forms of identity orchestration provide avenues by which form and function of emerging and established selves are found (Rice 2009). They also allow for more authentic approximations of Black male identity than those offered through rigid normative models that many times miss the depth and scope of who individuals internalize and represent themselves to be (Rice 2008).

There is an involved structural justification of identity orchestration from a theory-building base (Rice 2008) that places the construct squarely within personality psychology. McAdams and Pals (2006) significantly advance the concept of personality, suggesting that beyond the widely accepted Big Five (McCrae and Costa 1997)—openness, conscientiousness, extroversion, agreeableness, and neuroticism—there exists an alternative view of how persons are whole within and because of the world. Dispositional signature, characteristic adaptations, narratives/modern identity, and the differential role of culture are components of personality that McAdams and Pals (2006) put forward that help to govern tenets of identity orchestration.

Identity through purposeful, unitary life stories and the role of culture are two dimensions that help in exploring the form and function of Black male identity construction in this analytic exercise. Rakim's resolute and consistent knowledge of self-expressions on "wax," and Ice Cube's relentless and reasoned search for self across his recordings, provide a language of cohesive narratives that are prime for study. This allows contemporary artists similar visibility because of precedent. The visibility that Rakim and Cube demonstrate provides a fuller picture of Black males than is typical. The gendered and race-based orientation is context validated by and grounded through race self-complexity, the foundational theory from which identity orchestration is extended.

Race self-complexity is the first personality theory to integrate narrative theories of personality with psychological significance of race theories (Winston 2010; 2011). The theory finds utility in the embrace of Rakim, Ice Cube, the narratives of *Watch the Throne*, and hip-hop stories generally because of the assumptions it operates from in explaining race and the active role attributed to narratives in the defining of self. Within the discursive acts—language—of hip-hop expressions there is fundamental context. James Jones (2004) might suggest it is a universal context of racism that suggests visibility informed by self-protection and self-enhancement. Race self-complexity explains this race reality as consequent in how Black people consider themselves and in how they are considered by others. Cultural historical and biopsychological realities of race[6] within the United States further dictate self-defining behaviors and identification. This informs but does not define the master narratives of race that all Black folks confront. And this psychology work is at the core of hip-hop expressions and identification, where artists are seen defining and developing identities by "[engaging] in a process of negotiating affective, thematic and motivational internal and external stimuli relevant to race. This meaning-making process becomes selectively, synchronically and diachronically integrated into a person's internalized narrative of self, which is as important an element of human personality as the trait and characteristic adaptation dimensions" (Winston 2010).

RAKIM AND CUBE AND AN INITIAL PASS AT ORCHESTRATION

Accordingly, the themes that Rakim unpacks in the declarative recording "I Ain't No Joke" extend beyond superficial bravado. And Ice Cube's "angry Black man"–styled "Tha N—a You Love to Hate" is also more than what a contextual listen might suggest. At base both recordings articulate a racialized understanding of self relative to a universal other. This is in line with race self-complexity. There is the consideration of self within a field of racism, complicating an already complex self. There is also the working toward psychological balance with the public articulation of how Rakim and Cube are fitting themselves into a public that at best questions (Rakim) and at worst holds contempt for (Ice Cube) who they are.

Identity orchestration is present with the assumption of acute identity expression for Rakim. Asserting his dominance on the microphone with "I Ain't No Joke," he demands visibility with "So when you see me come up, freeze / Or you'll be one of those seven emcees."[7]

The last line establishing narrative continuity with Rakim's seminal "My Melody," where he legendarily hyperarticulates, "I take seven emcees put 'em in a line / And add seven more brothas who think they can rhyme." He concludes with, "Well, it'll take seven more before I go for mine / Now that's twenty-one emcees ate up at the same time."[8]

Rakim, though not obviously addressing a racialized environment within the presented lyricism, does operate within it. This is apparent in considering the reputation[9] that Black males without traditional access to capital[10] are charged to achieve with the imposition of a default patriarchal, hegemonic experience. Again, in defining a supremely proficient self across "I Ain't No Joke" and "My Melody" from the LP *Paid in Full*, Rakim is striking an orchestrated identity that elicits visibility from the listener so that the day-to-day invisibility experience is balanced.

Ice Cube's identity and race intersection is more conspicuous with his orchestrated and unadulterated presentation of self and burden of proof. McAdams and Pals (2006) talk of the differential role of culture and its potential to impact personality. As an extension of personality, the self is also consequent of culture. Understanding the threat that his being Black and a man elicits within a broad context, Ice Cube is agentic in his engagement of the stereotype. He co-opts it, utilizing it as strength, and exercises it in confronting the individual who holds the stereotype while simultaneously challenging institutional and cultural racism. A clear example of this activity is found in the narrative "The N—a Ya Love to Hate," the first song off Cube's first solo album, *AmeriKKKa's Most Wanted*: "Now who do ya love to hate."

This is a rhetorical start to a self-aware understanding of how Ice Cube understands himself as fitting outside of "proper" spaces. He explains, "'Cause I talk s—t and down the eight-ball 'cause I don't fake / You're begging I fall off."

Here Cube taps in to the social illustration of young and old Black men as perpetual stoop sitters who talk daily about neighborhood events with great animation, colorful language, and an accent of alcohol. But instead of letting the stereotype sit, Ice Cube extends his engagement with the cultural perception by juxtaposing it to "The crossover might as well cut them balls off."

With "crossover" and an illustration of the consequence "might as well cut them balls off," he suggests that he would rather remain the stereotype than compromise any cultural integrity, particularly if that compromise renders him ineffective in wielding whatever power he assumes.

Ice Cube's allusion to the castration of Black men that was rampant from slavery into the middle of the twentieth century is as in-your-face an assumption of unadulterated presentation of self as is entitling one's first solo studio album *AmeriKKKa's Most Wanted* or being a founding member of the group Ni—as With Attitude. Even if one understands employing cursing and "the 'N' word" as salacious attention-seeking language, or as age-appropriate anti-establishment behavior, there is still the function of this identity assumption to be considered, and this behavior is essentially activity toward visibility.

With the added "The N—a Ya Love to Hate" couplet "And get your ass ready for the lynching / The mob is droppin' common sense and . . . ,"[11] Cube's unadulterated presentation of self is pushed even further into identity orchestration, where the stereotype assumption is transmuted into a responsibility with "the mob is droppin' common sense and . . . " There is a burden that Cube assumes. He wants to prove there is more to him than simple stereotype, to use his position to educate on the most practical and relatable of levels.

COPING . . . IDENTITY AS ACTIVITY

With their life stories, Rakim and Cube represent the process of psychological development. The phenomenon often escapes consideration for Black men in popular culture and social science literature and is not generally recognized in the examination of hip-hop music. Identity expressions within hip-hop are limited to adolescent understandings of manhood because, typically, rappers are adolescents. Their station in development calls for anticipated, perceived, and aspirational identities, not static ones. Rakim and Ice Cube, in their hip-hop recordings and constructed and reconstructed narratives, demonstrate psychological growth. On their records, they are coping. With the presentation of their narratives, they are "doing" and "being." They are participating in the activity of identity while also occupying identities that substantiate a self-space that is working for the context at hand and toward contexts with which they are familiar or in which they hope to participate.

Coping is understood here as diminishing the physical, emotional, and psychological burdens linked with stressful life events and daily hassles (Snyder and Dinoff 1999). Through the authenticity of their narratives, Rakim and Cube highlight vulnerabilities and articulate perspectives as strategies that minimize psychological strain. This is done by employing a set of styles (Harrell 1979; Harding 1975), perspectives on motivation (Jones 2003), and activity of "being" a Black male (Spencer, Dupree, and Hartmann 1997). Through a personality lens (McAdams and Pals 2006), coping can also be considered in terms of characteristic adaptation through culture. The cultural attribute of resistance and the revelation of personal ethnosocial truths in Rakim-and Cube-styled hip-hop are illustrative of this type of cultural adaptation. This "doing" of identity (Cunningham 1999; Spencer, Cunningham, and Swanson 1995) sees the artist adapting his presentations of self to his expectancies relative to affirmation given his contextualized experience.

The psychological work that Rakim and Ice Cube enact on their beginning LPs, *Paid in Full* and *AmeriKKKa's Most Wanted*, respectively, support ideas about constructs of and relating to identity balance. The artists' multi-dimensionality of identity expression is significant; so too are the potential identities that the albums suggest. The initial works generated by Rakim and Ice Cube laid a working map for who and how Black men are, in part. They are suggestive of the artists' potential for personal growth as evinced in their respective catalogues and anticipated contemporary hip-hop and its adult perspectives on "being" and "doing."

NEGOTIATING THE THRONE

Two of the most popular and influential hip-hop lyricists of the twenty-first century are Jay-Z and Kanye West. They represent Black male lived experiences on different ends of a spectrum and, like Rakim and Ice Cube, overlap in their understandings and expressions of self. They are very much extensions of the golden era of hip-hop artists.

Says Rakim of Jay-Z's significance relative to hip-hop, "What I did and that feeling that I gave the game when I was at that forefront . . . is a feeling that Jay is giving to people today" (Langhorne 2011). That "feeling" is bound in narratives that have visibility as a shared thread. Within the life stories of Rakim, Ice Cube, Jay-Z, and Kanye West are reflections of self that are highly relatable across raced and gendered identities. Certainly, this is a contributing factor to their successes within and influence on popular culture. To understand the identity orchestration and the gendered and racialized negotiations of these Black men is to see reflections of self across a variety of statuses. Their stories and language have a common touch that affords understanding beyond pathology and stereotype.

Jay-Z and Kanye West's 2011 collaborative work *Watch the Throne* debuted at number one on the US Billboard 200 chart and ranked number two on *Rolling Stone*'s list of best albums of the year (Anderson et al. 2011; Caulfield 2011). With songs produced by West and others and emceed by both men, the album is replete with social commentary and stereotype. It anchors the self in both contradictory and complementary versions of identity that give voice to the complex nature of living across varied contexts. It is a Du Boisian album in this way.

Watch the Throne is also aggressively ostentatious with references to esoteric art, luxury cars, and expensive vacations. Riccardo Tisci of the French fashion house Givenchy designed an image of gilded, ornate embroidery for the album's cover artwork. This in combination with the implicit warning of the title could easily situate *Watch the Throne* as typically disposable hip-hop fare, but the collected songs demonstrate an important subversive declaration of Black man resistance. *New York* magazine's Nitsuh Abebe (2011) wrote in his review, "It's a portrait of two black men thinking through the idea of success in America; what happens when your view of yourself as a suppressed, striving underdog has to give way to the admission that you've succeeded about as much as it's worth bothering with; and how much your victory can really relate to (or feel like it's on behalf of) your onetime peers who haven't got a shred of what you've won."

Watch the Throne works as a thesis on what success means, or can mean, for Black men in America as they think and are active beyond the limited scripts set for them. Though there is only a single album between Jay-Z and Kanye West to date, the LP has aged well—performatively and perceptually—as social commentary. This is accentuated with the track "Jail" from West's tenth studio album, *Donda*. With public disagreements and distance between them, hearing Jay-Z and Ye (formerly Kanye) on one track was a significant pop-culture moment in 2021. And it reads even deeper considering the two reconciled "on wax" in the name of West's mother, Donda West, who passed in 2007. On "Jail," Jay-Z reaches past stereotypical expectations of how he might be connected to Kanye given the distance, committing, "Hol' up, Donda, I'm with your baby when I touch back road / Told him, 'Stop all of that red cap, we goin' home.'"

Here Jay-Z articulates an unbroken attachment to Kanye West that the two began with West's production of Jay-Z on *The Blueprint* and that they further formalized, publicly, with the *Watch the Throne* record.

"Otis," the lead single from *Watch the Throne*, was a commercial hook for the album. The track samples Otis Redding's crooning from "Try a Little Tenderness," providing a backdrop to the stylized braggadocio of Jay-Z and West. An unengaged pass at the single could easily miss messages present. Lyrics of hypermaterialism become more palpable with knowledge of Redding's contribution to the legacy of Black people in the music industry, having been one of few Black singers to maintain publishing rights for the songs he wrote. Redding's example is linked to the entrepreneurship that has afforded Jay-Z and Kanye West material gains. Jay-Z subversively boasts, "Driving Benzes, wit' no benefits / Not bad huh, for some immigrants."

This shows as Trojan horse–type braggadocio with the expensive car reference connecting to an awareness and assumption of the "immigrant" sociocultural status. This is especially powerful considering that the United States was more aggressively walling itself off from Mexico at the time, signaling a cold posture toward select immigrants. Jay-Z continues, fully assuming an identity of the marginalized but aligning with Western, capitalistic fundamentals with "Build your fences, we diggin' tunnels / Can't you see, we getting' money up under you."

West further employs a hip-hop bully pulpit–referencing impact with his breakout pop song of faith, "Jesus Walks" from his 2004 debut album, *College Dropout*: "I made 'Jesus Walks' I'm never going to hell / Couture level flow, it's never going on sale."

The substance offered by Jay-Z is extended by West and is then tempered with still clever but more stereotypical and less threatening descriptors: "Luxury rap, the Hermes of verses / Sophisticated ignorance, I write my curses in cursive."[12]

The teaming of the two here is reminiscent of the hardcore political and playful tension between Public Enemy's Chuck D. and Flavor Flav.[13] Lauryn Hill explains the dynamic with her couplet,[14] "And even after all my logic and my theory, I add a 'motherf—ker' so you ignorant ni—as hear me." The duo of West and Jay is built to be seen, but as a Trojan horse of sorts.

The video for "Otis" extends the artists' attempt at visibility. It's set in what looks to be an empty freight yard, where central images are an American flag hung from the side of a warehouse wall and a trashed Maybach—a German luxury automobile. The video opens with Jay-Z and Kanye West approaching the car with a welding torch and power saw in hand. Flash to a team of men in protective gear dismantling the vehicle. And then the hip-hop stars at once mock and endorse symbols of the American dream for the sub four-minute visual, speeding through the rail yard in the mangled auto with women in the backseat and a frame or two capturing a comedian du jour making quirky, funny hip-hop hand movements. The video's final frame is a written message explaining that proceeds from the auction of the car will go to East African drought disaster relief.

The whole of the video is exemplary of identity dilemma articulation. It is a form of identity orchestration that is interwoven throughout the album. Jay-Z and Kanye are developed men of "means." They have graduated beyond the initial insights of Rakim and Ice Cube, who now partner with them in their adult world. Whether through wealth or role modeling, these men now possess privileges that have the capacity to oppress or to provide access to those they represent and for whom they care. With "Otis," Jay-Z and Kanye West illustrate both respect and disdain for this dilemma.

Watch the Throne's "Murder to Excellence" provides a more direct social commentary. It places the lifestyles of Jay-Z and West beside those of Black men living in American cities with the consistent threat of murder. West uses as example his hometown of Chicago, Illinois, to demonstrate the tragedy that is the "murder capital," while Jay-Z opens the recording with "this is to the memory of Danroy Henry," a Pace University student killed in 2010 by Westchester County police officers in New York.

Jay-Z connects to visceral solidarity that links culture to cool to consciousness with "All-black everything, / Ni—a you know my fresh code" and underscores his attachment to community with "Ni—as watching the throne, / Very happy to be you."

He concludes his set of bars with an allusion to the Black power movement and, arguably, an invitation to activism, rallying, "Power to the people, / When you see me, see you."

Kanye West flatly extends that with "It's a war going on outside we ain't safe from," lamenting, "I feel the pain in my city wherever I go / 314 soldiers died in Iraq, 509 died in Chicago." But Jay-Z counters with a hope through Black death, explaining, "I arrived on the day Fred Hampton died / Uh, real ni—as just multiply" and concludes verse four, knowing he's escaped being a statistic, saying, "And they say by 21, I was supposed to die / So, I'm out here celebrating my post-demise."[15]

Jay-Z and Kanye connect their condition to that of young Black men across the country, Black men who are marginalized and challenged by what West questions, "Is it genocide?"

With their narratives, Jay-Z and Kanye are reorienting the listener's expectation of them as wealthy, famous, powerful, and distant through a connection to the circumstance of the Black everyman, everyboy. The artists are leveraging their visibility in an effort to make those they identify with more relatable. Jay-Z and Kanye West are orchestrating identity by demonstrating their relationship to the Black male whole through burden of proof. They affirm their connection to community with the articulation of a shared vulnerability to police brutality and other violence against them. When explaining, "I'm out here celebrating my post-demise," in the context of the album's other side of material gain, Jay-Z is further exhibiting orchestration with an unadulterated presentation of self, cognizant of his relationship to the identity dilemma that exists between his achievement and the killing of people who look like and are like him.

"Murder to Excellence" highlights the realities of violence with an understanding of persistent and epidemic murder rates, a nod to the armed resistance attached to the legacy of Black Panther Fred Hampton, and a professed unconditional love regardless of sociocultural station in the acknowledgment, "What up blood? What up cuz? It's all Black, I love us." This storytelling is a process of orchestrating psychological balance, an effort to make sense of competing realities in a public space. It is a desire for celebration of achievement and an overture for help in pulling and pushing those who are not as fortunate forward. Jay-Z and Kanye West give voice to self and to others with their insights and use *Watch the Throne* as a tool to understanding that is unapologetically contradictory. This allows for authentic engagement with vulnerable personal and public Black selves in an arena of social intimation of a departure from such humanness because of status achieved through wealth and fame.

CONCLUSION

Simply, Rakim, Ice Cube, and Jay-Z and Kanye West with their *Watch the Throne* LP represent for Black men and Black boys. Likely, this does not elicit much debate. The advance is in the significance attributed to this representation through identity orchestration. It is an advance in prioritizing identity form and function and in substantively engaging visibility present in the psychological work inherent in the language of hip-hop.

Form is found in the acute identity expression of Rakim's "I Ain't No Joke" and "My Melody" and in the unadulterated presentation of self that Ice Cube outlines. Cube illustrates additional identity form with the orchestration of race representation in the lyrics for "The N—a Ya Love to Hate." The *Watch the Throne* LP also demonstrates burden of proof with the recording "Murder to Excellence." Jay-Z and Kanye West further exemplify identity orchestration with the identity dilemma articulation of "Otis" and present a complex, unadulterated presentation of self in "Murder to Excellence."

Function is prevalent across identity orchestration examples here with a striving toward visibility that helps to establish a central argument of the piece. There is further function, however, that exists across psychological layers and personality levels—the "why" of visibility. The negotiation of self relative to context is an additional function found in the language of Rakim, Ice Cube, Jay-Z, and Kanye West, and in the stories they tell. A consideration of W. E. B. Du Bois's (1903, 46) *Souls of Black Folks* helps in summarizing the motivation—the function—behind the narratives offered by these artists: "to be a co-worker in the kingdom of culture, to escape both death and isolation, to husband and use his best powers and his latent genius."

The phrase "you can't see me" is late 1980s, early 1990s, hip-hop lingua franca. It is a statement indicating sophistication or a complicated self that is so far ahead or beyond as to be inaccessible. It is often a false statement, suggestive of a desire to be seen. We posit this desire for visibility is at the core of the hip-hop lyricist. Identity orchestration is a theoretical construct that provides an additional device by which to consider and to responsibly complicate Black men and Black boys beyond stereotype. It is a device by which to more richly see others in the everyday and, in the best of circumstances, affords an opportunity to see one's self and one's relation to others more effectively.

REFERENCES

Abebe, Nitsuh. 2011. "Watch the Throne: Uneasy Heads Wear Gaudy Crowns." *New York*, August 12, 2011.

Anderson, Stacey, Jon Dolan, David Fricke, Will Hermes, Monica Herrera, Jody Rosen, Rob Sheffield, and Simon Vozick-Levinson Kathleen. 2011. "50 Best Albums of 2011." *Rolling Stone*, December 28, 2011.

Baldwin, James. 1985. "If Black English Isn't a Language, Then Tell Me What Is." In *The Price of the Ticket*, edited by James Baldwin, 649–52. New York: St. Martin's/ Marek.

Bourdieu, Pierre. 1986. "The Forms of Capital." In *Handbook of Theory and Research for the Sociology of Education*, edited by John G. Richardson, 241–58. Connecticut: Greenwood.

Caulfield, Keith. 2011. "Jay-Z and Kanye West's 'Watch the Throne' Breaks U.S. iTunes Record." *Billboard*, August 15, 2011.

Charnas, Daniel. 2010. *The Big Payback: The History of the Business of Hip Hop*. New York: New American Library.

Cunningham, Michael. 1999. "African American Adolescent Males' Perceptions of Their Community Resources and Constraints." *Journal of Community Psychology* 27 (5): 569–88.

Du Bois, W. E. B. 1903. *The Souls of Black Folk*. Chicago: A. C. McClurg & Co.

Ellison, Ralph. 1952. *Invisible Man*. New York: Random House.

Franklin, Anderson J. 1999. "Invisibility Syndrome and Racial Identity Development in Psychotherapy and Counseling African American Men." *The Counseling Psychologist* 27 (6): 761–93.

Gordon, Edmund W. 2001. "Affirmative Development of Academic Abilities." *Pedagogical Inquiry and Praxis* (2): 1–4.

———. 2005. "Academic Politicalization: Supplementary Education from Black Resistance." In *Supplementary Education: The Hidden Curriculum of High Academic Achievement*, edited by Edmund W. Gordon, Beatrice L. Bridglall, and Aundra S. Meroe, 88–103. Lanham, MD: Rowman & Littlefield.

Harding, Vincent. 1975. "The Black Wedge in America: Struggle Crisis and Hope, 1955–1975." *Black Scholar* 7 (4): 28–46.

Harrell, Jules P. 1979. "Analyzing Black Coping Styles: A Supplemental Diagnostic System." *Journal of Black Psychology* 5 (2): 99–108.

Jam, Def, Bill Adler, Dan Charnas, Rick Rubin, and Russell Simmons. 2011. *Def Jam: The First 25 Years of the Last Great Label*. New York: Rizzoli.

Jones, James M. 2003. "TRIOS: A Psychological Theory of the African Legacy in American Culture." *Journal of Social Issues* 59 (1): 217–41.

———. 2004. "TRIOS: A Model for Coping with the Universal Context of Racism." In *Racial Identity in Context: The Legacy of Kenneth B. Clark*, edited by Gina Philogène, 161–90. Washington: American Psychological Association.

Knight, Michael M. 2007. *The Five Percenters: Islam, Hip-Hop and the Gods of New York*. Oxford: Oneworld.

Langhorne, Cyrus. 2011. "Rakim Respects Jay-Z's G.O.A.T. Honors, 'I Think It's Only Right.'" SOHH.com, December 10, 2011.

Linville, Patricia W. 1985. "Self-Complexity and Affective Extremity: Don't Put All of Your Eggs in One Cognitive Basket." *Social Cognition* 3 (1): 94–120.

McAdams, Dan P., and Jennifer L. Pals. 2006. "A New Big Five: Fundamental Principles for an Integrative Science of Personality." *American Psychologist* 61 (3): 204–17.

McCrae, Robert R., and Paul T. Costa. 1997. "Personality Trait Structures as a Human Universal." *American Psychologist* 52: 509–16.

Moynihan, Daniel P. 1965. *The Negro Family: The Case for National Action*. Washington, DC: US Department of Labor.

Perry, Imani. 2011. *More Beautiful and More Terrible: The Embrace and Transcendence of Racial Inequality in the United States*. New York: New York University Press.

Rafaeli-Mor, Eshkol, and Jennifer Steinberg. 2002. "Self-Complexity and Well-Being: A Review and Research Synthesis." *Personality and Social Psychology Review* 6 (1): 31–58.

Rice, David Wall. 2008. *Balance: Advancing Identity Theory by Engaging the Black Male Adolescent*. Lanham, MD: Lexington Books.

———. 2009. "Race Self Complexity, Identity Orchestration and Authentic Engagement: Positioning Visibility through Public Narratives." Boston College. Boston, MA. October 23, 2009. Manuscript presented at the Institute for the Study and Promotion of Race and Culture Ninth Annual Diversity Challenge Conference.

Rice, David Wall, Brenda Wall, and William M. Hayes. 2010. "Black Males, 'Church' and Supplementary Education: General Considerations." In *Educating Comprehensively: Varieties of Educational Experiences*, edited by Edmund W. Gordon, Herve H. Varenne, and Linda Lin, 69–93. Lewiston, ME: Edwin Mellen Press.

Robinson, Louie. 1975. "Bad Times on the 'Good Times' Set." *Ebony*, September 1975.

Snyder, Charles R., and Beth L. Dinoff. 1999. "Coping: Where Have You Been?" In *Coping: The Psychology of What Works*, edited by Charles R. Snyder, 3–19. New York: Oxford University Press.

Spencer, Margaret B., Davido Dupree, and Tracey Hartmann. 1997. "A Phenomenological Variant of Ecological Systems Theory (PVEST)." *Development and Psychopathology* 9 (4): 817–33.

Spencer, Margaret B., Michael Cunningham, and Dena P. Swanson. 1995. "Identity as Coping: Adolescent African American Males' Adaptive Responses to High Risk Environments." In *Racial and Ethnic Identity*, edited by Herbert W. Harris, Howard C. Blue, and Ezra H. Griffith, 31–52. New York: Routledge.

Winston, Cynthia E. 2010. "The Theory of Race Self Complexity and Human Personality: Is the Meaning of Race Processed Narratively?" San Diego, CA. August 14, 2010. Manuscript presented at the American Psychological Association 118th Annual Conference.

———. 2011. "Biography and Lifestory." In *Qualitative Research: An Introduction to Designs and Methods*, edited by Stephen D. Lapan, MaryLynn T. Quartaroli, and Frances Julia Riemer, 105–36. Hoboken, NJ: Jossey-Bass.

Winston, Cynthia E., and Michael R. Winston. 2012. "Cultural Psychology and Racial Ideology: An Analytic Approach to Understanding Racialized Societies and Their Psychological Effects on Lives." In *Oxford Handbook of Culture and Psychology*, edited by Jaan Valsiner, 558–81. New York: Oxford University Press.

NOTES

1. Within racialized societies, master narratives of race emerged as a cultural psychological mechanism to "story" dominance, subordination, and equality ideology (Winston and Winston 2012).

2. Imani Perry (2011), in her treatment of the critically acclaimed television drama *The Wire*, provides a succinct explanation of considerations of the show relative to Black men that parallel the dilemma found in the broad narratives of hip-hop. The HBO series and hip-hop en masse both offer "diversity and emotional depth of [their] representations of Black men" (47) and, as a result, also provide "multiple triggers of recognition" (48) that can either challenge biased assumptions or confirm stereotypes, dependent on the general beliefs of the viewer and listener.

3. Ralph Ellison's (1952) archetypal *Invisible Man* persists as a clean illustration of what it can mean to be a Black man—"people refuse to see me" (3)—at least within an American context. Distinguished psychologist Anderson J. Franklin makes even

more real this literary construct, offering "invisibility [as] a psychological experience wherein the person feels that his or her personal identity and ability are undermined by racism in a myriad of interpersonal circumstances" (761).

4. Beyond publicity around album releases, Rakim's image has been most accessible in mainstream outlets through references from other artists to his legacy and/or classic works.

5. Golden age hip-hop was a time of diverse lyricism and production within the genre that extended from approximately the late 1980s through the 1990s.

6. Winston (2011) presents two primary perspectives as a part of race self-complexity. The biopsychological perspective suggests psychological dealing consequences because of attitudes associated with phenotypic variation. The cultural historical perspective posits that unique historical experiences of Black people in the United States give race psychological meaning that is incorporated into cultured patterns of thoughts, feelings, and actions.

7. Eric B. & Rakim. "I Ain't No Joke." *Paid in Full*. 4th & B'Way/Island, 1987. CD.

8. Eric B. & Rakim. "My Melody." *Paid in Full*. 4th & B'Way/Island, 1987. CD.

9. E. T. Gordon (2005) positions respectability and reputation at polar ends of a continuum and at the core of a Black male cultural dilemma. Respectability is largely accommodative in that those who ascribe attend to others' perception of them, particularly the perspectives of those who represent mainstream society. Alternatively, reputation is deeply resistant and oppositional (Gordon 2005). The cultural practice transmutes Anglo practices of masculinity through Black urban expressions toward norms of "cool" and dominance.

10. Bourdieu (1986) via E. W. Gordon (2001) summarizes nine capitals—cultural capital, financial capital, health capital, human capital, institutional capital, pedagogical capital, personal capital, polity capital, and social capital—as spaces of existing or potential strength.

11. Ice Cube. "The Ni—a Ya Love to Hate." *Amerikka's Most Wanted*. Priority, 1990. CD.

12. Jay-Z and Kanye West. "Otis." *Watch the Throne*. Roc-A-Fella, Roc Nation, Def Jam, 2011. CD.

13. You needed Flavor because otherwise Public Enemy could have turned into a sermon. Flav made it funny and cool: "Let me joke with you guys, but really, we teaching you. Let me '*Yeah, boyyyy!*' in the midst of Chuck's 'Elvis was a hero to most.' You needed that" (Jam et al. 2011).

14. Fugees. "Zealots." *The Score*. Ruffhouse/Columbia Records, 1996. CD.

15. Jay-Z and Kanye West. "Murder to Excellence." *Watch the Throne*. Roc-A-Fella, Roc Nation, Def Jam, 2011. CD.

Chapter 3

I Stank I Can, I Know I Can, I Will

Songwriting Self-Efficacy as an Expression of Identity Orchestration

Jacque-Corey Cormier

Self-efficacy is a domain-specific concept in which one's perceived capability to perform a given task impacts one's performance and task-related outcomes. The definition of self-efficacy can be summed up by Walter Piper: "I think I can, I think I can, I know I can, I will"; however, Outkast's Big Boi stated this sentiment in the Dungeon Family's "Trans DF Express" song in a more interesting manner: "I stank I can, I stank I can, I know I can, I will." Big Boi immediately followed this declaration by stating that he is "knockin' players off the field, for real."

Hip-hop has commonly been positioned as a space for artists to speak on their perceived abilities and actual achievements related to their lived experiences. There is a presumption that the hip-hop artist is an individual with a high sense of task self-efficacy related to rapping, songwriting, or the content of their lyrical focus. Generally, if an artist states they are a top-tier performer of a given task, then the listener is supposed to assume that the artist feels a high capability to execute said task. The ubiquitous line "Ain't nobody f—kin' with me" and its many variations has been a statement made in reference to one's songwriting abilities, stardom, social capital, or hypermasculine prowess. Here, we will examine the ways in which identity orchestration relates to hip-hop artists' portrayal of songwriting self-efficacy. Identity orchestration as a process and state will be utilized as the lens by which self-efficacy research and hip-hop lyrics will be discussed.

I was kind of shy about telling people that I could rap for the longest. I never wanted anybody to know that I could even rap. Even when I got to college and I told my best friend I could rap, she'll be like, "OK. Well, then rap." She wanted me to rap and I wouldn't do it. But then we went to a kickback and I just started rapping.—Megan Thee Stallion, 2020

I DO THIS

Those familiar with Walt Piper's book *The Little Engine That Could* have been exposed to the concept of self-efficacy: "I think I can, I know I can, I will." Self-efficacy is the belief in one's ability to engage in a task in a manner that produces one's desired results (Bandura, 1997). For instance, I think I have the ability or skill to engage in task X, I have a cognitive schema and motive to believe I can complete task X, thus I will participate in task X. Afterward, I will reflect on the level of success I achieved for task X and decide to reset my goals and practice behaviors accordingly (Figure 3.1). Outkast's Big Boi stated this sentiment in the Dungeon Family's 2001 "Trans DF Express" song as, "I stank I can, I stank I can, I know I can, I will." Big Boi immediately followed this declaration by stating that he is "knockin' players off the field, for real." Hip-hop has commonly been positioned as a space for artists to speak on their perceived abilities and actual achievements related to their lived experiences.

Tsang, Hui, and Law (2012), in their conceptual review of self-efficacy as a construct, described it as "one's beliefs in one's capability to organize and execute the courses of action required to achieve given results" (p. 1). Kurtuldu and Bulut (2017) have linked task self-efficacy to motivation, which affects task mastery. Zimmerman (2000, as cited by Hewitt, 2015) illustrated how self-efficacy sources led to task self-efficacy, which affected motivation structures. Motivation led to the forethought stage of self-regulation, then to the task performance stage, self-evaluation, and self-reflection. These motivation-driven stages are critical to new goal setting such that the cycle

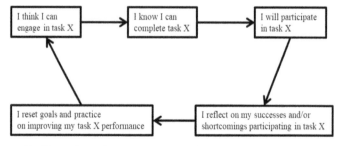

Figure 3.1 Self-efficacy for Task X. Image Created by Jacque-Corey Cormier.

of practice, performance, and evaluation repeat at a higher level than the previous period. Higher levels of self-efficacy have been a protective factor against quitting, for persevering through challenges, and for utilizing more critical thinking skills during tribulations (Zimmerman, 2000; Bandura, 1986; 2006, as cited by Ritchie & Williamon, 2012). "Those with high self-efficacy may choose more complex and risky tasks and set their goals high; and they may work ambitiously to achieve these goals" (Kurtuldu & Bulut, 2017, p. 837). For example, a "bookworm with two left feet" would be a person with high reading self-efficacy and low dance self-efficacy. That bookworm would display more endurance in reading difficult literary works than while learning a complex dance routine.

Self-efficacy initiates action and is a contributor to task outcome variance; nonetheless, it is important to note that perceived self-efficacy is not always an accurate representation or sole predictor of task output and quality. "Self-efficacy does not refer to how effective a person is in performing a particular skill, but to the person's belief in their ability to perform the skill" (Kurtuldu & Bulut, 2017, p. 836). Regarding self-efficacy of music performance, Ritchie and Williamon (2012) stated that "self-efficacy . . . representing beliefs about capabilities, that does not measure actual musical qualities or quantities" (p. 337). Think about the first round of the earliest seasons of *American Idol*. The purpose of the show was to "search for a superstar"; nevertheless, the network would often air the low-quality musical auditions for comedy, such as allowing a person who could not sing well to perform for the judges only to receive harsh criticism. The humor from those televised segments came from the singer's level of confidence being incongruent with their musical ability. Notably, the high perceived self-efficacy, low-quality performers who auditioned for *American Idol* still put themselves in a better position to become the next singing superstar compared to low perceived self-efficacy, high-quality performers who chose not to participate in the contest. In sports terms, one can only score if they shoot their shot; thus, a talented three-point shooter will never score a point if they do not try out for the basketball team.

Knapp and Silva (2019) examined how music-based interventions for underserved, stigmatized groups, such as people facing homelessness or home insecurity, created a space for those people to receive social support, sources of self-esteem, and self-efficacy building opportunities. Compared to people who were not band members, people in the band facing homelessness reported lower recidivism, improved relationships between them and their case managers, increased happiness, and changed perceptions of circumstances. One band member was quoted stating "that [fellow bandmates' encouragement] helped me out enormously ego-wise. You know, because people realized that I was important" (Knapp & Silva, 2019, p. 239). The researchers highlighted another band member's process of self-efficacy building when he stated, "It's kinda rough [at the shelter] to begin with, but I done accepted it now. I can handle it. . . . I like jamming with y'all man" (p. 240). The feedback from fellow bandmates and the affective state of the band members reflect two of the four sources of self-efficacy.

In a comparative study on music self-efficacy beliefs, Hendricks, Smith, and Legutki (2016) defined self-efficacy as "the ability to execute actions necessary to accomplish a particular task" (p. 918). They continued, stating how one's self-efficacy influenced task completion efforts and endurance during challenging obstacles. Two significant predictors of music performance quality were time spent practicing and level of performance anxiety (Kenny, Fortune, & Ackermann, 2009, as cited by Ritchie & Williamon, 2012). Ritchie and Williamon (2012) found that in both of their studies on undergraduate music students' self-efficacy and musical performance, self-efficacy was the only predictor of the students' self-report of performance quality ratings. Note that those findings were based on self-reports and not objective measures of music performance quality. Other researchers have also found music self-efficacy to be directly linked to music performance and that the interactions among self-efficacy building, past success, and skill development influenced self-concept (McCormick & McPherson, 2003; McPherson & McCormick, 2006). Thus, task self-efficacy for identity-associated activities would impact one's willingness to engage in tasks deemed salient to one's identity expression. When introducing the concept of musical identity, Hirschorn (2019) provided a definition for musical self-efficacy as "personal beliefs in one's musical capabilities that we bring into new musical situations" (p. 60). The researcher further went on to conceptualize musical self-efficacy as "a characteristic of an even deeper sense of one's musical self-image" (p. 53). Thus, Hirschorn (2019) asserted how a particular task self-efficacy could shape one's self-image related to a task. For example, a math professor's identity as a mathematician is inherently linked to that professor's perception of math-related abilities.

FREESTYLE OR WRITE DOWN WHATEVER, IT STILL COMES UP CLEVER

Songwriting self-efficacy is one's perceived ability to engage in songwriting and musical performance. Songwriting self-efficacy arguably differs from musical self-efficacy, just as mathematics self-efficacy differs from academic self-efficacy. Crafting lyrics is not the totality of songwriting, as songwriting is the creation of lyrics along with the musical composition and melodic aspects of the song. Musical self-efficacy differs as the term does not include the performers' sense of lyric and melody creation. For comparison, while *American Idol* highlighted musical self-efficacy, the more recent show *Songland* highlights contestants' songwriting self-efficacy as they perform original songs for established artists to decide if they will be chosen to become collaborative music partners with said artists. It is only recently that the term *songwriting self-efficacy* has been utilized in scholarly research, with all four of the references that show on Google Scholar being dissertations (Cooper, 2021; Richardson, 2011; Sigler, 2021; Usherwood, 2015). Most of the research on music-related task self-efficacy and music performance has been conducted in primary or secondary school settings, with instrumentalists, or does not incorporate hip-hop music (Girgin, 2020; Hendricks, Smith, & Legutki, 2016; Hewitt, 2015; Hirschorn, 2019; Kurtuldu & Bulut, 2017; Leung, 2008; Sarikaya & Kurtaslan, 2018). For instance, Hirschorn (2019) examined vocal music and improvisation with classical music as the genre of reference to the participants' music self-efficacy.

Some artists' songwriting process mirrors Wale's pen-to-paper style: "I don't just keep raps in my head or my phone. I write it on the spot." Continuing in his July 2019 interview with *DJBooth*, Wale emphasized locale and familiarity when writing: "Sometimes, I feel like my brain doesn't activate unless I'm in the studio." Jim Jones told *Revolt TV* in May 2019 that during studio sessions he prefers to feed off the energy in the room: "Some nights [in the studio], it could just be me and a couple of people in there. Some nights, it could be the whole gang in there walking in and out. I need to feed off that confusion. I need to feed off people talking. I need to feed off their conversation. I need to feed off their words." In contrast, Lil Wayne famously claimed to stop writing down his lyrics by the early 2000s, rapping in 2008's "Dr. Carter," "But I'm a doctor, they don't understand my writing / So I stopped writing, now I'm like lightning." During an October 2018 guest appearance on *The Jimmy Fallon Show*, Lil Wayne bragged about not writing down his lyrics and thanked Jimmy Fallon's staff for printing out his lyrics for him to perform a song that night. Nicki Minaj told *Hot New Hip-Hop* in August 2018, "I have written a song in my head in the shower. . . . I find it's confining to write in the studio."

Within the context of rapping, *songwriting* could be a bit of a misnomer as some hip-hop artists take pride in not writing down lyrics and instead improvising or freestyling verses. The phrase "off [the top of] the dome" has been utilized by many rappers in their songs and recorded freestyle appearances to illustrate their nonreliance on writing notes. Both approaches to songwriting require songwriting self-efficacy and awareness of the motivation-driven stages toward new goal setting.

LOSE YOURSELF IN THE MUSIC

Bandura (1977; 1997) identified four primary sources of self-efficacy development: mastery experiences, vicarious experiences, verbal/social persuasion (authority-based conviction), and physiological/affective states. Although other factors influence one's sense of task self-efficacy, the four previously listed sources have been linked to music self-efficacy (Schunk, 1991, as cited by Hewitt, 2015). These four sources of self-efficacy can be found in hip-hop artists' narratives and lyrics. Each source of self-efficacy will be supported with content from hip-hop artists.

Direct Experience

When citing Bandura (1977), Ojonugwa and colleagues (2015) referred to direct experience or performance outcomes as "if one has performed well at a task previously, he or she is more likely to feel competent and perform well at a similarly associated task" (p. 26). Ludacris's 2008 track "I Do It for Hip-Hop" featured Jay-Z recalling his experiences with rapping, which led Jay-Z to view music as a viable career path: "I used to rap to impress my friends / To pass the time while I was gettin' it in."

During his verse, Jay-Z mentioned his direct experience of rapping as a pastime. As his skill set for and confidence in songwriting increased, he decided to integrate hip-hop into his career identity and discontinue his illegal actions. As he stated, "I'm so illegal with the pen / They [his peers] ain't want me doin' anything illegal again."

In a January 2020 *Drink Champs* podcast interview, Lil Wayne talked about his early experiences rapping as a member of the Hot Boys group under Cash Money Records: "Being in Hot Boys was perfect, but I looked at it like school. That's a test: 'I'ma go pass the test when I get to that studio; my verse gon' be the hardest.'" When music engineer eMIX discussed working with Megan Thee Stallion on *Revolt TV* in March 2020, he described her as "a lyricist's lyricist and a rapper's rapper." eMIX further commented on the Houston-based rapper's work ethic: "She ain't there to play or waste time. She did [her single] 'Savage' on the spot . . . maybe took an hour. We [the song's producer J. White and Megan Thee Stallion] were building as the song was forming. While he was laying down the snares and the kicks, she was writing to the skeleton of the beat." These are references to how engaging in a task contributes to enactive self-mastery—that is, the experience of success in smaller tasks associated with greater goals.

In Hirschorn's (2019) mixed-method study on musical self-efficacy in vocal performers, the direct experience of engaging in an improvisational musical performance was emphasized by participants as "magical" and "the chance to be free and express myself and my feelings" (p. 58). Direct experience with a task over time through practice and trial and error increases one's self-efficacy. Kendricks, Smith, and Legutki (2016) found that high school orchestra students made comments and references to mastery experience mostly when asked about their increased sense of self-efficacy over time.

Vicarious Experience

It could be assumed that music artists, like most people, grew up listening to some form of music. The vicarious experience of watching or listening to someone rap can encourage others to engage in the activity. Within hip-hop, many artists have expressed an appreciation for collaborating with others as it entices them to work harder and to revise their work multiple times. In a May 2020 session on *Young Money Radio*, Drake said, "In rap there's no score to define a winner or there's no championship game. So, these are the moments of competition that we truly enjoy." When addressing whether the frequent *Young Money* collaborators would create more songs together, Lil Wayne stated in that same May 2020 session, "Me and Drizzy [Drake], songs that we do together, we are both perfectionists. So, it's not like, you send me a joint, I'm going to throw a verse on there. . . . I know this man's about to go crazy on me." Lil Wayne further discussed the legacy of their collaborations and the caliber of music expected from them not only from fans but for themselves as well.

Megan Thee Stallion was introduced to hip-hop music and the industry at an early age as her mother was a rapper in the early 2000s. She said to *Rolling Stone* in February 2020, "Every time she [her mother] put on a new song, [her mom would say] 'Put you on some real s—t right quick." She stated to Rolling Stone in March 2019 that listening to rap legends like the late Pimp C of UGK inspired her to bring a female's perspective to the male-dominated hip-hop industry: "[Songs like UGK's] 'Take It Off' made me feel so confident and cool. . . . I was like, 'If a girl was saying this stuff, this will probably go even crazier!' I feel like I have to put on for my city, because we have so many legends and so many greats. But I don't feel like we ever really had a female rapper come from Houston or Texas and shut s—t down. So that's where I'm coming from with it."

In an interview with the *New York Times* in March 2020, Megan Thee Stallion further highlighted how vicarious rap experiences led to her direct rap experiences: "I watched old DVDs of people in Houston and videos of guys in a circle, rapping, freestyling with each other. Showcases. I was thinking, I have to rap my a—off. Every time I had the opportunity to go somewhere and freestyle, I would do that, because that's what I was looking at."

Hirschorn's (2019) study revealed that the music-major undergraduate participants' peer vicarious experience was one of the strongest predictors of musical self-efficacy along with mastery/direct experience. One participant stated, "A stronger, more confident singer who sets a standard . . . some lead the way, and others follow similarly" (p. 58).

Verbal/Social Persuasion

Verbal/social persuasion, authority-based conviction, is the reinforcement or punishment individuals receive in regard to their task performance. Lupe Fiasco has a song entitled "Hip-Hop You Saved My Life" where he narrates the story of an aspiring rapper in the early beginnings of his potential music career. In the third verse, the protagonist learns that the local radio station played and praised his recorded freestyle: "They [the radio station] played it [his freestyle] two times say it might be crowned / As the best thing out the H-Town in a while."

Lupe illustrated the protagonist's excitement through physical descriptions and his connection with his family: "He picked up his son with a great big smile / Rapped every single word to the newborn child."

The protagonist has a reinvigorated mindset to continue pursuing a rap music career and consequently goes back to work on his craft: "Then he put him [his infant son] down and went back to the kitchen / And put on another beat and got back to the mission."

It is less challenging to put time and effort into skill building, and to be future oriented, after one's spheres of influence reinforce that behavior and mindset. Lupe positioned this verse in a manner that emphasized the importance of community feedback on identity development within hip-hop and arguably Black culture as a whole.

As a source of self-efficacy, being booed off a talent show stage would decrease the likelihood of a person continuing to practice and perform said talent; however, that would depend on one's perception of the audience as authority feedback. For some young, rising artists in the hip-hop industry, the authority-based conviction they have internalized comes from young fans and not as much from "old heads" whose reign, relevance, or nostalgia are based in the pre-2010s hip-hop scene.

Over the past two decades, it has become more commonplace to circumvent traditional music industry gatekeepers and receive direct audience reinforcement and feedback. Many up-and-coming rappers have acknowledged the fact that the internet and social media have changed how artists get fan bases and notoriety. Megan Thee Stallion bluntly told the *New York Times* in March 2020, "The main reason I am where I am today is because of the Internet. . . . My career does really well because of the Internet." Lil Yachty, self-proclaimed "King of the Teens," suggested in a 2016 *The Breakfast Club* interview that he was not concerned with the older stakeholders of hip-hop not liking him as he puts it, "because I'm not lyrical enough. . . . If you ever read comments and click on their profile, they're like super old." Streaming and free music promotion platforms have limited the necessity of record companies and radio station mediation between the artist and the consumer. What better authority to convince one to pursue music as a career than for one to receive revenue and fan recognition from a mixtape or single song?

Physiological/Affective State

Physiological states include but are not limited to one's mood, anxiety, fatigue, and emotional arousal. This source of self-efficacy relates to feelings of anxiety or excitement when performing a task. Big Boi of Outkast in 2000's "Xplosion" explained how one's emotional and physiological states are important to consider when freestyling in rap because "it's kinda hard to execute when you ain't feeling it that day." Eminem detailed the physical state changes that can occur while performing music in his 2002 Academy Award–winning single "Lose Yourself": "His palms are sweaty, knees weak, arms are heavy / There's vomit on his sweater already, mom's spaghetti."

Eminem opened the track with the duality of having sweaty palms and weak knees while still portraying himself as "calm and ready" because it is salient to his identity as a rapper to engage in his career-related task of rapping unbothered by the crowd: "He's nervous, but on the surface he looks calm and ready."

In the next lines, he demonstrated how the anxiety of live performance could manifest as "freezing" on stage or "choking" in front of a crowd: "But he keeps on forgetting what he wrote down, / . . . He opens his mouth, but the words won't come out."

All performers, from musicians and actors to spokespeople and teachers, can experience the daunting, exhilarating, and tranquil feelings of engaging in career-related tasks as a form of self-expression. Ludacris began "I Do It for Hip-Hop" with visual and visceral details on how crafting lyrics and songwriting made him feel: "Heart screams with emotion / It's my daily devotion."

He spoke on why he chose to continue to rap as a commitment to the culture and his community: "I do it for the front row; I do it for the stands / I spit it for the hood; I do it for the block."

For context, when Ludacris raps during the verse "I don't do it for the money," he is likely referring to his past successful albums and his ongoing acting career in movies such as 2005 Best Picture Oscar winner *Crash* and the

Fast & Furious multibillion-dollar movie franchise. Thus, Ludacris wanted to make it clear that he does not rap to pay bills or fuel his lifestyle, but rather "Luda do it cause it's art." One of the participants in Hirschorn's (2019) mixed-method study stated, "When I improvised, I felt amazing . . . the music was playing [and] it just found me. Rhythm was everywhere and I felt free" (p. 58).

RAP IS HERE TO STAY, AND THE SOUTH HAS SOMETHING TO SAY

The level of task dedication needed to persevere through difficult challenges requires an elevated level of task self-efficacy. Joey Bada$$ in October 2013 spoke on Complex TV's *The Process* about adjusting to his then budding rap career: "The only difficult part about it was breaking it down to my mom. I'm trying to go to the studio after school, putting in these hours, find this balance." Megan Thee Stallion expressed to *Rolling Stone* in March 2019 that although she was confident in herself as a person, she was hesitant to rap in public. Furthermore, even her former-rapper mother was not keen on her dropping out of college to pursue a hip-hop career: "I was confident in myself, but I didn't really know how people would react to how I thought about myself on the inside. . . . I went home and told her [mom] I could rap, and she was like, 'No you can't.' I'm like, 'Yes I can.' I started rapping and she was like 'Oh my god! No, you not coming out 'til you're 21!'"

Imagine telling a loved one that you wanted to be a ballerina only to have that person discourage you, stating if you want to be a professional dancer you should choose a more acceptable, respectable dance form. Those words may deter you from pursuing ballet or motivate you to hone your dancing skills; nevertheless, both options respectively contribute to your decreased or increased sense of dance self-efficacy. Aspiring hip-hop artists may be able to relate to the lack of support or negative assumptions others have of them for wanting to pursue a musical career, in particular as a rapper. Being a rapper is like being a ballerina, yet society tells you that performing ballet is not a wise choice even among the various professional dance styles.

Many hip-hop artists have expressed that it is a burden to negotiate their identity as legitimate musicians to the music industry and society. The pressure to be taken seriously as an artist has cultivated some of the best hip-hop artists' music and songwriting self-efficacy to achieve recognition and financial success. During his 2020 acceptance speech for the Industry Icon award at the Pre-Grammy Gala, Sean "Diddy" Combs spoke about discriminatory practices within the music industry, reflecting the oppression experienced by people of color on a societal level: "Black music has never been respected by the Grammys to the point that it should be. So, right now, in this current situation, it's not a revelation. This thing been going on and it's not just going on in music." More contemporary artists such as Drake and Tyler the Creator have expressed similar concerns about systematic biases within the music industry. Although he received two Grammys in 2017 for Best Rap Song and Best Rap/Sung Performance, Drake expressed confusion during his Apple Music *OVO Radio* show about his winning song's nomination: "I am referred to as a Black artist, like last night at [the Grammys], I'm a Black artist. . . . I'm apparently a rapper, even though 'Hotline Bling' is not a rap song. The only category they can manage to fit me in is in a rap category, maybe because I've rapped in the past or because I'm Black. I can't figure out why."

Regarding the album *IGOR*, for which he won the 2020 Grammy for Best Rap Album, Tyler the Creator stated, "It sucks that whenever we—and I mean guys that look like me—do anything that's genre-bending or that's anything they always put it in a rap or urban category. I don't like that 'urban' word— it's just a politically correct way to say the n-word to me. When I hear that, I'm just like why can't we be in pop? Half of me feels like the rap nomination was just a backhanded compliment."

These assertions are consistent with identity orchestration, specifically with the identity dilemma articulation and burden of proof constructs. The lack of respect, confusion, and backhanded compliments these artists highlighted are intertwined with knowledge of a system that devalues Black culture, positioning it as inferior to European culture or standards typical of pop versus rap. Further, many hip-hop artists feel pressured to consistently legitimize their craft to mainstream culture as an art form. For historical context, in 1989, the Thirty-First Grammys awarded its first Best Rap Performance Grammy during an untelevised part of the ceremony. The winners, DJ Jazzy Jeff and Will Smith, boycotted the Grammys when they found out that their win would not be aired. Will Smith called it a "slap in the face." While presenting the Best Rap Performance award at the Grammy preshow, Kool Moe Dee announced, "On behalf of all MCs . . . we express ourselves through rhythm and rhyme. So I think it's time that the whole world knows rap is here to stay."

In a 2017 interview with *Yahoo Music*, the first hip-hop inductee into the Rock and Roll Hall of Fame, Grandmaster Flash (and the Furious Five), talked about how he was honored to be in the company of music legends through his revolutionary use of turntables and how the induction was beneficial for hip-hop: "I thought it wasn't just good for us [himself and the Furious Five]—it was good for the [hip-hop] culture to be recognized. I think by this point in time we should have been recognized; [hip-hop] is not just a ship passing in the night. It was like, 'Now we are solid, we have followings, we matter.' Although we were the youngest of all the other genres, we did have the following that says, 'This is credible.' So to be honored was a groovy thing."

The burden of proof expressed by Grandmaster Flash and Kool Moe Dee is in their acknowledgment that hip-hop is a relatively young genre that nevertheless has staying power within society. Later in the interview, Grandmaster Flash goes on to bring up how some critics were apprehensive about the Rock and Roll Hall of Fame recognizing hip-hop artists. Interestingly enough, Rock and Roll Hall of Fame 2021 inductee Jay-Z expressed similar sentiments during his induction speech: "Growing up, we didn't think we could be inducted into the Rock and Roll Hall of Fame. We were told that hip-hop was a fad. Much like punk rock, it gave us this anti-culture, this subgenre, and there were heroes in it."

Once assumed to be a fringe or trend genre of music, hip-hop has woven itself into twenty-first-century pop culture across the globe due to hip-hop stakeholders and creators' persistence in seeking to be seen and respected.

Unfortunately, various rappers have had to face the challenge of proving their lyrical skills and musical approach as legitimate forms of hip-hop even within the genre. Within the context of the twentieth-century hip-hop landscape, southern rappers were not widely accepted or respected as "real" hip-hop artists. In 1995, Outkast was jeered by the audience while receiving the Source Award for Best New Rap Group. As the crowd, predominantly made up of New York City and West Coast hip-hop stakeholders, booed and ridiculed the southern duo, André 3000 closed their acceptance speech with his now celebrated phrase: "The South has something to say." Rice's (2008) evidence of burden of proof illustrated Outkast's 1995 declaration and many hip-hop artists' sentiments: "We always got to work twice as hard to prove them wrong, you know?" Atlanta native T.I. reminded his listeners in 2006 on his *King* album's first track, "King Back," of his particular influence on the 2000s hip-hop scene: "You need to get familiar with 'Dope Boyz' [single on his first album] and see where all these n—as got they style right now / See where that trap s—t came from."

Like West Coast rappers before them, southern rappers have had to assert their songwriting skills and relevance in relation to the assumption of where "real hip-hop artists" were born and raised. The influence of southern hip-hop culture is now vastly apparent in the twenty-first-century hip-hop landscape, so much so that the southern-originated term *trap music* is commonly used to describe the contemporary rap sound. T.I. continued in "King Back": "You need to go back and grab *I'm Serious* [his first album] you know / . . . Then you need to go to *Trap Muzik* [his second album]."

There are many components of personal and career identities that must be addressed and orchestrated. A hip-hop artist must contend with external forces of devaluation from mainstream culture and internal forces of competition and validation. This is why it is important to consider one's level of songwriting self-efficacy in relation to one's perseverance through tribulations and dedication to practice and songwriting skill building.

I AM A BEAST, FEED ME RAPPERS OR FEED ME BEATS

Defined as "defiance in the face of negotiation," unadulterated presentation of self relates to hip-hop artists' fidelity maintenance in internalizing their craft as a crucial component of personal identity. Lil Wayne began his 2005 *Tha Carter 2* album with "Tha Mobb," a song with no chorus but a plethora of wordplay and worldly references. Among the metaphors and similes are justifications for his musical style and declarations of his supreme status in hip-hop: "I'm awkward like Cartwright . . . / Shot ugly, but my arch right." Lil Wayne utilized his knowledge of basketball to compare his form and style to NBA three-time champion Bill Cartwright's shooting form. Although Cartwright's free-throwing form was unorthodox and "awkward," he ended his fifteen-year career with a 0.77 free throw percentage average. Music artists constantly have to negotiate how they approach their craft with the expectations and norms of their genre and the music scene overall. The line "Shot ugly, but my arch right" provides a visual metaphor of Lil Wayne internalizing that though he may not be a prototypical lyricist, he can still effectively perform at the level of his colleagues. This awareness of his identity as a hip-hop artist is similar to Cartwright acknowledging his unconventional approach to his free throw shooting technique.

In his 2008 song "Mr. Carter" featuring Jay-Z, Lil Wayne concluded the track asserting that he is lyrically of the same caliber as other hip-hop legends and should be respected as such: "And the next time you mention Pac, Biggie, or Jay-Z / Don't forget Weezy Baby [Lil Wayne]."

Tupac and Biggie Smalls are revered so much in hip-hop culture that newer rappers have received pushback for their flippant disregard of the pair's cultural impact and musical ingenuity. In August 2016, during a *Billboard* interview, Lil Yachty was quoted saying that he "honestly couldn't name five songs" by either Tupac or Biggie. He also stated in an interview with *Tidal* that same year that his music is "just fun, it's not serious. I hate serious rap. It's boring. Serious rap music puts me to sleep." When referring to "serious rap," the then nineteen-year-old rapper cited J. Cole's songwriting as an example. In March 2018, Lil Xan had to clear up his comment about how Tupac's music is boring and giving his music a low rating while interviewing with *Revolt TV*. These young men, of course entitled to their opinions, likely did not grow up listening to 1990s hip-hop music and most likely were introduced to hip-hop music in the 2000s. Lil Yachty and Lil

Xan's honest interview responses are these newer rappers' demonstration of fidelity and uncompromised stances. These rappers did not compromise how they expressed their musical identity and did not respond to interview questions on hip-hop history, craftsmanship, and preferences with pandering clichéd answers.

Unadulterated presentation of self is present in the "old heads" (pre-2010s hip-hop stakeholders) and the "new wave" of artists; nonetheless, many felt that newer hip-hop artists were dismissing those icons' contribution to the culture. Many hip-hop fans and some artists openly expressed their disappointment in both young men, with Waka Flocka receiving over one hundred thousand likes for a 2018 tweet calling to ban Lil Xan from hip-hop. In subsequent online posts, Waka Flocka explained that Tupac's music helped him "get thru childhood" and that it is problematic not to respect the "man that paved the way for all of us literally." The legacy of a hip-hop artist is salient to their identity and metaperception, as illustrated by Waka Flocka's following line in the same tweet: "I hope nobody overlook me [my] accomplishments when I leave." Lil Wayne's line in 2005's "Tha Mobb"—"I'm already a legend if I ever leave"—and his previously referenced closing lines in 2008's "Mr. Carter" match Waka Flocka's sentiments of wanting to be recognized and remembered for being proficient in the task that contributes to his identity.

Other artists have similarly recognized the role that hip-hop music and its potential career path has had on their lives. Jay-Z paid homage to hip-hop legends in Ludacris's "I Do It for Hip-Hop," implying that hip-hop literally saved his life. These sentiments further illustrate these artists' respect and knowledge of the culture that cultivated hip-hop: "Without your [Kool Herc] s—t I probably would've got murked / Shout out to Grandmaster Flash and to Caz."

Unadulterated presentation of self and acute identity expression are similar concepts as they are both about visibility within the broader context of oppression(s) compromising visibility. The critical difference between these constructs toward visibility is that while unadulterated presentation of self is rooted in a central identity marker or concept of self, acute identity expression leans more into one's conspicuous embellishment of strengths or weaknesses. A crude example: an unadulterated presentation of self would be one wearing braids or dreadlocks as a representation of their connection to their cultural roots. At the same time, an example of acute identity expression would be color dyeing those braids or dreadlocks to distinguish oneself from one's contemporaries. Think about T. I., Kendrick Lamar, J. Cole, and Jay-Z brandishing longer hairstyles compared to when they first started their careers. Now consider Lil Uzi Vert, Lil Pump, and the late Xxxtentacion incorporating color into their already long hairstyles for visibility and image branding.

This image branding is deliberate, as Lil Yachty pointed out in a May 2018 interview with *The Guardian*: "You've got to be like a cartoon character, you've got to be memorable. You see him and you know. SpongeBob wears a button-up shirt with a tie and brown pants. He opens his closet, he got the same thing."

The concept of acute identity expression emerged out of the examination of hypermasculine and hypervulnerable expressions of self. Tupac's line, "I ain't a killer but don't push me," in his 1996 song *"Hail Mary"* has been quoted repeatedly by other rappers and within pop culture to represent one's duality between not wishing to perpetuate violence but still being willing to do what is deemed necessary for survival. The hook on 8-Ball and MJG's 2004 single "Don't Make Me" is an example of acute identity expression of hypermasculinity with less vulnerability than Tupac expressed: "Don't make me kill, no mother—kin' body in here / . . . Somebody done made me hot."

That same year and album featured another one of the duo's singles, "You Don't Want Drama," highlighting a similar form of hypermasculinity minus Tupac's apprehension: "Lay it down, please remember, games we don't play them now / Disrespect, please remember, [blood] stains we gon' spray them round."

Regarding acute identity expression's relation to songwriting self-efficacy, some hip-hop artists purposefully tie their sense of lyrical prowess to their masculinity, thus linking their career/professional identity, musician, to their manhood. Previous researchers have studied the linkage between a man's career decisions and masculinity across multiple cultures and contexts, from primary school students' career interests and college major selection to job insecurity and coping with job loss (Akosah-Twumasi et al., 2018; Buschmeyer & Lengersdorf, 2016; Kågesten et al., 2016; Kluczyńska, 2017; Twomey & Meadus, 2016; Yi & Keogh, 2016). During diss tracks against fellow artists, many rappers have cited their opponents' lack of songwriting talent, financial gain, and/or notoriety as reasons for discounting competing artists. The Game's 2005 "300 Bars & Runnin'" song is over fourteen minutes long and one of his many diss tracks against 50 Cent and G-Unit. The Game had conflict with G-Unit members and attacked all of their personal and songwriting integrity: "B—h a—n—a [Lloyd Banks] need a rhyme dictionary, to rehearse his lines / . . . He [Lloyd Banks] got stuck, he called 50 [Cent], tried to borrow some lines."

The Game attacked 50 Cent, the founder of G-Unit Records, on a personal level, referring to his father and chosen rap moniker, which is based on the Bronx criminal Kelvin "50 Cent" Martin. "Then you lied about your pops, he ain't never bust no cap / . . . You ain't 50 Cent, he went out like a gangsta."

In July 2015, Meek Mill called out Drake, claiming he used a ghostwriter with the tweet, "He [Drake] don't write his own raps! . . . If you gonna be the mother—kin' greatest of this s—t just make sure you're doing your mother—kin' pen game, and keep it all the way a mother—kin' hundred." By hip-hop policy, Drake was compelled to address the accusation. Lupe Fiasco weighed in on the 2015 beef, discussing the living nature of hip-hop: "Meek Mill struck a nerve accusing Drake of having a ghostwriter and the entire rap world reacted on all sides of the fence because rap is alive. It's active and it feels. Its rules and traditions are vibrant and responsive."

Drake rapidly responded with two diss tracks against Meek Mill. In the second diss track, "Back to Back," Drake attacked Meek Mill's relationship power dynamics (then with Nicki Minaj) while simultaneously defending his own songwriting self-efficacy with self-awareness of his lack of gangster persona: "Is that a world tour or your girl's [Nicki Minaj's] tour? / . . . This ain't what she meant when she told you to open up more."

As a unique display of acute identity expression, Drake doubles down on both of their rap personas; Meek Mill comes off in his singles as a hardened "gangster," while Drake's singles typically position him as an emotional ladies' man (see his 2021 album entitled *Certified Lover Boy*): "Yeah, [Meek Mill's] trigger fingers turned to Twitter fingers / Yeah, you gettin' bodied by a singin' n—a."

Thus, Drake was attacking Meek Mill with pervasive notions of hypermasculinity through (1) Meek Mill's female companion being more successful than him, (2) Meek Mill's switch from physical to passive-aggressive behaviors, and (3) Meek Mill being outperformed in a task (rapping) that figures in his primary identity by someone, Drake, who associates that task with a secondary or tertiary identity.

A hip-hop artist's domination in the industry and on a record is a crucial element of lyrical bragging. It is difficult to convince an audience that one is the "hottest in the game" or "one of the greats" if one does not display lyrical skills or have chart-topping songs or albums. Jay-Z's 2003 *Black Album* included several songs in which he reflected on his legacy in hip-hop as not only a lyricist but also an award-winning artist. In "Dirt Off Your Shoulder," Jay-Z introduced the track with the decree, "You're now tuned into the mother—kin' greatest, Jigga! [Jay-Z]" and concluded the track with the phrase, "Best rapper alive." At the time, Jay-Z's lines may have come off as typical braggadocios raps; however, his self-proclamation was based on his perceived songwriting self-efficacy, tangible rewards earned from his musical efforts, and the feedback received from critics and fans alike. His "Encore" track is a matter-of-fact declaration that he has consistently shown that he was the best of his time, "with no pen, just draw off inspiration," and that usurping him would be difficult: "Who you gon' find doper than him? / . . . Soon you gonna see you can't replace him."

In 2017, Jay-Z became the first hip-hop artist to be inducted into the Songwriters Hall of Fame. Hip-hop legend Rakim said in regard to Jay-Z's induction, "For the last 20 years, Jay-Z has personified not only our hip-hop culture, but the definition of true lyricism. He remains a prolific MC getting my respect both in the booth and the boardroom."

OKAY, WELL THEN RAP

I was off-beat like a mother—ker. I had to learn to find a rhythm. The person who told me to keep rapping was [DJ] Clark Kent. I went with Cam[ron] to Hot 97. This was when [DJ Funk] Flex was doing freestyles back in the day. This was when we signed to Un Entertainment and Cam brought me up there to rap. Un [Lance Rivera] and them were mad, "Oh, you can't have that n—a rap." Clark Kent was like, "F—k them n—as, bro. You were hot. Listen . . . you need to keep rapping, Mr. Jim Jones."—Jim Jones, 2019

As direct experience is a primary source of self-efficacy development, the following section provides songwriting practice. This exercise does not aim to raise you to the status of musical legend or awardee. Please fill in the following blank spaces with your choice of words given the prompts provided. The outline of the four bars (lines) are excerpts from Rob Base and DJ E-Z Rock's 1988 hit single "It Takes Two."

I wanna _____ right now
(verb)
I'm _____ and I came to get down
(your name or rap moniker)
I'm not internationally known, but I'm known to _____

_____
(phrase with an ending that rhymes with "known" or "down")

Now practice rapping the completed four bars aloud. Listen to the original song for inspiration on the flow of words and utilize the "It Takes Two" instrumental track for tempo assistance. No matter how the completed prompt sounded when you rapped it, know that it was a great attempt, so good job!

Next, complete the following blank spaces with phrases in which the last word of each bar rhymes with one of the last words of another bar. Your last word will be the basis for the rhyme scheme. There are multiple ways to rhyme the last words of bars, so utilize the "A, B" letters for context. For novice MCs, one could use an "ABAB" or "AABB" rhyme scheme (the "It Takes Two" prompt is an AABB rhyme scheme). For more advanced MCs, consider incorporating internal rhymes as well.

(A)

(A/B)

(A/B)

(B)
_____

Now practice rapping the completed four bars aloud along with the previous four bars you created from the "It Takes Two" prompt. Congratulations, you can proudly claim to know how to "spit fire bars"!

Reflect on your experience completing this exercise and consider the following:

1. How did it feel, physically and emotionally, to create and rap these lyrics aloud?
2. Do you feel comfortable with your ability to perform this rap to a loved one, friend, or even a stranger?
3. Would you agree that you have the ability to build your songwriting skill with more time and practice?
4. Do you have a greater appreciation for the art of creating lyrics and rapping?
5. Do you now feel comfortable identifying yourself as a rapper if you did not already?

For many readers, this activity may seem too easy or, by contrast, too difficult to complete; nonetheless, this direct experience with the art of rapping is a source of songwriting self-efficacy. While the first three questions for consideration allude to the physiological/affective states and positive feedback sources of songwriting self-efficacy, the last two questions relate to the potential integration of the hip-hop artist identity.

Whatever you felt or experienced during this songwriting self-efficacy exercise is akin to the nervousness, excitement, confidence, and doubt that all music artists have felt at one point in time during their career. Perceived task self-efficacy is related to one's perseverance through task-related challenges and tribulations; thus, engaging in skill-building activities, self-reflection, and goal setting are protective factors against quitting a task. Whether you decide to take on the hip-hop artist identity or another skill-related identity, know that your mindset during training and setbacks is a greater predictor of your future success than your current task performance.

When you think you can succeed, you will eventually know that you can succeed, so you will succeed.

REFERENCES

Akosah-Twumasi, P., Emeto, T. I., Lindsay, D., Tsey, K., & Malau-Aduli, B. S. (2018). A systematic review of factors that influence youths career choices—the role of culture. *Frontiers in Education, 3*(58), 1–15.

Bandura, A. (1977). Self-efficacy: Toward a unifying theory of behavioral change. *Psychological Review, 84*(2), 191–215.

Bandura, A. (1986). The explanatory and predictive scope of self-efficacy theory. *Journal of Social and Clinical Psychology, 4*(3), 359–373.

Bandura, A. (1997). The anatomy of stages of change. *American Journal of Health Promotion: AJHP, 12*(1), 8–10.

Bandura, A. (2006). Guide for constructing self-efficacy scales. *Self-Efficacy Beliefs of Adolescents, 5*(1), 307–337.

Buschmeyer, A., & Lengersdorf, D. (2016). The differentiation of masculinity as a challenge for the concept of hegemonic masculinity. *NORMA International Journal for Masculinity Studies, 11*(3), 190–207.

Cooper, P. K. (2021). *Development and validation of a scale to measure songwriting self-efficacy (SSES) with secondary music students* (Doctoral dissertation, University of South Florida).

Girgin, D. (2020). Motivation, self-efficacy and attitude as predictors of burnout in musical instrument education in fine arts high schools. *Eurasian Journal of Educational Research, 85*, 93–108.

Hendricks, K. S., Smith, T. D., & Legutki, A. R. (2016). Competitive comparison in music: Influences upon self-efficacy beliefs by gender. *Gender and Education, 28*(7), 918–934.

Hewitt, M. P. (2015). Self-efficacy, self-evaluation, and music performance of secondary-level band students. *Journal of Research in Music Education, 63*(3), 298–313.

Hirschorn, D. N. (2019). Vocal improvisation and the development of musical self-efficacy and musical self-image in adolescent choral musicians. *The Choral Journal, 60*(5), 53–61.

Kågesten, A., Gibbs, S., Blum, R. W., Moreau, C., Chandra-Mouli, V., Herbert, A., & Amin, A. (2016). Understanding factors that shape gender attitudes in early adolescence globally: A mixed-methods systematic review. *PloS One, 11*(6), e0157805.

Kenny, D. T., Fortune, J., & Ackermann, B. (2009, December). What predicts performance excellence in tertiary level music students. In *Proceedings of the International Symposium on Performance Science*, 487–492.

Kluczyńska, U. (2017). Motives for choosing and resigning from nursing by men and the definition of masculinity: A qualitative study. *Journal of Advanced Nursing, 73*(6), 1366–1376.

Knapp, D. H., & Silva, C. (2019). The Shelter Band: Homelessness, social support and self-esteem in a community music partnership. *International Journal of Community Music, 12*(2), 229–247.

Kurtuldu, M. K., & Bulut, D. (2017). Development of a self-efficacy scale toward piano lessons. *Educational Sciences: Theory and Practice, 17*(3), 835–857.

Leung, B. W. (2008). Factors affecting the motivation of Hong Kong primary school students in composing music. *International Journal of Music Education, 26*(1), 47–62.

McCormick, J., & McPherson, G. (2003). The role of self-efficacy in a musical performance examination: An exploratory structural equation analysis. *Psychology of Music, 31*(1), 37–51.

McPherson, G. E., & McCormick, J. (2006). Self-efficacy and music performance. *Psychology of Music, 34*(3), 322–336.

Ojonugwa, O. I., Hamzah, R., Bakar, A. R., & Rashid, A. M. (2015). Evaluating self-efficacy expected of polytechnic engineering students as a measure of employability. *International Journal of Education and Literacy Studies, 3*(3), 24–30.

Rice, D. W. (2008). *Balance: Advancing identity theory by engaging the Black male adolescent.* Lexington Books.

Richardson, T. G. (2011). *The impact of training on music therapists' songwriting knowledge, self-efficacy, and behavior* (Doctoral dissertation, Indiana State University).

Ritchie, L., & Williamon, A. (2012). Self-efficacy as a predictor of musical performance quality. *Psychology of Aesthetics, Creativity, and the Arts, 6*(4), 334–340.

Sarikaya, M., & Kurtaslan, Z. (2018). Prediction of musical performance anxiety according to music teacher candidates' perfectionism and self-efficacy beliefs. *International Online Journal of Educational Sciences, 10*(4), 183–198.

Schunk, D. H. (1991). Self-efficacy and academic motivation. *Educational Psychologist, 26*(3–4), 207–231.

Sigler, S. Z. (2021). *A survey of literature on entrepreneurial experiences for classical musicians: Implications for training pianists* (Doctoral dissertation, The Ohio State University).

Tsang, S. K., Hui, E. K., & Law, B. (2012). Self-efficacy as a positive youth development construct: A conceptual review. *The Scientific World Journal, 2012.*

Twomey, J. C., & Meadus, R. (2016). Men nurses in Atlantic Canada: Career choice, barriers, and satisfaction. *The Journal of Men's Studies, 24*(1), 78–88.

Usherwood, J. (2015). *Music business and entrepreneurship: A graduate level course for performance students* (Doctoral dissertation, Indiana University).

Yi, M., & Keogh, B. (2016). What motivates men to choose nursing as a profession? A systematic review of qualitative studies. *Contemporary Nurse, 52*(1), 95–105.

Zimmerman, B. J. (2000). Self-efficacy: An essential motive to learn. *Contemporary Educational Psychology, 25*(1), 82–91.

PART II

Self-Complexity

Chapter 4

The Theory of Race Self-Complexity and Narrative Personality

Is the Meaning of Race Processed Narratively?

Cynthia Winston-Proctor

In racialized societies, race is part of a meaning-making system that extends reciprocally from the microecology of the individual to the macro contexts of social, economic, and political institutions. As interest in studying racial and ethnic diversity grows in the field of psychology in the United States and throughout the world, it is a critical time for psychological science to expand its engagement in rigorous, systematic, and collaborative race theory development. Such theory development should capture the complexities of the meaning of race in the lives of people whose narrative identity and personality develop in racialized societies.

Race self-complexity is a new personality theory that is the first to integrate narrative theories of personality with those of the psychological significance of race. Using autobiographical memories, this theory describes the narrative processing and autobiographical reasoning people engage in to understand the meaning of race in their lives and in racialized societies. In this theory, race is conceptualized as a scientifically invalid biological concept but one that has cultural-historical meaning in racialized societies. The key distinction is between what race "is" objectively and what race "means" in different cultures, periods of history, and lives.

The goals of this chapter are to identify key theoretical questions and challenges to be addressed by any narrative personality theory of race and to present a formulation of the theory of race self-complexity in terms of how it meets some of these challenges and guides future inquiry.

> I was fourteen years old, playing varsity soccer. Our team was very good; we were district champions. We were playing in a game against one of our rivals, Sherwood High School. It was cold and wet, not a very good night for soccer. I kept getting fouled in the game; the other team was brutal. I remember being kicked in the stomach too. There were only three black kids on our team, two of which started, me and a senior. After one bad foul, where I was elbowed in the back of my head, the coach from Sherwood said that I was diving like a monkey. He said it out loud to the referee. The referee did nothing but caution the coach. Is it a coincidence that Black people are often referred to as monkeys? Sherwood always gave some kind of trouble. They had the loudest, rowdiest fans. It was crazy being on the field. After a little longer, I went over to the sideline to play an outside position and fans started throwing bananas. There must have been like five or six peels on the ground. The fans started jeering me and making monkey sounds as well. It was electrifying; I wanted to beat Sherwood even more. I was motivated. I refused to let their ignorance and bigotry take me down. This was the first time I experienced racism on that level ever in soccer, and nobody saw it as racism on my team, they just thought that Sherwood was being rude to the only two Blacks on my team, as well as the rest of my team. Really everyone was getting joked, they just left the monkey jokes for me and Denise. Since that incident, I joined a group named Stand up, Speak Up. It is a group that promotes the stopping of racism in soccer.—Regina, earliest autobiographical memory of race

Race has meaning in the lives of people living in racialized societies. How does a person make sense of race? What are individuals' adaptive capacity for making sense of internal and external racialized symbols, images, and discourses? How is the meaning of race processed and incorporated into human personality development? In the field of psychology, studying race poses many conceptual, analytical, and methodological challenges (see Winston-Proctor & Winston, 2021). It is widely recognized in psychological science that there is no scientific validity to the concept of biologically distinct races. And yet, the use of the concept of race remains a common practice in developmental, personality, and social psychological research. Moreover, in everyday practices of living, the ideological use of the concept of race persists. A wave of national debates has illuminated the need for a much more complex and culturally and historically grounded analysis of the meaning of race. These racialized debates include but are not limited to those about education, public health, policing, immigration law, voting rights, and interpretation of the multiple races categories of the US Census Bureau. Taken together, these theoretical and practical realities highlight the important role of psychological science in informing complex analyses of the meaning of race in the cultures of racialized societies.

In this chapter, I present a formulation of the theory of race self-complexity, a new narrative personality theory that accounts for both systems (i.e., social, political, and economic institutions) and interindividual personality-level variables in describing the narrative processing of race in people's lives. In the theory of race self-complexity, race is conceptualized as a scientifically invalid biological concept but one that has cultural historical meaning within racialized societies. The key distinction is between what race "is" objectively and what race "means" in different cultures, periods of history, and lives (Winston & Winston, 2012).

In the theory of race self-complexity, the theoretical conceptualization of narrative personality is as follows: Narrative personality is a person's interpretive system for the narrative processing of lived experiences that unfolds across time, place, and energy with the cultural motion of the larger society in which the person's personality develops. The interplay of cognitive, affective, motivational, and neurobiological psychological systems propel and constrain a person's autobiographical reasoning levers as "their" narrative personality evolves. The individual's psychology necessarily involves emphasis on the whole person as curator of the meaning of life experiences that are dynamically arranged in the symbolic systems of culture and constitutive of culture (see Bruner, 1990). Narrative personality is a layer of a person's personality that intersects with dispositional traits and personality characteristic adaptations (e.g., motivation and personal goals, emotional intelligence, coping style). Autobiographical memory, life story, and narrative identity theoretical concepts have been developed by psychologists who work within and across a wide array of areas in the field of psychology (e.g., personality, developmental, cognitive, social, neuroscience). This work serves as fundamental to the theoretical conceptualization of narrative personality that is being offered in this psychobiography. Among these are the following concepts: the life story model/theory of identity (e.g., McAdams, 1985; Singer, 2005); narrative identity (e.g., Singer, 2004; McLean & McAdams, 2013; McLean et al., 2020); the cultural psychology of identity (Hammack, 2008; McLean et al., 2018; Winston & Winston, 2012); and self-defining memories, autobiographical memories, narrative processing, and autobiographical reasoning (e.g., Singer, 2004; Singer, 2005; Singer & Bluck, 2001; Conway & Pleydell-Pearce, 2000; Conway, Singer, & Tagini, 2004).

The theory of race self-complexity makes several contributions to the field of psychology generally and race theorizing specifically. Its storied theoretical perspective provides a heuristic for psychologists to use in both research and practice to elicit, interpret, and analyze the meaning of persons' lived experiences of race. It also creates an integration of two classes of theories, narrative theories of personality and psychological significance of race theories, which have not been conceptually integrated in either personality or race theorizing. Thus, the theory of race self-complexity provides an opportunity to guide future theory and empirical research. Most importantly, the theory provides future inquiry a process-centered conceptualization of the importance in personality research of aiming to describe and explain people's adaptive capacity to meet the demands of environmental presses of living within the culture of a racialized society. The theory of race self-complexity also allows for comparative research across different cultures and racialized societies, because it is not specific to any particular racial group. Instead, the theory focuses on core personality processes that are grounded in human nature concepts while also specifying elements of racial ideology, systems, and interindividual dimensions within the cultural-historical context of different types of racialized societies. In a nutshell, the theory of race self-complexity aims to describe the interplay of the neurobiological, affective, cognitive, and motivational systems engaged in the narrative processing and autobiographical reasoning of the meaning of race in the narrative personality development of individuals who live in a racialized society.

The goals of this chapter are twofold. First, I identify key theoretical questions and challenges to be addressed by any narrative personality theory of race. Second, I present a formulation of the theory of race self-complexity and describe how it meets some of these challenges as well as guides future inquiry.

NARRATIVE PERSONALITY RACE THEORY: KEY THEORETICAL QUESTIONS AND CHALLENGES

Contemporary personality psychology is an exciting subfield of psychology, with a complexity and variation of theoretical perspectives (see McAdams & Pals, 2006), levels of personality analysis, and vast methodologies (Robins, Fraley, & Krueger, 2007) to study the whole person. Winston-Proctor (in press) conceptualizes personality as a person's psychological individuality that unfolds as a behavioral pattern of dispositional traits, adaptive personality characteristics, and narrative identity complexly situated within culture, circumstance, and society. This theoretical conceptualization refines McAdams and Pals's (2006) conceptualization that has informed the evolution of the theory of race self-complexity in the Identity and Success Research Laboratory since its founding. They conceived personality as "an individual's unique variation on the general evolutionary design for human nature, expressed as a developing pattern of dispositional traits, characteristic adaptations, and self-defining life narratives, complexly and differentially situated in culture and social context" (McAdams & Pals, 2006, p. 204).

Given the wealth of knowledge about human personality and the multiple levels of analysis of a person, I have identified key issues that need to be addressed by any narrative personality race theory: (1) How is the concept of race defined? (2) Does the theory allow for human nature, individual differences, and human uniqueness levels of personality analysis? (3) Is theoretical consideration given to the complexities of the person as an active and goal-oriented organism developing within the opportunities and constraints of the culture of living in a racialized environment? These key ideas should also be addressed by theories that seek to describe or explain the personality development of individuals who live in the culture of racialized societies.

THEORETICAL CONCEPTUALIZATION CLARITY: HOW IS THE CONCEPT OF RACE DEFINED?

Any effective narrative personality race theory needs to include a definition of race. Such a definition needs to consider the cultural-historical evolution of the concept, use, and lived experience of race (see Winston & Winston, 2012; Winston-Proctor & Winston, 2021). It also needs to clarify how the definition reconciles the most recent research after the sequencing of the human genome that confirmed scientifically that there is no existence of biologically distinct races and that humans are 99.9 percent the same genetically (Bonham, Warshauer-Baker, & Collins, 2005).

Defining race is also particularly important in a narrative personality race theory because of the strong arguments that have been made about the imperative for the field of psychology to consider transforming the use and conceptualization of race. Helms, Jernigan, and Mascher (2005) argue that racial categories should be replaced as explanatory constructs in psychological research and theory. Based on analysis of historical, theoretical, and empirical factors, Teo (2009) argues that it is important to eliminate the term *Caucasian* as a category of race because it is obsolete. Cole (2009) argues for the need for psychologists to consider the meaning of race simultaneously with gender as they often conjointly depend on one another for meaning in persons' lives.

In the theory of race self-complexity, race is defined as a cultural-historical lived experience for persons living in the culture of racialized societies. At the level of the individual, race is primarily psychological in nature. It relies heavily on racialized phenotypic characteristics as "first sight markers" that have come to hold individual, systemic, and symbolic meaning. This can be defined as a biopsychological perspective of race in that there is a biological process in which melanosomes inside cells, called the melanocytes, produce melanin in the skin (see Winston et al., 2004). This in turn produces a wide spectrum of skin color among human beings, with individuals of African descent having the largest range of skin tone variation among human populations (Winston & Kittles, 2005). From a cultural-historical perspective, skin color has been the most common marker of racial group membership associated with psychological interindividual-and systems-level meaning across different historical periods and types of racialized societies (see Winston & Winston, 2012).

Beyond the interindividual level of personality, racial ideology influences the structural arrangement at the macro level of systems within racialized societies in the form of economic, social, and political institutions (Winston & Winston, 2012). One of the dynamics of the structural nature of race is that, culturally and historically, individual opportunities have been most typically structured within the culture of racialized societies by racial group membership. For example, in American culture the opportunity for excellence and equity in education has on the whole, with very few exceptions, systematically varied by racial group membership across history (Ladsen-Billings & Tate, 1995). Here racial group membership is conceptualized in terms of the racial categories that are recognized within the particular racialized society in which a person lives. In the United States, for example, these racial groups could be considered in terms of those used by the US Census. In 2020, the US Census was revised include a two question format to capture the races and ethnicity of the US population, which followed standards of the US Office of Management and Budget established in 1997. Thus, the Census measurement permits a people to choose to report "more then one race group. And people of any race may be of any ethnic origin" https://www.census.gov/topics/population/race.html.

*Mark one or more boxes **AND** print origins.*

1. White—*Print, for example, German, Irish, English, Italian, Lebanese, Egyptian, etc.* _____
2. Black or African American—*Print, for example, African American, Jamaican, Haitian, Nigerian, Ethiopian, Somali, etc.* _____
3. American Indian or Alaska Native—*Print name of enrolled or principal tribe(s), for example, Navajo Nation, Blackfeet Tribe, Mayan, Aztec, Native Village of Barrow Inupiat Traditional Government, Nome Eskimo Community, etc.* _____
   ____   Chinese
   ____   Filipino
   ____   Asian Indian

___   Vietnamese
___   Korean
___   Japanese
___   Other Asian—*Print, for example, Pakistani, Cambodian, Hmong, etc.* _____
___   Native Hawaiian
___   Samoan
___   Chamorro
___   Other Pacific Islander—*Print, for example, Tongan, Fijian, Marshallese, etc.* _____
___   Some other race—*Print race or origin.* _____

There are some important nuances of the interindividual and systems dynamics related to government-imposed racial group classifications and lived experiences. The US Census does not recognize Latino/a as a racial group but rather as an ethnicity. However, using a cultural-historical definition of race that centers on a psychological lived experience, Latinos/as of various ethnicities, because of skin color and language, typically have a racialized lived experience that is similar to that of other recognized racial groups with a history of oppression and domination in the culture of a racialized society.

Of course, at another level of complexity is the question of how the individual self-identifies with a specific racial group or not, irrespective of ancestry or phenotypic characteristics. Individuals who have parents who are from two different racial groups provide the most obvious example of complications in racial self-identification, though monoracial individuals may also have similar challenges given the overlap and distinctions between racial and ethnic group membership and associated lived experiences. The multiracial identity suppression theory is a new race self-complexity theory that has been developed to describe the multiracial lived experience in which the process of racial self-identification is complicated by presses for suppression of identification with one racial group over another (Terry, 2008; Terry, 2010; Terry & Winston, 2010).

The importance and complexity of defining race in any narrative personality race theory is further complicated by the distinctions and overlaps of the concept and lived experience of ethnicity in the more "fixed" categories of race. In the US, individuals who are Chinese, Japanese, and Vietnamese, for example, are considered Asian by official federal government racial classifications. And yet, as Philip (2007) highlights, these individuals may have lived experiences that are not only specific to their racial group membership, like interdependence and collectivism, but also distinguish their lived experience among other Asians based on their specific ethnic group membership. Similarly, Black is a racial group membership recognized in the United States, but many who belong to this racial group have lived experiences associated with their ethnic group membership as Trinidadian, Jamaican, or South African, for example. Interestingly, new biotechnology coupled with pioneering data collection of DNA from samples in present-day African countries has provided an unprecedented opportunity. More specifically, these advances have enabled individuals who self-identify as African American, Black, and/or multiracial to use their DNA to trace their African ancestry to specific countries and ethnic groups in Africa (see www.africanancestry.com; Winston & Kittles, 2005). This further expands and complicates the meaning, lived experiences, and definitions of race as well as racial group membership.

The theory of race self-complexity addresses some of these challenges, offering clarity about the definition of race and emphasizing narrative personality development in the culture of a racialized society. To some extent, this conceptual emphasis guides the work of other scholars, particularly those who study racial and ethnic identity specifically. Yet, often the concept of race itself is not explicitly defined in this scholarship, much in the same way it is not in most psychological research (Winston-Proctor & Winston, 2020).

With an explicit emphasis on the lived experience, cultural-historical context, and matrix of dynamics in a racialized society, the definition of race in the theory of race self-complexity provides a common language for scholars, practitioners, and laypersons. Hopefully, this will mobilize all of these human actors to move from a simple, often genetically based conceptualization to a more complicated psychological one grounded in culture and lived experience. This, in turn, may lead to questions, strategies of inquiry, and analysis that penetrates more deeply toward understanding the meaning of persons living race in a racialized society and its effect on the personality development of the whole person.

HUMAN INDIVIDUALITY: DOES THE THEORY ALLOW FOR HUMAN NATURE, INDIVIDUAL DIFFERENCES, AND HUMAN UNIQUENESS LEVELS OF PERSONALITY ANALYSIS?

Any narrative personality race theory needs to describe how it relates to the human nature, individual differences, and human uniqueness levels of personality. During the founding of the field of personality psychology, Kluckhohn and Murray (1953) characterized these different levels for understanding individuality and personhood in terms of (1) the human nature level or how a person is like all others, (2) the individual and group differences level or how a person is like some others, and (3) the individual uniqueness level or how a person is like no others. Interestingly, scholars often associate each of these levels with different epistemologies, worldviews, strategies of inquiry, and research methods (Winston, 2011).

Moreover, at different periods in the history of personality psychology, scholars have emphasized different levels of personality analysis. In the early period of personality theorizing, "grand theories" at the level of human nature were stressed, with the goal of trying to identify the "determinants of personality" (e.g., Kluckhohn & Murray, 1953). More contemporary personality theories and research focused more on individual and group differences levels of analysis of personality traits, personalized goals (e.g., personal projects, personal strivings) (see Emmons, 1986; Little, 1983), motivation (e.g., achievement, power, affiliation, intimacy motivation) (see Smith, 1992), and developmental tasks (see McAdams & Pals, 2006; McAdams & Pals, 2007; Robins, Fraley, & Krueger, 2007). The individual uniqueness level of personality analysis has characterized personality research throughout the history of personality research. Within personality psychology, analyses of persons at the levels of both individual uniqueness and human nature have been particularly influenced by the pioneering efforts of Murray and his colleagues in the development of the area of personology (see Winston, 2011). This has been defined as the scientific study of the whole person in biographical and cultural contexts (McAdams, 2001).

The theory of race self-complexity incorporates all three levels of personality analysis in its theoretical and methodological orientation. For example, ideographic and nomothetic research methods have been employed in race self-complexity pilot studies to examine human uniqueness of single cases' storied identity, traits, and personal striving configurations (Dawkins, Terry, Winston, & Mangum, 2010; Terry, 2008; Thomas, 2010; Thomas & Winston, 2018), as well as the thematic (Burrell, Winston, & Freeman, 2010; Wynn, Winston, & Freeman, 2010), affective (Mangum, 2010; Mangum & Winston, 2008), motivational (Anderson, Freeman, & Winston, 2010; Freeman et al., 2021), and trait (Burford, 2005) patterning of race experience across samples and discourse (Rice, 2008; Burford & Winston, 2005) of adolescents and emerging adults. This flexibility of levels of personality analysis that the theory of race self-complexity affords creates new possibilities for future personality and race theorizing. It also facilitates research that can capture a sophisticated understanding of the whole person in the context of living in the culture of racialized societies.

Though culture is significant in its incorporation in McAdams and Pals's (2006) conceptualization of personality, a large gap remains in personality theory and research. For example, personality scholars have a dearth of understanding about the person in a cultural context, particularly in those that are non-Western. With the increasingly global emphases of the economy and of everyday living, psychological theorizing about personality and culture at many different levels of analysis will be critical for the present and future inquiry of scholars. In the theory of race self-complexity, culture is considered in terms of the cultural psychology of the cultural-historical individual and systems-level lived experiences of race and racial ideology across both the macro and micro contextual ecology of racialized societies. Winston and Winston (2012, p. 566) describe the concept of racialized society in the following way:

> The racial ideas of the eighteenth century did not, of course, create independently the racialized societies of the nineteenth and twentieth centuries. In their time they were primarily speculative conjectures. They gained importance later, when race-based systems of dominance operationalized them by the application of governmental power and private institutions. A "racialized society" develops over time. It is not simply a society in which there is a sudden or transitory contact between different racial groups through conquest or immigration. In a racialized society, different groups, that have been socially identified as "races," are limited to social and economic roles according to their racial identification. Racialized societies are historically a phenomenon of the early modern world, (beginning in the sixteenth century) when western Europeans developed the technical and military means to conquer societies in Asia, Africa, and Latin America and extract mineral wealth and other natural resources from some of those areas using native labor. During a second stage, millions of laborers, either through slavery or contract labor systems, were moved to frontier societies, such as those in North and South America, the Caribbean, East Africa, and South Africa. There, Europeans imposed a caste system in which race was made a functional boundary for economic and social roles.

From this perspective, then, in the theory of race self-complexity, race and culture are not synonymous concepts. And yet they can be used in overlapping ways to describe individual-and systems-level experiences and structures in racialized societies. The key element that makes race a psychological concept as well as a structural one is the cultured patterns of thought in the form of racial ideology at the individual and structural levels of lived experience. Within the macro-and microecological contexts in which people develop, this can happen such that the ways of thinking about race can eventually become part of culture and personhood.

In the theory of race self-complexity, culture is defined as both personal and public meaning systems that define people, lives, values, identity, time, place, and traditions (i.e., food, dress, celebrations, ceremonies, rituals). Inherent in this conceptualization of culture is Geertz's (1973) idea that culture is interpretive and directed by a search for meaning. In other words, culture is not an objective reality out there to be revealed or discovered by psychologists. Rather, it is something that is invented, reinvented, and sustained by people in personally meaningful ways within the political terrain that frames their lives; it is dynamic, fluid, and emergent. This process takes place, to some extent, through discursive practice. Such practices do not emerge in a political vacuum but are influenced, perhaps even limited on occasion, by hegemonic forces across historical time. Valsiner (2009) describes culture in this way: "in terms of semiotic mediators and meaningful action patterns—it is the inherent core of human psychological functions, rather than an external causal entity that has 'effects' on human emotion, cognition, and behavior" (p. 5). Inherent in these conceptualizations is the central role of the person as an actor and the larger power of what is invented or given meaning by individuals to be scaled up, institutionalized, and symbolized to become part of the larger context of what is cultivated within a community, society, and the world. Tracing the evolution of racial ideology throughout the world for centuries provides an excellent cultural-historical example of this process (Winston & Winston, 2012).

NARRATIVE PERSONALITY ORCHESTRATION: WHAT THEORETICAL CONSIDERATION IS GIVEN TO THE COMPLEXITIES OF THE PERSON AS AN ACTIVE AND GOAL-ORIENTED ORGANISM DEVELOPING WITHIN THE OPPORTUNITIES AND CONSTRAINTS OF A RACIALIZED ENVIRONMENT?

It is well established within psychological science that persons have individual agency in many aspects of their development across the lifespan (see Heckhausen, Wrosch, & Schulz, 2010). What is less clear is how and when individuals who live in the culture of a racialized society engage their agency in critical life episodes to achieve personalized goals and to curate an internalized, integrative, and evolving narrative of self (i.e., narrative identity). Most theories of personality vary in their degree of emphasis on the person or the situation at work in influencing behavior. Any narrative personality race theory should attempt to describe the mechanisms of agency as well as the role of affect, personalized goals, and motives as contextualized facets of personhood.

   Current theories of racism provide an example of possible ways in which these types of mechanisms can be described in the lives of persons living in a racialized society, like the one found in the United States. Jones (1991), in the early development of his cultural theory of TRIOS (Jones, 2003), emphasized that the personality development of African Americans in part becomes an adaptation to racism, since all Black people who live in the culture of a racialized society experience what Jones (1991) terms "a universal context of racism."

Boykin (1986) has proposed a theory of identity dilemma in which individuals of African descent have to actively and simultaneously negotiate three realms of psychological experience: the mainstream, minority, and Afro-cultural orientation. Harrell (1997) also provides a theoretical orientation for describing an active process of resistance or embrace that people of African descent can engage in with respect to the negative psychological consequences of racism in the form of standards of beauty, European ideals, and miseducation.

At the heart of narrative theorizing is its emphasis and insight into meaning making as an active rather than passive process. Thus, rather than racism automatically being psychologically undermining, though it can be, a person also has the psychological agency to invoke active patterns of coping and response to create psychological stamina, resilience, and flourishing. Jones offers that this can be achieved through deployment of culturally appropriate psychological resources (see Jones, 2003).

The theory of race self-complexity identifies types of goal-directed behaviors a person can draw on in a culture of a racialized society. These include, but are not limited to, self-protection, self-enhancement, and narrative reconstruction. Psychological agency casts the person onto center stage. There the person can orchestrate a meaning-making process about racialized lived experiences (see Rice, 2008; Rice, this volume) that afford an opportunity to author an inner story of self that represents a uniquely personalized configuration of narrative identity. As such, the theory of race self-complexity allows for theorizing that can span a continuum of individual difference realities such that living in the culture of a racialized society creates numerous psychological constraints, largely due to racism, as well as stimulates some opportunities to develop unique psychological strength and stamina grounded in cultural assets.

THE THEORY OF RACE SELF-COMPLEXITY FORMULATION: FOUNDATIONS AND NEW DIRECTIONS

The theory of race self-complexity integrates two classes of theory: narrative personality theories and psychological significance of race theories. Examples of these theories are as follows: narrative personality theories such as script theory (Tomkins, 1979), acts of meaning (Bruner, 1990), the life story theory of identity (McAdams, 1985; Singer, 2005), autobiographical and self-defining memory theory (Singer, 1995; Conway & Pleydell-Pearce, 2000; Conway, Singer, & Tagini, 2004), and narrative identity theory (Singer, 2005; McLean & McAdams, 2013; McLean et al., 2020); and psychological significance of race theories such as nigrescence theory (Cross, 1971; 1991; Parham & Helms, 1985), microaggression theory (Pierce, 1977; Sue et al., 2007), universal context of racism (Jones, 2003), stereotype threat (Steele, 1995), triple quandary (Boykin, 1986), whiteness theory (Lewis, 1994), Manichean psychology (Harrell, 1997), multidimensional model of racial identity (Sellers et al., 1997; Sellers et al., 1998), Atunwa: authenticity theory (Nobels, 1998), invisibility syndrome (Franklin, 1999), and TRIOS (Jones, 2003).

At its inception, the theory of race self-complexity described how the meaning of race adds a layer of complexity to the individual, relational, and collective layers of self-system (see Autry, 2010; Burrell, Winston, & Freeman, 2011; Jones, 2012; Rice, 2008; Mangum, 2010; Terry, 2008; Thomas, 2010; Winston et al., 2004; Winston, 2009). Over the last eight years, the theory has evolved to describe how the meaning of race can be processed narratively as a routine dynamic of personality development for individuals who live in the culture of a racialized society (see Winston & Winston, 2012; Winston-Proctor & Winston, 2022). Concepts of emotional intelligence, storied cognition, and acts of race meaning are central to this theoretical evolution. Equally important is the very recent formulation of a new theoretical question in the Identity and Success Research Lab: What is the interplay of the neurobiological, affective, cognitive, and motivational systems in autobiographical memories and narrative identity development?

In the Identity and Success Research Lab, we have launched a series of independent (Miller, 2021) and team science (Hill, Miller, Boney, Cotton, Freeman, & Winston-Proctor, 2021) projects to systematically explore this question. We also aim to incorporate a more explicit theoretical conceptualization of the culture of living in a racialized and gendered society. Our theoretical, methodological, and practice considerations will lead to the development of new race self-complexity instruments and design-based research design innovations. This scientist-practitioner focus will make a meaningful contribution to multiple Identity and Success Research Lab affiliation projects: (1) the Narrative Personality Health Psychology Collaborative, (2) the NSF Broadening Participation Research Center for the Development of Identity and Motivation or African American Undergraduate Students in STEM, (3) and the NSF Howard University ADVANCE Institutional Transformation Cooperative Agreement.

The theory of race self-complexity creates a heuristic for understanding questions of how and why it is natural and useful for researchers, practitioners, and people in their everyday living to process the meaning of race narratively. As a theory, it also allows for illumination of balanced themes of psychological negotiation. In other words, the theory of race self-complexity affords theoretical space to consider the continuum from narrative identity struggle to narrative identity equanimity (Winston-Proctor & Winston, in preparation). In so doing, the theory recognizes the complications of narrative identity processing and autobiographical reasoning. These complications take the form of contradictions and multiplicities for making meaning of race within the multiple social ecologies of a racialized society.

In sum, the goal of the theory of race self-complexity is to describe how race adds a layer of psychological complexity to the self-system and how the meaning of race is processed narratively within individual lives. The evolution of this theory has been led by early career and midcareer scholars in the Identity and Success Research Lab as they engage in critical thinking about theory, research design, and practice. Race self-complexity theory, like all psychological theory, is tentative (Fiske, 2004; Wyer, 2004). As new problems to be solved emerge in the society and the world, and as new data are collected and analyzed, complicated dynamics will emerge to strengthen the theory of race self-complexity.

CONCEPTUALIZING IDENTITY IN HUMAN PERSONALITY: WHAT IS THE STORIED NATURE OF IDENTITY IN THE NARRATIVE PROCESSING OF THE MEANING OF RACE?

In psychological science, there are multiple theories and conceptualizations of identity (Erikson, 1968; McAdams, 1985; Stryker & Serpe, 1994). Conceptualizations of identity as storied are useful to advance understanding of the meaning of race in lives because of the human capacity for individuals to think in storied terms. Moreover, as a part of human nature, this storied cognition cuts across cultures, making this storied form of identity understandable and accessible to study participants, scholars, practitioners, clients, and everyday citizens in the community. Within McAdams's (1985) life story model, identity is conceptualized as storied. More specifically, the life story model explains that persons engage in identity work of selective synchronic and diachronic integration of experience in the form of a story of self. From this perspective, human personality is not only composed of dispositional traits and adaptations characteristic of the person in time, place, and role but also includes an internalized and evolving narrative of self (McAdams & Pals, 2006). To bring unity and purpose to life, a person has the interpretive power as an author of their story of self to internalize, dismiss, incorporate, and/or combine internal and external stimuli that answer the question "Who am I?" From this perspective, Bruner (1990) argues that a person's narrative construction and symbolic meaning depends on the existence of language and the human capacity to internalize language and to use a system of signs for interpretation.

In racialized societies, the lived experience of race at the macro and micro levels of ecology demands that persons engage in symbolic meaning making and narrative processing to make sense of race. The theory of race self-complexity asserts that there is a process of the self-system by which autobiographical memories of race are remembered and narratively organized in storied form as part of identity development. Autobiographical memories refer to long-term memory for personal experiences and personal knowledge of an individual's life (Conway, 2009). Emotion enhances memory encoding (Singer & Salovey, 1993). Conway (2009) describes the process of auto-biographical memory construction in the following way: "When a specific autobiographical memory comes to mind then a rememberer has 'recollective experience.' That is, they experience remembering consciously and have what is termed 'auotonoetic consciousness.' Typically, images enter the conscious awareness, often visual in nature, attention turns inward, other highly specific knowledge may also feature too, and there is a strong sense of the self in the past. Additionally, there is a distinct 'feeling of remembering'; a feeling that what is in consciousness is a memory. Such experiences are part of a class of mental experiences that have been termed 'cognitive feelings'" (p. 77).

Building on Conway's (2009) and others' (Singer & Bluck, 2001) description of processes characteristic of autobiographical memories generally, the theory of race self-complexity posits that in the construction of auto-biographical memories of race, memory encoding of remembered emotions of race experiences launch two core processes of the self-system: narrative processing and autobiographical reasoning (Mangum & Winston, 2008). The theory of race self-complexity asserts that such processing engages narrative sequencing and the negotiation of the emotional significance of race with a particular emphasis on the emotional density (Mangum, 2010) of these narratives.

NARRATIVE PERSONALITY LEVELS OF ORGANIZATION: WHAT ARE THE PSYCHOLOGICAL MECHANISMS OF THE COMPLEXITY OF THE MEANING OF RACE IN LIVES?

The theory of race self-complexity posits that there are three core psychological mechanisms of the complexity of the meaning of race: the human nature to categorize, master narratives of race, and the universal context of racism. Each of these mechanisms operates at multiple levels of the individual, structural, and institutional levels of organization.

It is well established that it is human nature to categorize persons and objects (Prentice & Miller, 2007). This processing of psychological essentialism of humans can include racial and ethnic categories as well as the implicit association of cultural-historical symbols of race, racism, and ethnicity (Goff, Eberhardt, Williams, & Jackson, 2008). For example, this act of categorization plays out in skin color judgments. As a result of such categorization and automatic processing, skin color serves as a cue that has symbolic meaning in American society and can become attached to assumed behaviors, values, and life experiences.

In American society and culture there are master narratives of race, many of which have historically been based on white supremacy. In part, these master narratives of race hold symbolic meaning and have the goal to advance racial ideology that positions individuals who are Black as intellectually inferior, immoral, and generally inferior to other races. Master narratives of race operate both as impositions and opportunities in a person's life. As an imposition, they demand that the person respond to or accept being positioned by others. At the same time, master narratives of race can act as opportunities for a person to create psychological resilience in crafting an altered interpretation that is adaptive and functional for that person.

With respect to race self-complexity theoretical development, what is interesting and important to understanding lives and personality development is how a person constructs their own identity claims about the meaning of race in answering the question "Who am I as a person?" The inherent complexities and intricacies in accomplishing such a task span a lifetime and incorporate a large repertoire of experiences and meaning-making opportunities. Exploring this requires attention not only to the content of these autobiographical memories of race and the representation of master narratives of race within these personal narratives. It also demands more specific attention to identifying the discursive resources a person employs in trying to work up a sense of self, purpose, values, and identity in the lived experience of race.

Autobiographical memories of race are a vessel for such psychological action of crafting and reflection. They can also serve as a psychological spark for redirecting, reinterpreting, and creatively cultivating the meaning of race within a particular racialized society as well as in the person's life on their own terms. In many respects, master narratives of race, because they are learned, are part of a process of racial socialization. At the same time, the representation of master narratives of race in autobiographical memories of race in any form reflects another act of racial socialization in the countering, resisting, or crafting of something completely different.

The key to these master narratives of race having life is a pervasiveness of racism in racialized society. According to Jones (2003), this universal context of racism operates in important ways that have implications for autobiographical memories of race. From this perspective, racism is psychologically accessible at any given time, especially for those who are its targets. As such, racism is also an explanatory construct because individual and collective histories of its targets are psychologically available at any given moment. In other words, because it is accessible, it is part of the situation that can influence behavior, including a person's construction of a narrative identity. In terms of time dimensionality, therefore, living in a universal context of racism has past, present, and future orientation.

Using Lewin's field theory, Jones (2003) proposes that in American society there is a universal context of racism in which human development progresses. For individuals who are Black, for example, he argues that this universal context of racism has such a profound impact that there is a "Black personality" that is in large part an adaptation to racism (Jones, 1991). Similarly, scholars who advance whiteness theory argue that there is a relationship between ideological and material components of race that afford white individuals automatic privileged social status within a societal racial hierarchy, as well as psychological entitlement. Lewis (2004) asserts, "whether Whites have self-conscious racial identities may or may not matter as much for their life chances as external readings of them as White" (p. 624). The theoretical orientation of whiteness research suggests that race has meaning for individuals who are white living in American society. However, the degree of complexity, consciousness, and level of psychological negotiation may be distinctive and based on notions of privilege and entitlement (Bonnett, 1996; Murano, 2004). It also may depend on identity choice and suppression, especially in the case of multiracial individuals (Terry, 2008; Terry & Winston, 2010; Terry, 2010).

NARRATIVE PERSONALITY UTILITY: WHAT IS THE PSYCHOLOGICAL FUNCTION OF THE NARRATIVE PROCESSING OF RACE?

The theory of race self-complexity posits that one psychological function of autobiographical memories is to organize events of past life experiences of race in a temporal sequence and meaningful internal portrait of people, places, and happenings (Winston, 2012). In this regard, narrative personality is an organizing structure of personality, an idea advanced by the narrative identity concept of both Singer (1995) and McAdams and Pals (2006). Autobiographical memories can be thought of as what Singer (1995) refers to as "events of the past or images of previous events that return to our attention and consciousness" (p. 432).

The theory of race self-complexity predicts a relationship between the meaning of race and motivation. From this perspective, another psychological function of autobiographical memories posited by the theory of race self-complexity is self-regulation of the internal and external stimuli that operate within a universal context of racism for the purpose of self-protection, self-enhancement, and psychological balance (see Rice, 2008). Autobiographical memories of race can provide a mechanism for both internal psychological sight and narrative construction for revealing and engaging these types of motivational processes.

Self-protection and self-enhancement motivational consequences of racism can operate at the individual or collective level. Jones (2003) argues that individuals are psychologically oriented toward avoiding, detecting, protecting, and/or conquering episodes of racism. As a result, he suggests that self-protection motives are more likely to be individually based and dependent on the person's construal of the psychological moment, stimulating an adaptive response to an anticipated experience of racism. Self-enhancing motives are more likely to be collectively based and more oriented toward sustaining, defending, and enhancing one's self-worth and humanity (Jones, 2003).

The agentic nature of human personality and the forms that stimuli take are important to understanding the psychological functions of self-protection, self-enhancement, and psychological balance. Stimuli related to the meaning of race are not only external to the individual but internal as well. There is empirical research that describes internal stimuli in narrative processing and explains "thinking human beings do not only have one attentional field—the physical world outside of the body; we attend to our own thoughts independent of that world" (Singer, 1995, p. 431). Master narratives (and those about race in this case) do not automatically or simply position the way a person thinks about who they are as a person. But what is most interesting and important to understanding lives and personality development is how a person is an agent giving meaning to race, as well as in their own construction of their own identity claims. The degree of psychological escape that a person can have from the imposition of master narratives of race, especially those with negative, racist, or outrageous plotlines, character descriptions, and evaluations, depends on how the person chooses to position themself with respect to the main storyline or characters within the narrative. Other dimensions of personality, including dispositional traits as well as motivational, social cognitive, and developmental characteristic adaptations that define a person's personality, likely shape this choice. Taken together, all of this suggests that there are inherent complexities and intricacies in accomplishing this lifespan task that includes a large repertoire of experiences and meaning-making opportunities.

Another psychological function of autobiographical memories of race posited by the theory of race self-complexity is to achieve emotional longevity, *optimal* psychological well-being and health through active positioning of the self within and/or outside of master narratives of race, as well as a location in other forms of negative, self-defeating, and problematic storyline that a person identifies as self-relevant. Narratives of race experiences allow the person to act as author with interpretive power. As such, the person has the agency to decide what both master narratives and personal narratives of race mean to them and how this meaning gets incorporated into an evolving narrative identity in a way that is adaptive for positive regard for self and buffering of stress or other forms of physiological assault on health (see Pieterse, Todd, Neville, & Carter, 2011). Autobiographical memories of race can also serve as a psychological canvas for the individual to create a mindset of success that is adaptive in its expandability and applicability in achieving educational, professional, and personal success outcomes. Both the models of emotional longevity (see Anderson, 2003) and life synergy illustrate the beneficial well-being and health functions of autobiographical memories of race. For example, the Winston synergy model of life transformation and balance is a new narrative personality model (www.winstonsynergy.com) that integrates principles, techniques, theories, research, strategies of inquiry, and methods of assessment from the fields of narrative psychology and personality psychology as well as from the identity and success life story research method (Winston, Philip, & Lloyd, 2007). The primary goal of the Winston synergy model is to help individuals gain self-knowledge about their dispositional traits, characteristic adaptations, and narrative identity, as well as train them in narrative reconstruction as a form of life transformation and balance. Given the universal context of racism characteristic of racialized societies, these processes often demand that individuals who are not white have to frequently make sense of the meaning of race in their lives and proximal environment.

Therefore, the race self-complexity theoretical approach to understanding how race is processed narratively is not an exercise that only has utility for the research scientist and their respective theories and methods of inquiry. Instead, this approach to understanding the narrative meaning of race has inherent value for the insight and transformation of persons in their everyday lives, including guiding the training of those professionals and community-appointed leaders who are responsible for the management, coping, and transformation of the lives of others. In other words, autobiographical memories of race have import and value not only to create a better research base but also to craft better versions of lives. A person's self-knowledge building can work toward the achievement of both identity balance and life synergy. And the narrative processing of race through narrative construction of autobiographical memories of race is part of the process of a person learning more about self and the meaning of specific life experiences. In a racialized society, the basic premise of life synergy is that a person cannot change their life experiences but can reconstruct the meaning of these life experiences through autobiographical reasoning and narrative processing to create a psychologically adaptive form of self-understanding and living.

CONCLUSION

The significance of the theory of race self-complexity is multifaceted. It advances narrative personality theory, research design innovations, and practice. Moreover, it explains an individual's adaptive capacity to meet the psychological demands of environmental presses within a racialized society. Jones (1991) suggests that there is a Black personality formed as an adaptation to living in a universal context of racism. However, there is no personality theory per se that is explicitly described as a narrative personality race theory. This does not make the contribution of the theory of race self-complexity in and of itself important. Instead, its significance is the novel integration of two classes of well-established theories with their distinctive methods of inquiry and collection of research findings. Another point of significance is that the theory of race self-complexity offers a heuristic for future exploration of narrative personality, lived experience, the meaning of race, and the dynamics of the racialized social ecologies of human development. The theory of race self-complexity was initially developed as broader than an identity theory (see Winston et al., 2004). Its current formulation anchored in narrative processing and autobiographical reasoning can inform debates about identity centrality, salience, content, and psychosocial stages of development. The theory of race self-complexity is also poised to stimulate theoretical evolution and methodological development about McAdams and Pals's (2006) principle of the differential role of culture in an integrative science of personality. Within personality psychology, research centered on personality and culture is severely underdeveloped. And yet, Sarbin (1986) has characterized narrative as the root metaphor for psychology.

At this stage in the development of the theory of race self-complexity, there are several important considerations. Unlike many other theories, it is not introduced as an endpoint but rather strives to stimulate interest among others to explore, refine, reconfigure, and apply the theory. Also, the theory of race self-complexity should be judged based on its viability to explain how the meaning of race can be processed narratively and not based on a particular ideological position about race. Moreover, the theory should not be discredited because it includes the term *race* even though there is no validity to the concept of "biological races." The cultural-historical significance of centuries of systematic racism that endures today makes the name and intent of the theory relevant to future theorizing and application. We must strive to create a reality for the next generation in which they can play a game of soccer without the experience of monkey jokes and thrown banana peels. The theory of race self-complexity offers the next frontier for narrative personality psychological theorizing that celebrates human agency, narrative personality orchestration, psychological well-being, and human flourishing.

REFERENCES

Anderson, A. A., Freeman, K. E., & Winston, C. E. (2010). *Exploring racial identity and racial socialization as sources of academic self-efficacy in science for African American middle school students.* Manuscript submitted for publication.

Bonham, V., Warshauer-Baker, E., & Collins, F. (2005). Race and ethnicity in the genome era: The complexity of the constructs. *American Psychologist, 60*(1), 9–15.

Bonnett, A. (1996). White studies: The problems and projects of a new research agenda. *Theory, Culture and Society, 13*(2), 145–155.

Boykin, A. W. (1986). The triple quandary and the schooling of Afro-American children. In U. Neisser (Ed.), *The school achievement of minority children* (pp. 51–92). New Jersey: Lawrence Erlbaum.

Bruner, J. (1990). *Acts of meaning.* Cambridge: Harvard University Press.

Burford, T. I. (2005). *Race narratives, personality traits, and race self complexity: Towards an understanding of the psychological meaning of race* (Unpublished master's thesis). Howard University, Washington, DC.

Burford, T. I., & Winston, C. E. (2005). *The guided race autobiography.* Unpublished instrument.

Burrell, J. O., Winston, C. E., & Freeman, K. E. (2010). *Race-acting: The varied and complex affirmative meaning of "acting Black" for African American adolescents.* Manuscript submitted for publication.

Cole, E. (2009). Intersectionality and research in psychology. *American Psychologist, 64*(3), 170–180.

Conway, M. A., & Pleydell-Pearce, C. W. (2000). The construction of autobiographical memories in the self-memory system. *Psychological Review, 107*(2), 261–288.

Conway, M. A., Singer, J. A., & Tagini, A. (2004). The self and autobiographical memory: Correspondence and coherence. *Social Cognition, 22*(5), 491–529.

Cross, W. E. (1971). The Negro-to-Black conversion experience. *Black World, 20,* 13–27.

Cross, W. E. (1991). *Shades of Black.* Philadelphia: Temple University Press.

Dawkins, E., Terry, R. L., & Winston, C. W. (2010, August). *What does it mean to be multiracial: An exploratory case study of the narrative processing of race within autobiographical memories*. Poster presented at the American Psychological Association Annual Meeting, San Diego, CA.

Du Bois, W. E. B. (1945). *Color and democracy: Colonies and peace*. New York: Harcourt Brace.

Emmons, R. A. (1986). Personal strivings: An approach to personality and subjective well-being. *Journal of Personality and Social Psychology, 51*(5), 1058–1068.

Erikson, E. H. (1968). *Identity, youth, and crisis*. New York: Norton.

Fiske, S. (2004). Mind the gap: In praise of informal sources of formal theory. *Personality and Social Psychology Review, 8*(2), 132–137.

Franklin, A. J. (1999). Invisibility syndrome and racial identity development in psychotherapy and counseling African American men. *Counseling Psychologist, 27*, 761–793.

Frazier, E. F. (1957). *The Negro in the United States*. New York: Macmillan.

Freeman, K. E., Winston-Proctor, C. E., Gangloff-Bailey, F., & Jones, J. M. (2021). Racial identity-rooted academic motivation of first-year African American students majoring in STEM at an HBCU. *Frontiers in Psychology, 12*, https://doi.org/10.3389/fpsyg.2021.669407.

Geertz, C. (1973). *The interpretation of cultures*. New York: Basic Books.

Goff, P. A., Eberhardt, J. L., Williams, M. J., & Jackson, M. C. (2008). Not yet human: Implicit knowledge, historical dehumanization, and contemporary consequences. *Journal of Personality and Social Psychology, 94*(2), 292–306.

Harrell, C. J. P. (1999). *Manichean psychology: Racism and the minds of people of African descent*. Washington, DC: Howard University Press.

Heckhausen, J., Wrosch, C., & Schulz, R. (2010). A motivational theory of life-span development. *Psychological Review, 117*, 32–60.

Helms, J. E., Jernigan, M., & Mascher, J. (2005). The meaning of race in psychology and how to change it: A methodological perspective. *American Psychologist, 60*(1), 27–36.

Jones, J. M. (1991). The politics of personality: Being black in America. In R. L. Jones (Ed.), *Black Psychology* (pp. 441–468). Berkeley, CA: Cobb and Henry.

Jones, J. M. (2003). TRIOS: A psychological theory of the African legacy in American culture. *Journal of Social Issues, 59*(1), 217–241.

Kluckhohn, C., & Murray, H. A. (1953). Personality formation: The determinants. In C. Kluckhohn, H. A. Murray, & D. Schneider (Eds.), *Personality in nature, society, and culture* (pp. 53–67). New York: Knopf.

Ladsen-Billings, G., & Tate, W. F. (1995). Toward a critical race theory of education. *Teacher College Record, 97*(1), 47–68.

Lewis, A. E. (2004). What group? Studying whites and whiteness in the era of color blindness. *Sociological Theory, 22*, 623–646.

Little, B. R. (1983). Personal projects: A rationale and method for investigation. *Environment and Behavior, 15*(3), 273–309.

Mangum, A. M. (2010). *Race self complexity and emotion: "How does it make you feel" to be Black in American society and culture?* (Unpublished doctoral dissertation). Howard University, Washington, DC.

Mangum, A. M., & Winston, C. E. (2008, August). *Race self complexity and emotion: How does it feel to be African?* Paper presented at the annual meeting of the Association of Black Psychologists, Oakland, CA.

McAdams, D. P. (1985). *Power, intimacy, and the life story: Personological inquiries into identity.* New York: Guilford Press.

McAdams, D. P. (2001). The psychology of life stories. *Review of General Psychology, 5*, 100–122.

McAdams, D. P., & McLean, K. C. (2013). Narrative identity. *Current Directions in Psychological Science, 22*(3), 233–238.

McAdams, D. P., & Pals, J. L. (2006). A new big five: Fundamental principles for an integrative science of personality. *American Psychologist, 61*(3), 204–217.

McLean, K. C., Lilgendahl, J. P., Fordham, C., Alpert, E., Marsden, E., Szymanowski, K., & McAdams, D. P. (2018). Identity development in cultural context: The role of deviating from master narratives. *Journal of Personality, 86*(4), 631–651.

McLean, K. C., Syed, M., Pasupathi, M., Adler, J. M., Dunlop, W. L., Drustrup, D., Fivush, R., Graci, M. E., Lilgendahl, J. P., Lodi-Smith, J., McAdams, D. P., & McCoy, T. P. (2020). The empirical structure of narrative identity: The initial Big Three. *Journal of Personality and Social Psychology, 119*(4), 920–944.

Miller, J. (2021). An exploration: Cognitive and motivational processes within autobiographical memories of African Americans. White Paper: The Identity and Success Research Lab.

Miller, Hill, Cotton, Boney, Freeman, & Winston-Proctor (2021). Theoretical and practical considerations: What are the cognitive, affective, motivational, and neurobiology processes engaged in the narrative personality of African Americans? White Paper: The Identity and Success Research Lab.

Murano, J. (2004). *Roots of "whiteness." Labour/Le Travail.* http://www.historycooperative.org/journals/llt/54/munro.html.

Philip, C. L. (2007). *Asian American identities: Racial and ethnic identity issues in the twenty-first century.* Amherst, NY: Cambria Press.

Pieterse, A. L., Todd, N. R., Neville, H. A., & Carter, R. T. (2011, November 7). Perceived racism and mental health among Black American adults: A meta-analytic review. *Journal of Counseling Psychology, 59*(1), 1–9. doi: 10.1037/a0026208.

Prentice, D. A., & Miller, D. T. (2007). Psychological essentialism of human categories. *Psychological Science, 16*, 202–206.

Rice, D. W. (2008). *Balance: Advancing considerations of self and identity by engaging the Black male adolescent.* Lanham, MD: Rowman & Littlefield.

Robins, R., Fraley, R. C., & Krueger, R. F. (2007). *Handbook of research methods in personality psychology.* New York: Guilford Press.

Sarbin, T. R. (1986). The narrative as a root metaphor for psychology. In T. R. Sarbin (Ed.), *Narrative psychology: The storied nature of human conduct* (pp. 2–21). New York: Praeger.

Sellers, R. M., Smith, M. A., Shelton, J., Rowley, S. J., & Chavous, T. M. (1998). Multidimensional model of racial identity: A reconceptualization of African American racial identity. *Personality and Social Psychology Review, 2*(1), 18.

Singer, J. A. (1995). Seeing oneself: Locating narrative memory in a framework of personality. *Journal of Personality, 63*, 429–457.

Singer, J. A. (2019). Repetition is the scent of the hunt: A clinician's application of narrative identity to a longitudinal life study. *Qualitative Psychology, 6*(2), 194–205.

Singer, J. A., & Bluck, S. (2001). New perspectives on autobiographical memory: The integration of narrative processing and autobiographical reasoning. *Review of General Psychology, 5*(2), 91–99.

Singer, J. A., & Salovey, P. (1993). *The remembered self: Emotion and memory in personality.* New York: Free Press.

Smith, C. P. (Ed.). (1992). *Motivation and personality: Handbook of thematic content analysis.* New York: Cambridge University Press.

Steele, C. M. (1997). A threat in the air. *American Psychologist, 52*(6), 613.

Stryker, S., & Serpe, R. (1994). Identity salience and psychological centrality: Equivalent, overlapping, or complementary concepts? *Social Psychology Quarterly, 57*(1), 16–35.

Sue, D., Capodilupo, C. M., Torino, G. C., Bucceri, J. M., Holder, A. B., Nadal, K. L., & Esquilin, M. (2007). Racial microaggressions in everyday life. *American Psychologist, 62*(4), 271–286.

Teo, T. (2009). Psychology without Caucasians. *Canadian Psychology, 50*(2), 91–97.

Terry, R. L. (2008). *Race self complexity within multiracial college students: Negotiating the suppression of multiracial integration* (Unpublished dissertation). Howard University, Washington, DC.

Terry, R. L. (2010, August). *Multiracial integration suppression: Implications for the multiracial lived experience.* Paper presented at the annual meeting of the American Psychological Association, San Diego, CA.

Terry, R. L., & Winston, C. E. (2010). Personality characteristic adaptations: Multiracial adolescents' patterns of racial self-identification change. *Journal of Research on Adolescence, 20*(2), 432–455.

Thomas, C. (2010). *An exploration into the personality and life of an African-American male incarcerated as an adolescent within an adult correctional facility: A psycho-biography* (Unpublished doctoral dissertation). Howard University, Washington, DC.

Valsiner, J. (2009). Cultural psychology today: Innovations and oversights. *Culture and Psychology, 15*(1), 5–39.

Winston, C. E. (2011). Biography and lifestory. In S. Lapan, M. Quartaroli, & F. Riemer (Eds.), *Qualitative research: An introduction to designs and methods.* New Jersey: Jossey-Bass.

Winston, C. E. (2012). Human personality: Race self complexity and symbolic meaning of persons living race in American society and culture. In A. U. Branco & J. Valsiner (Eds.), *Cultural psychology of human values* (pp. 163–194). Charlotte, NC: Information Age.

Winston, C. E., & Kittles, R. A. (2005). Psychological and ethical issues related to identity and using human genome research to infer ancestry of African Americans.

In T. Turner (Ed.), *Ethical issues in biological anthropology* (pp. 209–229). New York: SUNY Press.

Winston, C. E., Philip, C. L., & Lloyd, D. L. (2007). Integrating design based research and the identity and success life story research method: Toward a new research paradigm for looking beyond the digital divide and race self complexity within the lives of Black students. *Journal of Negro Education, 76*(1), 31–43.

Winston, C. E., Rice, D. W., Bradshaw, B. J., Lloyd, D., Harris, L. T., Burford, T. I., et al. (2004). Science success, narrative theories of personality, and race self complexity: Is race represented in the identity construction of African American adolescents? *New Directions for Child and Adolescent Development: Social and Self Processes Underlying Math and Science Achievement, 106*, 55–77.

Winston, C. E., & Winston, M. R. (2012). Cultural psychology of racial ideology in historical perspective: An analytic approach to understanding racialized societies and their psychological effects on lives. In J. Valsiner (Ed.), *Oxford handbook of culture and psychology* (pp. 559–581). New York: Oxford University Press.

Winston-Proctor, C. E. (in press). Personality: A Very Short Introduction. Oxford University Press.

Winston-Proctor, C., & Winston, M. R. (2021). Psychology and race in racialized societies. *Oxford Research Encyclopedia of the History of Psychology.*

Winston-Proctor, C. E., & Winston, M. R. (2022). Narrative identity equanimity. Unpublished manuscript.

Wyer, R. (2004). A personalized theory of theory construction. *Personality and Social Psychology Review, 8*(2), 201–209.

Wynn, M. E., Winston, C. E., & Freeman, K. E. (2010). *What is the nature of African American adolescents' implicit theories of intelligence?: An exploratory study.* Manuscript submitted for publication.

Chapter 5

Reflections on Black Women, Family, Offline Archiving, and Identity

Asha Grant

In the spring of 2018, a billboard went up atop an East Liberty building in Pittsburgh. In black-and-white capital letters, it read simply: "There are Black people in the future," the work of Alisha Wormsley, a local Black woman interdisciplinary artist and cultural producer. What followed is what always seems to follow—an uproar, removal by the powers that be, another uproar, a town hall, a statement, another statement.

On her website, Wormsley gave us a definitive last word: "However you might feel, whatever you might think, THERE ARE BLACK PEOPLE IN THE FUTURE." It was a reminder of an age-old fact—despite the world's attempts to delegitimize and subsequently remove Black existence on both a fundamental and universal plane, Black folk have always understood, located, and situated our identity within a deracialized space-time continuum.

To put it plainly, future making is, and has been, the business of Black people.

DEFINING RADICAL BLACK FAMILIAL ARCHIVING

I believe Black people carry and nurture a rich archiving tradition that supersedes even the definition of archiving itself. A simple internet search suggests the definition of *archive* as "a collection of historical documents or records providing information about a place, institution, or group of people." We know the history of Black life in America begins with no acknowledgment of life or personhood at all—an archive of handwritten receipts and drawn advertisements documenting flesh for labor, runaway slave reward posters as requests for the return of property, cursive diary entries describing wench and not woman. With these "archives," there is little room for visions of a Black interior identity, life, or truth; we have had to piece together those things on our own to anchor a collective identity named by ourselves, for ourselves, outside of exclusivity and the confines of Western archival standards and practices.

For Black folk, archiving our families' stories, histories, and traditions remains one of our most radical acts, as the very concept of archiving lends itself to an identity worth capturing—or countering—as well as an inherent belief in a purpose, a lifespan, a *future* already set in motion for someone along the way. In a world where the value of Black life is up for debate and at risk by the state even before conception, how remarkable and awe-inspiring is it to believe there will be "someone along the way" at all?

To borrow a sentiment from the episode "N*ggas Die Different" from the Black spirituality podcast *A Little Juju*, Black folk archive different. This essay journeys through the impact of radical Black familial archiving on the identity orchestration of Black women and the increasing desire to continue preserving our stories offline even in today's contemporary increasingly digital world.

BACKGROUND/MOTIVE

adrienne maree brown (2019) opens *Pleasure Activism* by lending herself to the reader first. Black women guide my steps, so first I note that I am a twenty-seven-year-old queer Black woman from Los Angeles, California, a bookstore owner and digital media producer. I found myself in Dr. Rice's Black Men, Black Boys, and the Psychology of Modern Media class at Morehouse College in the spring of 2014, my last semester at Spelman College. As an English major, women's studies and African diaspora studies minor, I was relatively new to the psychology world and even more new to the concept of identity orchestration—a theory that seemed to almost speak directly to my experience as an intersectional and marginalized person. This idea of striking an identity balance, finding "homeostasis" in the body and the self, was a concept I have wrestled with namelessly throughout my matriculation from Black girlhood and into womanhood, the "psychological equilibrium" providing a sense of relief, peace, and protection from toxic and conflicting tales around how my Blackness and woman-ness interact to shape and define me. My maternal family's personal archives have been a huge participant in much of that relief, peace, and protection.

My grandmother is the archivist of our immediate family. Her mantle serves as a public gallery of images of biological and chosen family throughout time. She has her children and grandkids' art projects filed neatly away in labeled, faded folders, and a wooden box of handwritten letters from our late cousin Sydney, who was away in Paris in the 1980s, on her dresser. I spent the majority of my childhood taking in each bit of information about our collective lives that my grandmother left for us to view and remember. She's worked hard to preserve and to share.

My grandmother's dementia diagnosis in 2018 woke me up to the realization that all we've got as Black folk is what we can hold in our hands and the things we can share. It's all we've ever had. As my grandmother's primary caregiver, I ask myself a series of questions around Black mortality and immortality almost daily: some meta (How does Blackness continue to cheat death, transcending time and space again and again?), some worrisome (What will we do when cursive is eliminated completely and future generations are so digital they're unable to decipher Nellie Johnson's loopy handwritten sweet potato pie recipe?), some fleeting quotes from my millennial attempts to preserve moments with her ("Print those photos out soon and give them to me; that phone isn't real").

In *Art on My Mind*, bell hooks (1995) writes, "When the psychohistory of a people is marked by ongoing loss, when entire histories are denied, hidden, erased, documentation can become an obsession." As a Black American woman grappling with my grandmother's fading mental and emotional history, this is a phenomenon felt on both a very personal and structural level. Over the past few years, archiving has become an obsession. I save little notes my grandmother leaves me on the back of receipts, pamphlets from my cousin's plays, baby shower invitations, even the calendars from years past remain, containing a year's worth of clues to a life lived. With *shadow banning*, a recent term acknowledging the intentional erasure of a person or group's online content, on the rise, technological redlining (Noble, 2018), and constant global threats to our digital security, I'm getting old school with it—and I'm not alone.

I invited three Black women between the ages of twenty-four and forty-three to reflect with me on their personal family archives, how it informs their identities as Black women, and how they are continuing the tradition, offline. Our phone conversations were relatively informal, my questions remaining open-ended to allow for responses to take their natural form. I spoke with Jehan Giles, an educator, librarian, full-spectrum doula, and multimedia artist based in Los Angeles, California; Tasneem Nathari, a twenty-four-year-old hip-hop head, R&B diva enthusiast, and creative from East Orange, New Jersey; and Ayana Jamieson, a professor in the Ethnic

Studies Department at California State Polytechnic University–Pomona and founder of the Octavia E. Butler Legacy Network.

Our conversations, averaging about an hour and a half each, presented me with more depth and nuance than I had anticipated. Combing through the transcriptions of each interview reminded me that, while connected through the shared experience of being both Black and women, our histories and relationships to the two are dynamic. Following are a few of my reflections.

GRANDPARENTS AND THE SPIRITUAL ARCHIVE

In 2000, a national study was conducted with data from the Census 2000 American Community Survey to "determine the prevalence, sociodemographic characteristics, and service utilization patterns of African American grandparents raising grandchildren." It found that out of 890,000, over 500,000 estimated African American grandparents aged forty-five-plus were raising grandchildren. These numbers, though shocking to some, feel right to me. They tell the story of my life, certainly, and the lives of many Black kids I knew growing up in households with varying familial structures. I began each interview inquiring about family placement, and each participant quickly located a grandparent as a primary influence in their life, as a contributor to their understanding of identity, and as both keeper and teacher of family history.

> My grandmother would wake us up for school every morning. She would have food ready when we got home because my mother worked far from home. So she was like the closest person to us growing up. And I would sit in her room every day and she would just tell me the same stories over and over and over and over and over again. And she would tell me, my brother, my sister. But I was the one who was really listening so that I would never forget.

Tasneem's recounting of her grandmother reciting her family's stories to her and her siblings illustrates beautifully an example of spiritual archiving. I first encountered this term while listening to filmmaker Sophia Nahli Allison discuss Black death and the conjuring of Black life through African oral traditions during a talk at the California African American Museum in October 2020. Allison explains that oftentimes, Black folk don't have access to the "tangible evidence" of our lives and family's lives, our stories being "the only piece of archive available to us," placing the spiritual archive as a critical component in Black collective memory making. She names Ty and Shanice, the best friend and cousin to Latasha Harlins and two main contributors in her Netflix documentary *A Love Song to Latasha*, as spiritual archivists who are gifted with the ability to preserve and protect Latasha's story through the conviction and energy bestowed in their voices alone. In this sense, the spiritual archive acts as a medium through which we negotiate—*orchestrate*—the terms of personal narratives against that of the dominant narrative. Allison does this respectfully by choosing to leave out the public archives made available to us—the footage of fifteen-year-old Harlins's murder by convenience store clerk Soon Ja Du—and instead offering us the voice-over of Ty recounting the story of her death against abstract animation and music.

If we locate oral storytelling traditions as a part of this greater spiritual archive, this re-conjuring of life and narrative, we open a portal to an archival practice that stretches out beyond any institutional container or influence. We can include music, melodies never captured on paper, family prayers, new rules to old games, advice passed down on how to properly care for cast iron cookware. Before the media's chokehold on Blackness, we archived our histories like Tasneem's grandmother did, one story at a time, to ground ourselves in nothing but ourselves. That has never left us.

Hip-hop keeps this radical tradition going. In Dr. Rice's essay "Rakim, Ice Cube, then *Watch the Throne*: Engaged Visibility through Identity Orchestration and the Language of Hip-Hop Narratives," (2013) he notes that hip-hop artists use this oratory art form as a way to identify and affirm their identities as racialized individuals in this world. I believe storytelling—spiritual archiving—has served as the number one proponent in the quest for striking a leveled and self-assured identity balance. Repetition in music and tale massage and download centuries of everyday Black interior life into the Black psyche.

ON BLACKNESS AND BEAUTY

Black women's relationship to beauty is a complicated one, having historically not been afforded the graces and benefits of a femininity informed and defined by whiteness. As Black women talking among ourselves about identity and familial archival practices, the preservation of intergenerational Black beauty quickly became a common theme. Objects of adornment—clothes, jewelry, hair pins, and the like—were all noted as meaningful ways of orchestrating, connecting, and maintaining a sense of self.

> [The women in my family] don't have pictures, but they still have the clothes. Oh, and the shoes! There are these knit, I would say, three inch round toe platforms that are just so beautiful that I love. So those types of items . . . we're all pretty tall women, so I can wear their clothes and I've been able to see myself. Like, Black women have adorned themselves, they hold on to things that make

them feel beautiful. And I was like that's something I try to keep in my practice, in my daily ritual. What is going to make me feel beautiful, what is going to make me feel good? What do I like?

The questions Jehan poses to herself at the end of her reflection on the significance of centering Black beauty in her life ("What is going to make me feel beautiful? What do I like?") speak directly to the ways archiving plays an active role in this negotiation of presentations of self. Rice notes Winston-Proctor's race self-complexity, explaining this race reality as "consequent in how Black people consider themselves and in how they are considered by others" (Rice, 2013). Jehan's reclamation of beauty through her aunts' and grandmother's clothes and shoes is also a reclamation of the self. It's a remembering, a growing consideration of an identity that loops back around and around through Black time and legacy. Where archives are often discussed in past-tense terms, for us, these bits of history are critical components in how we get through each day and create new futures for ourselves. To borrow language from Melissa Harris-Perry, they help us stand upright in a crooked room.

GROWING CONCERNS OVER DIGITAL SPACE, LESSONS FROM OCTAVIA E. BUTLER

Like many facets of Western culture and media, the digital cyberspace was not designed to authentically capture Black folk. Ayana Jamieson, archivist and founder of the Octavia E. Butler Legacy Network, reminds us "that even the Kodak film was not really made for us to be developed so that we were visible . . . we are still left out of so many official histories." And while the film and photography industries have evolved somewhat in their ability to properly capture our depth and tones, the internet's ability to capture, preserve, and distribute Blackness among the ethers without alarming bias presents a new challenge for Black creators and consumers of digital media alike.

Safiya Noble's *Algorithms of Oppression: How Search Engines Reinforce Racism* tackles data discrimination stemming from a personal reflection of searching the phrase *black girls* with her daughter on the internet and finding pages of sexually explicit sites and discussions around stereotypes of Black girls being "sassy," "difficult," and "aggressive." These associations and tropes, though centuries old, are replicated digitally along with other modes of Black exploitation. Minstrel performances are now enacted on the screen of white users using Black reaction GIFs as representations of their emotions, now referred to as "digital blackface," and more drastic algorithmic acts like shadow banning are preventing Black people from being discovered and amplified online altogether.

Despite the narrative that the internet serves as a great equalizer, the battle of striking an identity balance for Black folk (particularly Black women's) lives on and in more insidious ways. Talks with both Jehan and Ayana circled back to a growing concern and distrust of the digital space as a safe and reliable source for Black information. Jehan explains, "I don't trust Google; they don't tell us the truth. Like, you know, you can google one thing and your responses will be totally different than someone else's Google responses based on your, you know, checking internet habits. And that's not okay. So what's the right answer?" Each of my participants took a moment to reflect on the ways digital infrastructures can be compromised, wiping out everything along with it, shattering the veil of safety of "the cloud" and "back-ups." Ayana offered a rare and insightful perspective on her observations of Octavia E. Butler's concern over the emerging digital sphere:

> When [Octavia E. Butler] finally started using the computer, for example, there were all these like random papers, like things that her mother's employer would throw out or like books or different things she'd bring for her daughter to read. But then when she started using computers, she would print out whatever she had written that day and file it because she didn't trust early Microsoft Word. . . . She didn't trust it, because she would sometimes lose her data. So she was like, forget this, I'm printing this out, right? Or she would print out her emails the same way she would keep a carbon copy of letters like 1970, so she knew what she wrote to other people. She would write down a list of which Christmas card she sent to whom and who was on her list. Right. Or, you know, her groceries or her phone messages—there's so much stuff there that we, in our everyday surroundings, take for granted that are actually artifacts that could tell someone in the future about who we are and how we function. And that's one of the things that's been really apparent to me as I go through those objects that are sometimes everyday objects, right? Mass produced, bleached copy paper or whatever. And yet something really valuable is typed onto this paper. And I would not have it if not for her printing it out, because the disks are like three and a half by three and a half floppy disks that the data is on, but they don't have a drive like that to read it.

I think it's interesting that a world-renowned science-fiction writer, in her own process of archiving and future making, actively rejected technology as the primary medium for preservation. "Octavia knew" is now a common phrase given the prophetic, apocalyptic nature of 2020 (attributed to Butler's *Parable of the Sower*). Though true, I also hear "Black women knew." Our existence and identities are threats to the state in every sense. Often the only things we can rely on are ourselves and the worlds we create for ourselves to pass on, the only things we can rely on being birthed from our own mouths and hands.

Time, space, and place are all uniquely interlocked through our archiving practices. Archiving offline serves as a deep source of identity balance striking throughout history and well into our present and future. We see evidence of it all around us—in Negro spirituals promising a never-ending afterlife for Black folk, Afro-futurist elements that arise in nearly every facet of our creative expression, and television shows like HBO's *Lovecraft Country* illustrating the power of a conjured collective memory. We see it in the glittering Black babies tucked into the stars, tiny ornaments suspended among the deep, dark, Black galaxy in *The Wiz*; in Betye Saar; in Robin Coste Lewis's (2016) *Voyage of the Sable Venus*; on T-shirts sold on the corner of Crenshaw and King declaring "We Are the New Ancestors" to passersby on the street in waves of brilliant purple and gold. On altars, in Black spells, Black prayers that time travel back and forth, boomeranging safety and healing, pilgrimages to the ocean, the chorus of "Almeda," Jehan's inherited heels, Tasneem's collection of Black Barbies she is saving for her daughter, Ayana's vision boards.

Word to Aisha Wormsley.

REFERENCES

brown, am (2019) *Pleasure Activism: The Politics of Feeling Good*. Chico, CA: AK Press.

Coste Lewis, Robin (2015). *The Voyage of the Sable Venus*. Knopf.

hooks, b. (1995) Art On My Mind: Visual Politics. New York: The New Press.

Minkler, M., & Fuller-Thomson, E. (2005). African American grandparents raising grandchildren: a national study using the Census 2000 American Community Survey. The journals of gerontology. Series B, Psychological sciences and social sciences, 60(2), 582–592. https://doi.org/10.1093/geronb/60.2.s82.

Noble, S. U. (2018). Algorithms of oppression: How search engines reinforce racism. New York: NYU Press.

Chapter 6

Writing Wrongs

Identity Orchestration and Coping in Prison

Carlton Lewis

Intellect, innovation, and creativity as paths to the "American dream" are cornerstones of the Black cultural experience. Shirley Chisolm, LeBron James, W. E. B. Du Bois, Dave Chappelle, Howard Thurman, Prince, Fannie Lou Hamer, Jay-Z, Barack Obama, Martin Luther King Jr.—the narratives of each present as maps to ways that we, Black people in particular, can place our identities such that they can be seen, felt, heard, and available to make the American context better for those alongside and who might follow. But what of incarceration? How might these narratives be shifted or erased if being imprisoned was a reality for those above? To be sure, being jailed as a tool of protest for human rights is a component of MLK's history, and El-Hajj Malik El-Shabazz provides a righteous way forward from prison into the fight for American freedoms. Then there is my narrative. I center it here as an example of how identity can be balanced toward health and contribution even when mistakes are made and social contracts are violated.\

IDENTITY ORCHESTRATION, A PRIMER

As my professional environment shifted to spaces where psychological equilibrium became more difficult to achieve passively, I found myself mentally taxed. It wasn't until I developed active, healthy coping strategies that I was able to return to psychological balance. At some level, this is work that all Black men and boys (all Black people, really) are charged to engage. And if not done well, there is a stretch to find balance and affirmation beyond acceptable social norms. For clarity here, Jay-Z and his music catalogue with narratives documenting his rise from drug dealer to a legitimate "business man" can be helpful.

Identity orchestration (Rice, 2013) is understood as a personality theory that seeks to clarify the motives of the self-system as an ego-balancing mechanism to strike psychological health. The theory began as an attempt to illustrate work by Black men and boys to maintain psychological equilibrium. Identities naturally strive for psychological balance, and identity orchestration is the process by which the person navigates their environment in an effort to fit identity to it. This was work that I was doing, unbeknownst to me, in an effort at figuring out who I was across contexts. An unadulterated presentation of self—an expression of identity orchestration that positions an uncompromised demonstration of self no matter the contextual response—is where I understand much of my identity as being figured. I continue to cope, to strive to be understood, while navigating the gendered and racialized strain of just being a Black man.

PROFESSIONAL STUDENT

For the majority of my life, I have been a student. After high school I attended Morehouse College, where I enjoyed broad and deep opportunities to be me without consequence. There were many ways for me to express my unadulterated presentation of self. In class conversation, in the café, and across other college activities, I was able to be "many mes." From expressing my street persona to articulating with my laboratory acumen, I was embraced for who I was. I did this without having to give any thought to how my actions would be perceived or if I should buffer or suppress them in any way. I felt psychologically sound without making any overly conscious efforts to be so. Morehouse College, of course, is not a permanent context, and in my next environment it would prove more difficult to remain psychologically stable.

The University of Georgia, where I began graduate school, and Morehouse couldn't be more different. Morehouse was a small, tight-knit community with a student body of about 2,500 students. It was all Black men there, just like me. Conversely, the University of Georgia is a big, sprawling campus with a student body numbering 29,000. Black people there made up about 2 percent of those attending, which was cut to much less when counting only Black men. As a doctoral student at the University of Georgia, the cognitive strain I experienced was also different than when I was at Morehouse. In pursuing this advanced degree, the coursework, competition, stereotypes, and being a "fish out of water" combined in a way that required many techniques to figure identity orchestration.

In my doctoral program, we were ranked and pitted against one another to show who was more competent and thus worthy of more praise and recognition. In the Psychology Department of sixty-plus graduate students, I was one of two Black men. And in my incoming cohort of six, I was one of only two men and the only "minority." With pressures to keep up with my equally competent peers, and being in a space where my marginal status was more apparent than ever, I felt misfit to my context. As a result, I began coping in ways counter to psychological and physical health. I drank a lot, used sex to feel better about myself, and eventually began pursuing criminal activities.

This adaptation to my new context demonstrated strained and compromised identities that had me "being" through fictionalized identities that incorporated vices to convince my larger self of my worth. This misplaced adaptation at the University of Georgia proved to have far-reaching consequences that altered the trajectory of my life.

BECOMING A STATISTIC

In December 2011, I was sentenced to seventy months of incarceration in the Federal Bureau of Prisons. I served sixty months. I was a statistic. And I was with brothers once more. We were the majority, but, again, it was not at all like at Morehouse. Prison is not a place for rehabilitation and certainly not an environment where one can easily establish psychological equilibrium.

In federal prison, your identity is stripped from you. Your name is substituted for an inmate number, and you're forced to work an assigned job that pays you meager wages. My first job was as a food server in the chow hall. I worked five days a week and was paid $5.25 for the entire month. Most things are shared, and limits are established in everything so as not to create marked differences between the less financially able inmates and those at the other end of the spectrum. We all wore the same uniform, and there were caps on phone minutes and on how much money you could spend at the commissary, the inmate's equivalent of a grocery store.

There was a TV room with a limited number of televisions, so inmates had to cooperate with one another in deciding what shows to watch. The Bureau of Prisons couches this, contending they are making everything equitable and fair so no one inmate has an abundance of resources compared to another. Really, it's more of a holding area where they allow you to graze and move around like cattle, under constant supervision.

Again, in federal prison, your individuality is stripped from you. There is no privacy. It's a communal living space. All in all, the experience blasts holes in a person's psyche, making it very difficult to find any semblance of balance:

> Wake up and take a piss, I hear 'em sharpening knives
> Main focus every day is make it out here alive (Lawd)
> Take a shower in my boots and go to sleep in my shoes
> Last night, I had a dream some killers ran in my room (Ah)

These lines from Gucci Mane's "1st Day Out tha Feds" is an unfortunate, but accurate illustration of how stressful and uncomfortable I felt in prison. The last line reveals a pervasive paranoia that made it difficult to do even the simplest of things, like sleep.

Failing to find healthy coping mechanisms while incarcerated compounds the struggle. Being removed from our neighborhoods and contexts of fit, further strained in figuring new fit with groups that are not in concert with authentically orchestrated identities, can lead to participating in criminal behavior, drug abuse, and violence while in prison in attempts to adapt.

My experience at University of Georgia, in many respects, was similar to my prison experience, at least in terms of the psychological strain. But, then, there was increased opportunity for avenues toward identity orchestration because of the racial and gendered opportunity for an authentic unadulterated presentation of self. In prison there are Black men quite capable of successfully coping with the horrible context. I found them because this was who I needed to be like.

We found psychological balance in self-expression through sports, making music and rapping in the band room, cooking and making crafts, and storytelling. The prison would occasionally host talent shows, and guys would showcase their special skills. In prison, I heard some of the most impressive singers and rappers I've ever come across. I also witnessed a softball "savant" who hit a home run virtually every time he stepped up to bat.

But my most impactful experiences while incarcerated were found in the psychological unity I struck with those Black men who shared their life stories. I'm unsure if I felt such a powerful connection with these Black men because we could relate, simply because I was yearning to hear stories about a Black neighborhood similar to my own, or because the narratives were told so vividly that they freed me from the bars I was behind, if only for the moments the stories were being told. Whatever the case, these connections led me to actively search for my own healthy ways of coping.

COPING

Though it can present as stereotypical, I took up basketball in prison. I played when I was younger to relax, and it translated well. Whenever I was feeling frustrated or stressed out, I would grab my basketball, lace up, and go to the court to shoot the rock and practice drills. I preferred to be alone on the court. Having the freedom to do any creative move that came to mind without onlookers allowed me to feel a sense of peace. I would emulate my childhood basketball idol, Kobe Bryant, and the way he contorted his body in the air while trying to make a basket. This identity expression invigorated something inside of me and allowed me to focus my energies on something other than negative emotions. Playing ball became difficult, however, when the weather was inclement or when the temperature dropped. We only had an outdoor court, and one time when attempting to play basketball in the cold, I broke a finger because the cold weather made the ball hard to the touch. That left me seeking another coping technique. And I found it in writing.

I wrote every evening while I was in prison. It allowed me to be me, to orchestrate my self by developing characters and stories that had traces of my life and my identities; most importantly, writing allowed me to tap in to the creativity and intellect that was central to the free and balanced me I'd been at Morehouse College. Having an outlet to express myself, to feel connected to my Black community, and to liberate my mind from the structured, highly ordered environment I was in was therapeutic. I was coping through my writing.

Understanding storytelling as a process of orchestrating psychological balance (Rice 2013), I was doing just that. Some of my writings during this period were made into a book of fiction that I published upon my release. Without writing as an outlet, I don't know what would have become of me in prison. Writing and storytelling afforded my mind order while incarcerated, giving me the form of expression I needed to coordinate my many identities even when confined to the worst of spaces. Imagining and telling self stories allowed me to persist and, in many respects, allowed me to be free.

REFERENCES

Gucci Mane. 2016. "1st Day Out tha Feds." *Everybody Looking*. Guwop Enterprises/ Atlantic Records. Apple iTunes.

Livingston, G. 2018. "The Changing Profile of Unmarried Parents: A Growing Share Are Living with a Partner." Pew Research Center: Social and Demographic Trends. April 25, 2018. https://www.pewsocialtrends.org/2018/04/25/

the-changing-profile-of-unmarried-parents/#:~:text=Among%20solo%20
parents%2C%2042%25%20are,cohabiting%20moms%20(30%25%20vs.'

National KIDS Count. 2020. "Children in Single-Parent Families by Race in
the United States." The Annie E. Casey Foundation: The Kids Count Data
Center. Accessed January 2, 2020. https://datacenter.kidscount.org/data/tables/107-
children-in-single-parent-families-by-race#detailed/1/any/false/1729,37,871,870,5
73,869,36,868,867,133/10,11,9,12,1,185,13/432,431.

Rice, D. W. 2013. "Rakim, Ice Cube, then *Watch the Throne*: Engaged Visibility
through the Identity Orchestrations and the Language of Hip-Hop Narratives." *The
Journal of Popular Culture, 46*(1), 173–91.

Rice, D. W., Wall, B., and Hayes, W. M. 2010. "Black Males, 'Church' and
Supplementary Education: General Considerations." In *Educating Comprehensively:
Varieties of Educational Experiences*, edited by Edmund W. Gordon, Herve H.
Varenne, and Linda Lin (69–93). Lewiston, ME: Edwin Mellen Press.

Snyder, C. R., and Dinoff, B. L. 1999. "Coping: Where Have You Been?" In *Coping:
The Psychology of What Works*, edited by Charles R. Snyder (3–19). New York:
Oxford University Press.

Chapter 7

From Corporate to Camera

Identity Orchestration and Finding Purpose

Mikki Kathleen Harris

In my senior year of high school, I was working at a local Mexican restaurant as a host, earning thirty-four dollars a day, a significant step up from my three years as a busser. I used the money earned to buy gas and to go out with friends. All was right with the world.

Then, one evening after school, my parents sat me down with paperwork on the table. "You need to think about your future," they said. "You need to have a job that will lead you to a career, not just one that makes money." My mother handed me a brochure for INROADS. "This program prepares you for an internship that will set you up for a career."

This conversation was about more than the present moment. My parents were pouring into me based on their lived experience and how they were informed about identity, position, and success. We come from a proud line of domestic and factory workers from New York, Philadelphia, Camden, New Jersey, and the Caribbean, people who positioned my parents to have a drive that allowed them to create access not only for themselves but also for their children. That access was in education and corporate America.

My parents asked me what I wanted to do for a living, and I had absolutely no idea. I'd not thought about a corporate career, or any other for that matter. There was no internet search for me in 1992, so I thought of the television ads and sponsorship placements that were familiar. Arthur Andersen had a commercial that stood out, even though I knew nothing about accounting or the other services that the company provided. Nevertheless, I answered my parents with "I want to be an accountant."

By the time Dori Ray, the INROADS recruiter, showed up at my school for an information session, I could name the Big Six firms, the employee counts, and the cities they were in, and, after an afternoon shadowing a partner at Ernst & Young, I knew the dress code and to not assume *audit* and *tax* were the same thing.

I was accepted into the INROADS program, and when I entered Spelman College as a freshwoman, I was confident that I was on a good path, one where I was set up with an internship for four summers, training to make me a strong candidate in corporate spaces, and potential for a full-time offer at Arthur Andersen after a successful four years. No pressure.

I majored in economics with a minor in management and organization. It required two semesters of accounting. The first semester of my sophomore year, I sat in Accounting 101. Filling out the first general ledger was similar to when I had done inventory of Brio trains for my mother at her toy store, The Village Owl, as a kid. I was completing work to get to the fun, except there was no toy for me at the end of the ledger. I asked myself, "How do I keep my internship and never take another accounting class?" There was no answer, so I enrolled in Accounting 102 that spring and went back to Arthur Andersen for my third summer interning.

TWO WORLDS EMERGE: IDENTITY DILEMMA ARTICULATION 101

Andersen Worldwide of Philadelphia was on floors twenty-six to thirty-two of 1601 Market Street in Center City, Philadelphia. Five floors were Arthur Andersen, one floor was Andersen Consulting, and an additional floor was for shared services. I found my way to every floor at some point in the internship. It started with the copy room and reception desks my first summer, human resources in the second summer, and then marketing for the third summer. I was told that my final summer would be in audit, and I would need to apply what I was learning in my accounting classes.

This is when I decided to explore other options. I took the back stairs down to the thirtieth floor to find the office recruiter. She was positive and full of energy. I let her know that I was interested in switching from Arthur Andersen to Andersen Consulting, the caveat being I needed to know what consulting was. She explained, "At Andersen Consulting, it's using technology to be solutions-driven; it's something you actually have to be in and doing to know what it is."

I signed up. It felt like a years-old weight had been lifted. I was out of accounting and into an area of corporate work that had something to do with computers. I spent the summer before my senior year of Spelman at Andersen

Consulting, working on software design at a client site. The most memorable part of the internship was using the intranet on a laptop and having an email address. I didn't have anyone to email, but learning the basics of networks, front-end design, back-end build, and communication through data was interesting. My closest friends spent their summers working for KPMG Peat Marwick, AT&T, the 1996 Olympic Games, AR Sports, Sam's Club, and Upward Bound. I was excited to have a sense of what consulting was, as we compared notes and talked about our future with plans to break glass ceilings.

The fall of my last year at Spelman, I audited a computer science class so that I would know a software language before starting work full time. By spring semester, I had room for an additional class, so I tried to take photography. I loved the disc camera that my nana gave me in 1985 and that free Burger King camera I got with the kids' meal way back when. I wanted to hold a "real camera" in my hand and learn how to use it, but I only had a 35mm point-and-shoot that was set to full auto. And the only photography class, at Clark Atlanta University, was full.

I registered for Dr. Gloria Wade Gayles's Images of Women in the Media class instead. The course was incredible. It opened my eyes to the appropriate use of language—Who knew you pronounce *the* as *thee* before a vowel? The course introduced me to words like *hegemony*, *pedagogy*, *intersectionality*, *objectification*. Most of all, Dr. Wade Gayles situated us to "claim your space" and to examine media in ways that push against the white male gaze.

The class was my "time off" from the real world. It allowed me to think and to be critical of ever-present advertisements, billboards, music videos, television shows, magazines, movies, and news. Class projects encouraged us to lead by change. So, as a tennis player on the road with the Spelman and Morehouse teams, I borrowed a video camera and began to gather team perspectives on stereotypes across media.

I graduated from Spelman labeled a feminist—a dig by those throwing the words but a compliment to me as I had labels put on me all my life, and this one didn't feel limiting. This is where *the* real world and *my* real world began distinguishing themselves from one another.

My career in the consulting world began in fall 1997 with a tight-knit group of recent undergrads and MBA grads coming from schools in the Philly area, and me from Spelman. Our first six weeks flattened our layers. It didn't matter what we studied or where we came from; we learned to code and to use a solutions-driven approach to work with a team. Process was prioritized. Identities were stripped. Learning curves were high. There was no space for creativity and expression, but I appreciated the training that had history majors and economics majors learning a new language of coding that could take us to new horizons.

We were still under a business attire dress code with suits, stockings, and dress shoes required. This changed with the introduction of business casual, but I still had a client ask where we bought our uniforms. I hadn't thought of the mold that we matched to, but when I see those shared cobalt-blue shirts today, I know it all too well. I'd fit into my job, but at what cost?

As a consultant, you don't work in the office; you work with a consulting team at a client site, helping that client with a solution implemented through technology. I was told by a supervisor on one of my teams that to work eight to five was considered "teller hours," and we were not bank tellers. Consultants get to work before the client and stay at work until after the client goes home. My project team would become the people I spent most of my time with. We worked in gray cubicles pieced together in one large room. We were in each other's conversations, took lunch breaks to delis together, paused for the occasional happy hour, and formed tennis and flag football teams that we never had time to play on.

I tried to keep a separate life on weekends, but with no real success. A good friend of mine said, "You've sold your soul to this job." Friday evenings at home I was on conference calls, Saturdays were spent preparing for Monday's work, and Sunday was spent packing and getting ready for travel to the client on Monday. When Andersen Consulting was retooled as Accenture in 2001, with a new logo, brand statements, and a future-focused vision, I asked myself, "Who am I? What is *my* vision?" I couldn't answer those questions and was disturbed because I knew the answers were in spaces quite separate from the life I was plugging through.

There was no way for me to figure out who I was while working. I needed to get away from work, from home, from everything to find answers. During a performance evaluation with my supervisor, who was a partner, I said that I wanted to take a few months off at some point to do a service project. She was supportive, but there was nothing like that available, even if unpaid. I'd have to figure things out with the built-in five weeks of paid time off, time that we were actually expected not to use. I felt stuck, slowly losing myself to a career that offered little more than money and innovative ways of doing, but not for myself.

Then, one Thursday night while checking my email, I found a message offering six-and twelve-month sabbaticals to employees with the promise of job security at the end of the time away. We could keep our benefits and computers and receive a small percentage of our salary, as long as we met the conditions set in the agreement. I closed my computer, packed up to get on Amtrak, and traveled from Thirtieth Street to Union Station for the weekend. Once in DC, I told my friend about the opportunity. He asked me when I'd be signing up. "I need to think about it and to figure things out," was my response.

My mind raced with how I would pay my rent and student and car loans, and then I had no idea what I would do while away. My life as a consultant was all I knew. My identity had not only become attached to the job, it mostly was the job. My friend said, "Mik, if you don't take this sabbatical, you're slapping God in the face." Certainly, I hadn't thought of it that way.

I signed up, and on Monday morning my supervisor checked in with me to see if I had everything straight with the sabbatical. "You talked about this during your evaluation, so you were technically the first person to sign up."

I gave up my apartment, leased my car to someone, and put student loan payments on hold. I had enough saved to eat and to travel for six months, but I needed to figure out where to go. I grew up in a house of Spanish speakers who referred to me as *gringa*, so I figured my first trip should allow me to immerse myself in Spanish and become fluent. I was going to Panama, set to leave September 12, 2001.

Of course, with the September 11th terrorist attacks, that trip to Panama was put on hold, and so was I for the moment, but then the need to "find myself" felt even more necessary. Life is to be lived.

When air travel was back up a few days later, I flew with my entire family to the Virgin Islands. Tickets were under $200, and we had enough extended family there for me to stay and figure out next steps. While in the Virgin Islands, I had my parents, sister, aunties, uncles, cousins, and friends discussing my "midlife crisis."

To be sure, from the outside looking in, this "crisis" could be minimized as little more than a crisis of juggling privilege. But in looking at identity balance, we also know that no matter our station or access, the duality of being Black in the Western world, with the intersection of being a woman, pulls on the Black psyche universally while negotiating Du Bois's double-consciousness. The complications are even more acute when lifting the veil and recognizing that the baubles, bangles, and beads of promised success are misfit to a Black woman-ed you that is rooted in Barbuda. These are the echoes I was trying to source.

I left the Virgin Islands on a flight and booked a thirty-day car rental in San Juan, Puerto Rico. I enrolled in a Spanish immersion school and stayed with a family elder, Cajita. I was named for her son, Mickey, who died during the Tet offensive in the Vietnam war. And though I'd not seen her since I was a young child, Cajita embraced me as her own.

I knew of Mickey as a person everyone loved: a loyal friend, a great athlete, a devoted son. Staying with his mother, who wore an "Actividad Mickey Ojeda" T-shirt, clutched his oversized Morris High School ring on her finger, prayed for me daily, and sipped Cafe Bustelo in between stories of her children, was an immersion class all its own. At the end of my time there, I walked away with a fluency in Spanglish and an even greater appreciation of how we live our lives and the legacy we leave behind. My identity was being pulled from the cubicles and cobalt-blue shirts that had suspended it from a full self for some time.

I purchased my first real camera, a Canon Elan 7E, and traveled. Between September and February, I touched eleven Caribbean islands and Australia. Buddy passes and homestays carried me to and through each stay. I spent the majority of my time "off the grid," connecting to ancestral cultures that I previously knew only through food, music, and oral tradition. Now I found it through *my* lived experience. I stayed local, ate local, studied local, and discussed politics. Within each new space, I began to look at daily life, people, and events through my own lens, not one shared with others. I knew the montages I was photographing could speak important truths to a larger society that needed to know them. It was through my camera that I began to document the lives of others and began to demonstrate mine.

AN UNADULTERATED PRESENTATION OF SELF

I returned to Accenture in February 2002. I was at the same client site, working in the design stage of computer application development, my favorite stage of work. In March, I sat down for my performance evaluation full of confidence. My friend, a colleague that I'd started with, was now supervising me because my peers had moved up a level while I was on sabbatical. The eval was not the A+ I knew I'd earned. Ratings for a few areas were low because I was now being rated against my now-advanced peer group. I was performing at a top consultant level, but since my peers were now managers, I was being rated by a manager metric.

It made no sense. On the other side of defining myself as an individual, I was being pulled back to a uniform context where my identity was, again, reduced to flattened layers. I couldn't have that. I researched opportunities that fit my skills and interests, places where I could blend information technology, travel, and photography.

A great opportunity appeared in the Digital Village project, sponsored by Kodak and established by the NGO Africare. Bono of the music group U2 was a spokesperson, and the job was to establish information technology education and research centers in townships in South Africa. I applied, interviewed, and was accepted. I bought the largest suitcase I could find and started communicating with the previous fellow, who had just returned from her stint in South Africa. I had a start date and was waiting on travel information so that I could give notice at work. As I approached my timeframe, I became a bit concerned that I had no information on logistics. Time passed, and I eventually found out that Kodak could no longer sponsor the project. Stuck again. Not even the perfect fit was an option.

The morning alarm would buzz in my corporate apartment at 5:30 a.m. I'd hit snooze multiple times, calculate how many minutes I actually needed to get ready and commute to work, then hit snooze again. I'd search my mind for motivation to get out of bed, but the motivation thinned. I didn't want to get up. I had my sabbatical days on my mind, and I imagined meditating in the Caribbean Sea with the sun on my face. That sea was far from Pennsylvania, so I embraced what I could. I grabbed my camera in the morning and captured images of anything I could find outside.

The photos were not the best, but the exercise was beautiful. It gave me energy before heading to work. So, I doubled down, signing up for a Monday/ Wednesday night photography class at the Art Institute of Philadelphia. I attended two classes the entire semester and developed black-and-white images I took of a mural of Jackie Robinson in North Philly, but work was too demanding to take the evening break. I showed up at the end of class on the last day of the semester to share with the instructor some of my photographs from the sabbatical. I had twenty images tucked into plastic photo sleeves. I flipped through each, then asked for feedback. The professor carefully went through the collection, explaining, "This is photojournalism, not fine art."

Her statement hit different, connecting to something I'd always known but hadn't formalized. I am a storyteller.

I moved through the work weeks knowing there was an end in sight. It gave me renewed energy as I applied for graduate programs in photojournalism. I was accepted to Boston University's School of Communication and prepared for a change in career starting August 2003. In the weeks leading up to my leaving work, I had one-on-one lunches with coworkers I'd known since my days as an intern and those at the client site. Everyone expressed support, and those I knew well explained they wanted to do something different too but didn't know how to figure beyond the corporate catch. "This is all I know," one friend said.

I entered journalism school, and a friend from home connected me with Ayanna Pressley, who was working for John Kerry's campaign. Ayanna set me up with press passes for local events, and I used the access as my beat for coverage that year. Covering the Democratic primaries threw me into the photojournalism and political coverage that I find thrilling today. Both the National Association of Black Journalists and the Poynter Institute introduced me to a network of journalists and opportunities that have shaped my career as a photojournalist. For the past eighteen years, I've had front-row access to major events, remote towns, and people who I am able to approach because of the job.

Covering sports taught me how to use the camera in the same way you drive a manual transmission car. Do it enough and it becomes second nature. Study the sport, analyze players to anticipate plays, place the camera, and focus on what is about to happen. Athletes like LeBron James make that anticipation strategy tricky, but sports coverage made me technically stronger. Covering politics challenges me to find the unique angle and the details that not every camera composes. Concerts (I could do without) helped me understand lighting and how to make the most of the ninety seconds to three minutes allowed for capturing images.

I used my assignments to learn and to grow to become a better photojournalist, but I felt like my daily assignments were preparing me for something else, and I didn't quite know what that something else was. I began to think about the stories that I'd worked on, the events and people I'd covered: Rosa Parks's funeral, Coretta Scott King's funeral, the NCAA Final Four, NBA playoffs, Stanley Cup playoffs, NASCAR Cup series, Belmont Stakes, MLB, NFL, WNBA, PGA, 9–11 survivors, US veterans, the Democratic National Convention, the Republican National Convention, Democratic primaries, the Georgia governor campaign trail, Civil Rights Walk of Fame, Martin Luther King papers at Sotheby's, US presidents, a Liberian president, senators, congressional members, US Capitol coverage, athletes, educators, students, CEO portraits, concerts, plays, crimes, high school sports, and features.

The coverage I've been a part of has allowed me to witness and to document life that I can fully articulate through the visual moments captured. I've gained knowledge through lived experience. My world has expanded with firsthand access to major events and people. And I have learned that the "big" experiences are only as impactful as the authenticity attached. The meaning of the moments are the big experiences, no matter how much mass media is attending.

Brittany O'Connell was a high school student living in a motel with her mother, training in preparation for the United States Military Academy Prep School. At the time, she needed money for uniforms and incidentals, and after the story ran, more than two hundred people sent letters of encouragement and close to $30,000 in donations. Brittany became a cadet, and six years later graduated from West Point Academy.

Vonetta Flowers was the first Black woman in the world to win a US Winter Olympic gold medal. I covered Vonetta as she was competing in a bobsled qualifying event in Lake Placid, New York, so that she could compete in the Winter Olympics in Turin, Italy. The story was about more than the Olympics and her athletic genius. Her twin sons were born premature, and one of the boys had an undeveloped ear and ear canal. The only doctor in the world who could perform the surgery to build his ear was located near Turin.

The coverage of Vonetta was of a mother juggling family and career, but most importantly, a woman motivated by her family and led by God.

Katrina Poe was the only doctor in her town of Kilmichael, Mississippi. Dr. Poe had a medical practice, was the doctor for the hospital, worked in the nursing facility, was on call for school sports, and did house calls. A Black woman, she had white patients refuse her services until they realized she was the only person who could treat them. I shadowed Dr. Poe, who at the time had a newborn son and toddler and slept just a few hours a night. Her husband, parents, and sister were supportive in her life, but documenting Dr. Poe helped me to see how someone can do what seems impossible.

Celeste Waddell was a respiratory therapist working at Charity Hospital in New Orleans during Hurricane Katrina. Celeste manually pumped air into a patient to keep him alive throughout the night as the floodwaters rose in the hospital. She thought of her own son, who had died prior to Katrina, as she helped to save the life of this young patient. Her connection to the patient and his mother was a chapter in the series "Through Hell and High Water."

Adia Fields was a Spelman student who graduated from college after surviving a car accident that forced her to begin again, relearning to walk and eat, and ultimately regaining independence. I covered her as she walked across the stage at her graduation.

And there are so many more narratives: the "Lost Boys of Sudan," an undocumented immigrant who suffered third-degree burns while saving neighbors from a fire, families split apart at the border of Mexico and Arizona, the many people coming to the United States with a strong spirit who struggle to adjust and fit in to the United States, and on and on.

I often ask people I document what keeps them going, where and how they find the motivation to do what they do. Each of the women mentioned above said that it all comes from God. There is a connection to spirit that allows each of them to live in purpose as they overcome challenges, inspire goodness, and create meaningful change as decent human beings.

This is where I find the significance in sharing self stories and of realizing the self stories of others. They are identity salvations, maps and magnifiers of who we are and who we can be.

I connect to immigrant voices because of my family. In 2006, I took my camera gear with me to the island of Barbuda to record oral history narratives and to capture the stories of my paternal family's homeland the year after my grandmother passed away. Most of the interviews started with stories about my grandmother, grandfather, uncles, aunts, great-grandparents, or my father, but they all transitioned to the island, its history, and for some, issues around environmental destruction and greed. This time documenting people transcended storytelling, which had felt so right for me since I picked up that first camera.

There was the discovery of self through the context of family heritage and fight that I use to inform and motivate me today as I employ storytelling to preserve and protect culture. Understanding my family members as communal owners and stewards of their land, as subsistence fishers who used their hands to make everything their family needed, who immigrated for opportunities and made sacrifices that I would later benefit from, positions an orchestrated identity that allows me to appreciate my parents' guidance while putting my authentic self into the work that I do. I was able to deepen their instruction, "You need to have a job that will lead you to a career, not just one that makes money" to mean, "find yourself in the work that you do so that there is meaning and purpose attached." I've come to know that in doing this, there is a freedom that corporate access and money alone cannot match. It is a freedom to be, an elusive identity that we all look to bring closer to self.

Chapter 8

A Picture of James Baldwin Dancing for Freedom

Social Dance and Identity Orchestration

Asha L. French and C. Malik Boykin

PREFACE TO A HOUSE PARTY

In *Balance: Advancing Identity Theory by Engaging the Black Male Adolescent*, David Wall Rice (2008) invokes James Baldwin in his explanation of two facets of the Black male identity: the nature of Blackness in America (as described by Baldwin) and the experience of being a Black male (as described by Ellison). An existentialist lens allows Rice to conceive of Black identity in a way that pulls from both sets of descriptions. He defines identity stasis/identity orchestration as "the balance of this Black identity with other identities."

This balance depends on consciousness of ego depletion and replenishment. According to this theory, identity static occurs when there is "dissonance between self, related identities, and the context." In this lyric essay, we incorporate music and personal narrative to suggest that Black social life contributed to Baldwin's ultimate identity orchestration—the balance he struck between his individual self, his cultural self, and his racial self. Baldwin's work bears out the difficulty of integrating the individual and cultural identity into the oppressive prescriptions for Black identity in his America. White-authored biographical works on Baldwin (such as *I Am Not*

101

Your Negro) tend to emphasize this difficulty, cloaking Baldwin in what Rice calls a "dire film of hopelessness" associated with studies of Black men.

What follows is a house party in words. The house party essay is a form of the lyric essay, a hybrid that combines academic theory with creative writing.

Our house party combines memoir, music, identity, and literary analysis to gather loved ones with no agenda other than to be. In this essay, we are just two people in a living room, moving fluidly between concepts and thinkers who nod to us from across the room. The theme of this party-in-prose is the relationship between social dance and Black identity orchestration.

We get the party started with Malik's song "Dancing for Freedom." The song is the call. The response is our joint meditation on freedom, dance, and identity. Baldwin is the party guest we spend the most time with, as his life-long body of work helps us think about how Black men create healthy identities while navigating a pathological context. Most of us know that James Baldwin read the construction of whiteness for filth. What few of us know is how dancing helped him manage his relentless confrontation with white American myth making while retaining his own sense of self.

We lovingly use the form of the house party to vibe on these questions while connecting with our kin.

> It was an amazing thing
> when I found out why the caged bird sings. (Boykin 2021)

Maya Angelou wrote *I Know Why the Caged Bird Sings* at the behest of her brother and friend James Baldwin. In the documentary *And Still I Rise*, Angelou describes meeting Baldwin: "He was small and *hot*, dancing himself. He had the movements of a dancer. I mean his movements were always the movements of a dancer. So when I met Jimmy, well, we liked each other." Theirs was a glance of recognition; Angelou met Baldwin when she was in the process of "dancing [her]self." She'd been a dancer, an actress, and a Calypso singer. Baldwin must have known that the autobiography would propel her to the stardom and financial security she'd sought for herself. He was right. The first volume of what would become a serial autobiography *I Know Why the Caged Bird Sings* was a coming-of-age story describing the first leg of Angelou's remarkable journey.

The title alludes to Angelou's coming to voice after a self-imposed period of silence. Family members had killed the man who raped her, and Angelou blamed her own telling, not the rapist's choices, for his death. At eight, she decided that if words could get a person killed, she would not use them. Throughout her entire autobiography series, Angelou sticks to this refusal to indict with words, describing the ways racism impacted her without pointing a Baldwinian finger at the purveyors of racist logic.

Unlike the bird in "Sympathy," the Paul Lawrence Dunbar poem from which Angelou borrowed her title, her narrators do not sport bloodied wings from beating against the constructions that could have curbed her potential. Instead, she emphasizes her own resilience, leaving the politics and the polemical to her big brother James. Angelou published her first book just a couple of years after the three assassinations that would haunt Baldwin for the rest of his life: Martin Luther King Jr., Malcolm X, and Medgar Evers. The popularity of her autobiographical series and poems like "Still I Rise" is an indication that a culture-war-weary America preferred testifying to signifying.

Angelou may have been signifying on the act of signifying when she wrote "Caged Bird" in 1983. For Dunbar, the caged bird's song is "not a carol of joy or glee" but instead a heartfelt prayer, a "plea, that upward to Heaven he flings—." Where Dunbar's bird sings prayerfully, Angelou's bird sings a "fearful trill" while standing on "the grave of dreams." For both Dunbar and Angelou, freedom is a fixed state that exists outside of the cage. While Dunbar's speaker identifies with the bloodied bird who continues to beat against the bars of his cage, Angelou's speaker seems to have removed herself from the bird and his rage. In "Caged Bird," Angelou compares the plights of the free and caged birds but seems to indicate that the caged bird suffers more from his own rage than from the cage that holds him back. Were they not friends, one might think the following lines were signifying on big brother James himself:

> But a bird that stalks
> down his narrow cage
> can seldom see through
> his bars of rage
> his wings are clipped and
> his feet are tied
> so he opens his throat to sing

In 1983, this bird-that-might-be-Baldwin would have been standing on the grave of dreams born in the civil rights movement, and, if our read of Angelou's poem is onto something, she believes his rage has blinded him. In her documentary, she said (without judgment), "What Jimmy was, was angry. He was angry at injustice, at ignorance, at exploitation, at stupidity, at vulgarity. Yes, he was angry." The unjust, ignorant, exploitative, vulgar, stupid people who clipped his wings or tied his feet are mysteries buried beneath a promise Angelou made to her eight-year-old self not to name the perpetrator while telling the story of how she got over.

Baldwin made a speaking career of naming the perpetrators of the American nightmare. A novelist at heart, he imagined America as a series of interconnected stories, all fiction, all featuring clear antagonists and protagonists. The fiction of America, with its European immigrant antagonists, was crystal-clear to him and headed toward a tragic end. No wonder he often wrote and spoke about rage. In "Stranger in the Village," Baldwin writes, "The rage of the disesteemed is personally fruitless, but it is also absolutely inevitable; this rage, so generally discounted, so little understood even among the people whose daily bread it is, is one of the things that makes history. Rage can only with difficulty, and never entirely, be brought under the domination of the intelligence and is therefore not susceptible to any arguments whatever. . . . Also, rage cannot be hidden, it can only be dissembled" (165).

In Baldwin's essay, rage seems to be a force unto itself. Baldwin spoke and wrote about rage in white-facing venues and publications that required the passive voice. Hence, Black rage is "discounted" (by whom?), "little understood" (not by us) even by the rageful, and must "be brought" under domination. Further, it can't "be hidden" but must "be dissembled." By employing the passive voice, Baldwin focuses attention on the rage, not the rageful. By focusing on an "absolutely inevitable" rage, Baldwin de-essentializes an emotion that the mythmakers conveniently attached to Blackness during Reconstruction. The space offers room for Baldwin to replenish the ego depleted by American racism and the limited control over Black male possibilities. Before emancipation the mythmakers denied Black rage, selling instead the story of the happy, dancing darky. The incessant revolts were written off as anomalous, disconnected from the dancing witnessed by onlookers. This was an expensive misinterpretation of Black sociality, as the people who could not recognize the practices of freedom were unprepared for the moment it would be taken by force.

"Dancing for Freedom" gives a new interpretation of the caged bird's song. He sings to remind himself that he is a free bird, caged. "Free" is the essence. "Caged" is the situation. Dancing for freedom is celebrating one's essence despite the situation. Rice writes that "ego-replenishment is the 'building up' of a muscle that was strained as a result of the depletion" (2008, 29). Similarly, the essence is a muscle that, when exercised, will sometimes break the bars that bind you. This is especially true for social dance, since the self's relationship to the kinship group is such a huge component of Black identity. Like Baldwin, we first learned this lesson in church.

> Then when I started to move
> it was a spiritual awakening. (Boykin 2021)

Daddy was the piano player at our family church, where his father, my grand-father, was the pastor. Our church was small. There was no band. If Daddy was moved by the spirit to dance, the congregation had to keep the music going with their voices, their hands, and their tambourines. We called it "get-ting happy" with the same synecdoche that substitutes "bread and butter" for the rest of what a person affords with income. We knew, really, that he was doing more than just getting happy.

Jacqui Malone (1996), American dance historian and author of *Steppin' on the Blues: The Visible Rhythms of African American Dance*, would call Daddy's dancing an African retention of spiritual practice: "on both conti-nents [Africa and North America] black dance is a source of energy, joy, and inspiration; a spiritual antidote to oppression" (24). Malone traces the deep culture of Black dance to the Kongo, where "dancing was rarely done for pleasure alone; spiritual power itself could not be summoned itself without the influence of designated dances" (24).

Baldwin nodded to the Kongo origins of "getting happy" in *Go Tell It on the Mountain*, his first semiautobiographical novel:

> While John watched, the Power struck someone, a man or woman; they cried out a long, wordless crying, and, arms outstretched like wings, they began the Shout. Someone moved the chair a little to give them room, the rhythm paused, the singing stopped, only the pounding feet and the clapping hands were heard; then another cry, another dancer; then the tambourines began again, and the voices rose again, and the music swept on again, like fire, or flood, or judg-ment. . . . One day, so everyone said, this Power would possess him; he would sing and cry as they did now, and dance before his King. (6–7)

For Baldwin, the spirit is a promise, "this Power" that will find him even when he is feeling ugly and worthless. The spirit first found Baldwin in church, but it would also find him in secular spaces. There are only two pic-tures (that we know of) that bear this out.

They both capture James Baldwin dancing in the living room of a New Orleans home dubbed "Freedom House" by the activists who found shelter (and a clearing) there. The home belonged to John and Virgie Castle, a long-shoreman and waitress whose daughters became Freedom Riders. In support of a movement they didn't always understand (who would want to sit at those funky counters anyway when Dooky Chase, the Black restaurant with the best fried chicken, was right up the street?), the Castles opened their home to comrades of their daughters, Oretha and Doris Jean Castle.

In the first picture, Baldwin and Doris Jean Castle face each other. They could be doing any variation of the two-step, that classic ingredient of any house party worth writing home about. If dance is a conversation, the two-step captured in the first picture is a polite "hello." By the second picture, Baldwin and Castle know each other better. Baldwin has done away with his suit jacket, unbuttoned his collar, and loosened his tie. Castle found a cigarette *and* a lighter somewhere, and she's throwin' it back at her new friend (although, to be fair, there is still enough room for the holy ghost to slide between them). After all, they aren't dancing alone; they have company.

The pictures of Baldwin and Castle dancing in a cleared space in the living room were taken by freelance photographer Steve Schapiro. One of them would appear in the May 24, 1963, issue of *Life*.

> When things gets overwhelming,
> gotta dance till you break morning. (Boykin 2021)

Journalist Jane Howard followed James Baldwin on his first tour of the South. Baldwin's parents were displaced southerners who'd likely told horror stories about the white folks they left behind. That the South would be the birthplace of what Baldwin later called the "new Civil War" was a surprise and an inspiration. In the early 1960s, he decided to find out how he could be of service to the movement. The trip was white-magazine-newsworthy because Baldwin had won critical acclaim for his novels and essays.

Jane Howard was a white woman. She dropped subtle hints of her whiteness, of her cultural disconnect, dehumanizing Baldwin in her descriptions (if she wrote the captions to the photo essay). She called him "gnomelike" and later emphasized his "huge, protruding eyes." Another hint was her attempt at categorization; she called the dance captured in the first picture "The Hitchhiker." There wasn't a thumb in sight.

The final clue was a critical misunderstanding of the function of social dance in Black culture: "To unwind from the strain of speaking publicly," she wrote, "Baldwin drinks and dances and subjects himself to painful motel-room bouts of introspection" (36b). The list makes drinking look like the catalyst for Baldwin's dancing and thinking, the white imagination of just what went on at the Savoy anyway. She also imagines him "wound up" from speaking publicly, a task he described as "too easy," rather than from confronting a people whose myths authored his misery. Howard imagines that dancing is stress relief from being an "articulate" Negro, an exercise in mindlessness that precedes the "real" intellectual work. Howard may be employing a Du Boisian double-consciousness model to a man whose self-construction would better be understood through the filter of what A. Wade Boykin calls the triple quandary (Boykin 1986). Rice argues that Boykin matures Du Boisian double-consciousness by "emphasizing an African cultural ethos and interrelated dimensions of spirituality, harmony, movement, verve, affect, communalism, expressive individualism, oral tradition, and social time per-spective" (2008, 22).

Howard didn't know what was going on in Virgie Castle's house. Baldwin and Doris Jean Castle were creating an otherwise world with an "African cultural ethos." To borrow Angelou's phrase, Castle and Baldwin were *dancing themselves* anew.

> Move until the break of dawn
> if you feel like tomorrow ain't coming. (Boykin 2021)

This line carries us to Morrison's clearing space, as it is one of the first directives in the song. The first two lines are testimony: the speaker shares his process of finding meaning, then tapping into spirit. But in the gentle transition to the declarative (from "[you] gotta dance til you break morning" to "Move[!!!]," Malik gets downright sermonic, becomes a shaman, a twenty-first-century Baby Suggs, holy.

In *Beloved*, Toni Morrison's Pulitzer Prize–winning neo-slave narrative, Baby Suggs, holy, is a character who presides over the clearing ceremony for the enslaved. "In the heat of every Saturday afternoon," Morrison writes, "she sat in the clearing while the people waited among the trees" (87).

Like a DJ calling dancers to the floor, she begins to draw people out of the woods and toward the clearing space, a bridge between Boykin's triple quandary and Rice's identity orchestration. The fields of Sweet Home could represent the "minority realm" of the construct, where Black folks must negotiate their identities in the context of their oppression while being policed by racialized others who consider themselves superior. According to Rice's definition, the space is also a site of ego depletion, where there is definitely a "too-high tax" placed on the individual's limited range of personal choices. The clearing, on the other hand, is the Afro-cultural space that provides ego replenishment for the individual, a place to exercise all the muscles disal-lowed in white space.

The clearing space has also been theorized as a hush harbor, a place that is just under the radar of the oppressors who are near but ignorant to the codes Black people are speaking with their bodies. Baby Suggs, holy, has an embodiment task for all of the gathered. She wants the children to laugh until their parents smile. She wants the women to cry, releasing grief for the dead and those still living on what Angelou called the "graves of dreams." Finally, she calls the men to dance. "'Here,' she said, 'in this here place we flesh; flesh that weeps, laughs; flesh that dances on bare feet in the grass. Love it. Love it hard. Yonder they do not love your flesh. They despise it. . . . *You* got to love it, *you*!'" (88).

There is another picture of Doris Jean Castle in which she is wearing her "yonder" face. In a photo in the archives of the Congress on Racial Equality (CORE), Castle sits stiffly in a chair that four police officers carry down a flight of steps. The description says, "This is a 1963 photo of New Orleans CORE member Doris Jean Castle being removed by police from a demonstration at the local City Hall."

Castle looks over the edge of her chair as if she needs to prepare herself for the moment the police officers will abandon decorum and toss her to the ground. She wears sensible, close-toed shoes, a skirt, and a jacket. She is the very picture of the minority representative, the nonviolent Negro ideal, one weapon in an arsenal of tactics that would move the needle on segregation.

At her mama's house, the Freedom House, she is less composed. She is home. She wears house shoes, smokes a cigarette. She laughs and smiles. She turns around, looks back at James as if asking him if he can handle what she's putting down. The question seems honest, and his answer is affirmative. In that place, they are flesh. Loving themselves. Dancing themselves holy and free.

> I know what I'm bout (Ah Ha)
> Can't fill me with doubt (No No)
> I'm holding my clout (Ah Ha)
> And dancing it out (Boykin 2021)

In this essay, Malik and I are practicing identity orchestration by integrating the parts of ourselves that we usually reserve for various clearing spaces. While the nature of this collection is its own sort of clearing (for which we are grateful), we spend much of our academic lives out "yonder." By integrating our art forms in the academic task of expounding on the concept of identity orchestration, we model and practice the multiple negotiations that Black people face on a daily basis.

Earlier drafts of this essay find us pitching to the yonder crowd, trying to build a bridge between our art and our scholarship in stuffy language that didn't dance. But we returned again and again to the song that inspired this essay, dancing so much that the form of the essay announced itself. We've danced it out. At the end of the day, what we've created is a clearing space where we celebrate the elements of our artistic expression that we've been (poorly) advised to keep separate from our academic selves. This essay is Virgie Castle's living room floor, a place where we invite you to loosen your tie and hope you can pick up what we're putting down.

REFERENCES

Baldwin, James. *Notes of a Native Son*. Beacon Press, 2012.

Boykin, A. W. *The Triple Quandary and the Schooling of Afro-American Children*. Lawrence Erlbaum, 1986.

Malone, Jacqui. *Steppin' on the Blues*. University of Illinois Press, 1996.

Rice, David Wall. *Balance: Advancing Identity Theory by Engaging the Black Male Adolescent*. Lexington Books, 2008.

Starx, Malik. *Dancing for Freedom*. 2021.

Chapter 9

Eleven Days Older Than

Riffs on Reflexivity, Teaching, and the Global Exercise of Being Whole

David Wall Rice

BEGINNING THOUGHTS

This essay is a mixtape of sorts—a crossfading of ideas.

It was Wednesday, August 28, 2013—fifty years to the day since the historic March on Washington for Jobs and Freedom. The Sunday just before Robin Thicke and Miley Cyrus misappropriated appropriated pieces of sexualized Black-pop stereotypes on MTV's Video Music Awards,[1] cyclically reinforcing errant norms of how Black people are: Black men as hypersexual predators, Black women as objects to be controlled and fetishized.

It was forty-six days after George Zimmerman was found to have legally killed Trayvon Martin.[2] President Barack Obama spoke from the White House about it.[3] He said, "Trayvon Martin could have been me thirty-five years ago." The truth is, as writer Donovan X. Ramsey demanded, President Obama *is* Trayvon Martin. The de jure racism seemed too close to times that prompted the 1963 March on Washington.

That morning I came into the office early to reconcile some administrative stuff and afterward went next door to a lab that was being taught by a well-meaning young doctoral student who I had the opportunity to sit and talk with for some time a few weeks prior. We'd talked about her program of research and how she planned to integrate it into the coursework for our students in the coming academic year. I was going to class now to discuss the numbers for those enrolled in her section. They were low.

111

As I planned to be in and out of the office just before the proper school day started, and was going to my boxing class after my morning on campus, I was dressed in athletic clothes. I had on a pair of sneakers, black socks pulled to the knee with a favorite pair of baggy black Jordan shorts draped just atop them, and a black T-shirt with the Hawaiian Islands sketched in white across the chest.

The door to the classroom was open. I walked in and smiled, and the adjunct faculty extended her arm to me with what I assumed to be a syllabus in hand and said, "Research Methods Lab, right?" I was confused. I looked at her quizzically and said, "Right." Then I realized what was going on.

She motioned that the class had already started and for me to have a seat. The three young men seated in the room, one who was enrolled in a Tuesday/Thursday class of mine for the semester, looked up casually, and one matter-of-factly explained, "He's the department chair."

This was said over my stuttered, "No, I work here."

The instructor was noticeably embarrassed. "I'm so sorry. You look like . . . You're dressed like a student."

I thought about when A. Wade Boykin[4] taught me what microaggression was in graduate school. Then I reflected on when my not so well-meaning high school chemistry teacher said to me, "You people really like those," noting my super dope, all-white Jordan 11s.[5] Then I put together a lecture for my personality theories course using all of the above and taught with special focus. The contours of my experiences and perspectives I understood as being crucial to the psychology majors at Morehouse—at least as crucial as what classic theorists tell us of human behaviors.

PERSISTENT DILEMMA

Black boys and Black men are understood as, and are conditioned to be, invisible. Black masculinities abound throughout the American pop-culture context, but we are most easily recognized as "only my surroundings, . . . figments of *their* imagination, indeed, everything and anything except me."[6] The lived experiences mashed up above illustrate this type of potentially identity-debilitating racism. And we often adopt these marginal slivers of visibility as authentic selves, despite our natural distance from them. At best we implicitly cosign Miley's twerk and Robin's objectifying as validation of who we are as Black folk. We want to be post-racial because the reality of contemporary racism and white supremacy is hard to admit to.

No matter the sociopolitical gains that Black people and Black men, in particular, have demonstrated over the past decade, there remains a cosmetic tone to our advances that has us leaning a bit heavy into a type of Black exceptionalism that privileges distance from the larger Black community. President Obama's talks to Black men just before and throughout his time in office have been a painful watermark of this curious rift.[7] The premise is that we "common Black men" are below the norm, and those above the line need to tell us how to best be part of the world. I, and many others, reject this practice of exclusive Black exceptionalism[8] out of hand.

The norm for Black men and boys is healthy, nondeficient, and nonpathological. This is not to suggest that there are not ills and experiences that disproportionately impact Black men and boys within the context of the United States. However, these are not the identities of Black men and developing Black boys. Further, the "talented tenth"[9] orientation to helping to develop and recognize full, capable Black identities is a contextual to the collectivistic[10] default that is frequently attached to Black cultures.

FIGURATIVE AND LITERAL GLOBAL
WORK AT BEING HEALTHY

This involved patchwork of a preamble demonstrates the sensibilities that have governed my work with college students going to and throughout Ghana over several years. The pedagogy and praxis of the reflexivity here is situated in an effort to understand the visibility of a healthy self as typical, if not typically communicated.

The course Black Men, Black Boys, and the Psychology of Modern Media was piloted across Ghana and into Burkina Faso during the summer of 2011 with three Morehouse College students and one Spelman College student.[11] The class was part of the Morehouse Pan-African Global Experience (MPAGE) program that was designed as a community-centric travel abroad experience. The course stressed identity awareness—more so than identity development—by examining the familiar within the unfamiliar. For that first summer, the familiar was the deftly articulated text *Decoded* by Shawn Carter (and dream hampton).[12] The unfamiliar was the context that is West Africa.

The idea for the course was to have as homebase a narrative of Black masculinities by way of the deconstructed rap lyrics of Jay-Z that are found in *Decoded*. This was anchored by scholarly sociological, anthropological, and psychological writings and was vetted by way of the students' lived experiences as represented through participatory exercises with Queen Mothers,[13] secondary school visits, a cross-cultural dialogue course, and reflections on back home.

It is undeniable that thinking around the course was a combination of my relationship to hip-hop, my scholarship, the Morehouse College "mission,"[14] and the deep impact that traveling to Ghana had on me during my first visit in the winter of 2005. Further, the great success of student travel was largely due to my partnering in the process of self-discovery and academic learning with the students. The summer experience was a close cousin to advocacy participatory and participatory action research[15] that privileges the experience and persons in considering a phenomena in question. Here the phenomena was the crucial awareness that Black men and boys, and the students themselves, are complete people who have agency and a democratic space and who exist far beyond assumed deficit and pathology.

The students did well in the course that summer. More importantly, they took seriously their experiences and applied them back home in continued coursework toward graduate school and community involvement projects and seemed to internalize identity wholeness that was stressed in formal and informal interactions shared since that summer, through graduation from college and beyond.

In the summer of 2012, I traveled back to Ghana with the MPAGE program, not to teach the same course but to lecture from it. The week spent in Cape Coast with students and local artists was buttoned with a reference lecture from a to-be-published article[16] that students from the previous year helped to write. The piece (represented as chapter 2 in this text) discussed assets of Black men as self-described on "wax." The lyricists of note were Rakim, Ice Cube, Jay-Z, and Kanye West. They represented the familiar. A student from the previous year, Robert Shannon—now a Morehouse College graduate and aspiring diplomat—was embedded with the students throughout the summer and worked at actualizing the whole person/asset scholarship that was stressed during my seven days in the country.

A product of this work was a hip-hop record with me, Robert, MPAGE students, and local artists Lucy, 2Seeriyos, and Dabo, that talked of self-actualization, empowerment, and of being Black as good. With Black men and boys commonly understood as an engine to modern rap music, the song "Red, Black (Gold) and Green" proved a strong example of jilting a too-frequent colonized Africa orientation toward an affirming Black African and US Black American identification. This example was of special interest to students because the song garnered significant radio play throughout the region.

In the summer of 2013, I returned to Ghana as site coordinator for MPAGE's program there. This time all thirteen of those traveling—three Spelman students and ten from Morehouse—took Black Men, Black Boys, and the Psychology of Modern Media. Many of the same scholarly articles were used as in summers prior, but *Looking for Leroy: Illegible Black Masculinities* was used as the core text. Again, West Africa provided the broadening context, but popular culture was even more widely considered with Mark Anthony Neal's thorough explication of the meaning and impact of Black men in popular culture that were against the understood norm.

This very contemporary address of complete and capable Black men and boys was complemented in an interesting way with lectures from my mother[17] on W. E. B. Du Bois, on a redefined talented tenth, and on the psycho-religious fundamentals for Black Americans that find a beginning in West Africa and that can be seen in the everyday Ghanaian culture. Indeed, the lectures that Mom offered were of great significance in the developing scholarship of the students, but what seemed of equal value was the modeling of a relationship between grown son and mother who traveled together, who loved one another, and who referenced a healthy Black family. The impact here was illustrated in the way Mom was engaged by the students while traveling, and in inquiry about her, and about us, by students at the beginning of the next academic year.

This quick run through the course on Black men and boys that was taught in Ghana is not put square to demonstrate a type of prediction, control, and understanding that traditionally substantiates good works in science. Rather it is offered as a threaded example that builds to demonstrate how our own life story narratives and reflexivity are able to make an impact, however modest, on those who are learning by way of traditional scholarship and lived experience, and more. Ghana, of course, is not utopia. But the country allowed for a change in context that pushed and pushes the students we worked with toward innovative thinking that is necessary in how we know Black men and boys as whole people. And this impact is exponential. The notions, in sum, are vey liberally adopted from my mentor, Edmund W. Gordon, who says, "Liberation is a value worthy of science. That should be the perspective from which minority scientists seek to advance multiple perspectives, and methodological rigor: not for the purpose of simply predicting, controlling and understanding, but for the purpose of emancipating (liberating) the bodies, minds, communities, and spirits of oppressed humankind."[18]

REFLECTIONS

Even before I was taught Kurt Lewin's field theory and the politics of personality,[19] and before Michelle Fine showed me her awesome brand of participatory action research, I was of the opinion that context matters. I didn't know quite how to frame it when I was a kid having moved from DC to Los Angeles to Arlington, Texas. But I *knew* that if in junior high and in high school I could have had the cultural experiences of my cousins in Washington, DC, or the quasi-hippie private school life my mom sacrificed so much to expose me to me while we lived at Twenty-First and La Brea in Los Angeles, I just knew that things would have been better for me. These spaces at that pivotal time would have reinforced the psychological foundations that my mother and father insisted that I reference when there was the inevitable and, in Texas, the consistent abuse of my identity through racism. This is an awareness that I carry into the academy.

Again, this is a mixtape. And trust, a few editors didn't quite know what to make of it. Certainly, a casual read or a careful one with an unwavering set of assumptions might understand the words herein as providing little more than a loose stringing together of tangents. Others of us have similar, or better, experience-framing constructs. We should use them—Black men especially, because authentic reflexivity is needed from Black men who are researchers and practitioners for the good of Black boys and men and, by extension, for the greater good. The staid, objective, and removed approach too often practiced to maintain respectability[20] within the academy and to fit with a thin positivist lens presents as ever more ineffective. Authentic engagement, shifting contexts, and the positioning of nonpathological, healthy selves is crucial in developing paths to understanding and accepting whole Black men and Black boys who do exist and who are, in fact, the norm.

In writing all of this, I was given pause even though these were ideas that I've wanted to blend together for some time now. When I was tempted to stop, I was introduced to a piece on National Public Radio that pointed to August 11, 1973, as the start of hip-hop.[21] "Cool," I thought. I was born on July 31. "I'm eleven days older than hip-hop. This pushing against and crossfading of ideas comes honestly. I am whole and complete and normal."

NOTES

1. The 2013 VMAs had the former Disney teen sitcom star turned wanton YouTube bottom-popper, Cyrus, paired with Justin Timberlake light, Thicke, singing the latter's Marvin Gaye "Got to Give It Up" rip-off "Blurred Lines." Each desperate star grinded on and shook one against the other in what were poor passes at dancing, sensuality, and/or eroticism, proving much spectacle over substance.

2. Trayvon Martin was a seventeen-year-old Black high school student who was shot and killed by George Zimmerman in Sanford, Florida, on February 26, 2012. Zimmerman was a night watchman for a gated community and thought of and acted on Martin as a suspect. Martin was wearing a hooded sweatshirt and sneakers and was found shot through the heart, having been armed with a pack of candy and a soft drink.

3. President Obama spoke about Zimmerman being found not guilty of second-degree murder and manslaughter of Trayvon Martin from the James S. Brady Briefing Room in the White House on July 19, 2013. This after pronounced public concern about the verdict, particularly from Black communities.

4. A. Wade Boykin taught me developmental psychology at Howard University while I was in graduate school. He developed the triple quandary, a psychological extension of W. E. B. Du Bois's double-consciousness. Where Boykin's theoretical construct retains the Black cultural and American cultural tenets of Du Bois's thinking, there is the added "minority" experience that must be balanced in the negotiation of identity.

5. The Nike Air Jordan 11s were arguably the best ever of the iconic shoe. The patent leather base was what made them dope to me. I had the all-white with Carolina blue accents. I always wanted the black-and-white Concords but never found them. Tragically, I ruined the ones I had while trying to clean the upper with bleach.

6. Quote taken from Ralph Ellison's *Invisible Man*. New York: Random House, 1952. Emphasis mine.

7. President Obama's Father's Day Speech for the NAACP in 2008 and, arguably, his talk to the graduating class of 2013 at Morehouse College are examples of the exclusive Black exceptionalism that seems to be employed when the president speaks of and to Black men. His remarks at the fiftieth anniversary celebration of the March on Washington for Jobs and Freedom is another, broader example.

8. The exclusive Black exceptionalism that I explain gives a respectful nod to James Peterson's *All Black Everything* as explained in his TEDx Talk published on April 23, 2013. Here Peterson discusses the relationship between Black exceptionalism and success and the way that success obscures the pain and suffering of the Black community.

9. The term *talented tenth* refers to a leadership class that was coined by white philanthropic missionaries in the late nineteenth and early twentieth century. Though given notoriety with the 1903 writings of W. E. B. Du Bois, the towering intellect distanced himself from the elitist concept in later life, noting that development of the race could be found in a variety of spaces within the community.

10. Wade Nobles, Na'im Akbar, Kobi Kambon, John Mbiti, and other progressive Afrocentric psychologists have written extensively on the communalism that is most inherent in African cultures and civilizations. This includes Black American cultures and is in tension with the Eurocentric norms of individualism frequently practiced in the United States.

11. Brielle McDaniel, Malachi Richardson, David Robinson, and Robert Shannon were the brilliant students who comprised that pilot class. The following academic year, they joined the research lab and proved to be the best cohesive team of students with whom I have ever worked.

12. Though Shawn Carter wrote *Decoded*, it is commonly accepted that writer-activist dream hampton contributed heavily to her dear friend's book.

13. In Ghana, queen mothers are "culture carriers." In the Central Region, queen mothers are responsible for cultural vitality and for selecting chiefs.

14. The mission of Morehouse College is to develop men with disciplined minds who will lead lives of leadership and service.

15. I understand participatory action research through the lens of the Public Science Project. They explain it as positioning those most intimately impacted by research as

leaders in shaping research questions, framing interpretations, and designing meaningful research products and actions.

16. D. W. Rice. 2013. "Rakim, Ice Cube then *Watch the Throne*: Engaged Visibility through Identity Orchestration and the Language of Hip-Hop Narratives." *Journal of Popular Culture* 46, no. 1: 173–91.

17. My mother is Brenda Wall, PhD, a clinical psychologist and the best mother in the world.

18. From Carol Camp Yeakey (ed.). 2000. *Edmund W. Gordon: Producing Knowledge, Pursuing Understanding (Advances in Education in Diverse Communities: Research, Policy and Praxis)*. Vol. 1. Stamford, CT: JAI Press.

19. In his essay "The Politics of Personality: Being Black in America," James M. Jones talks of the psychological acrobatics necessary to maintain equilibrium within a racialized context.

20. In his writing *Academic Politicalization: Supplementary Education from Black Resistance*, E. T. Gordon positions respectability and reputation at polar ends of a continuum and at the core of a Black male cultural dilemma. Respectability is largely accommodative in that those who ascribe to it attend to others' perceptions of them, particularly the perspectives of those who represent mainstream society. Alternatively, reputation is deeply resistant and oppositional. The cultural practice transmutes Anglo practices of masculinity through Black urban expressions toward norms of "cool" and dominance.

21. The NPR piece points to Kool Herc's flyer for an August 11, 1973, Back to School Jam to be held in the recreation room at 1520 Sedgwick Avenue in the Bronx, New York, as an artifact indicating the birth of hip-hop.

PART III

Orchestration

Chapter 10

Complicating Black Boys

David Wall Rice

The familiar and debilitating phenomena of "missing" Black men is a calculus of census undercounting, disproportionate incarceration, and early death, among other social cues, that render us functionally invisible in community strength and community building. Achievements that break beyond spates of us as unseen demonstrate us as exceptional rather than as a norm.

The national school-to-prison pipeline trend is a socioeconomic through line that informs the missing/invisible Black man status. It is a construct that succinctly explains, through description and implication, problems of and relating to Black people that turn largely on Black boys and men stepping outside and beyond this stereotyped explanation of who and how we are. There is disconnectedness no matter the turn. If we perform to stereotype, our individuality is of no account. If we perform beyond stereotype, our selves are of no account because of the need for others to keep us in spaces that are familiar to them.

This problem of disconnectedness is very much a problem of narrative scope. Familiarity with the singular story of Black cultural deficit yields a default of Black men and boys as "missing" even where they are absolutely present.

BIKO, STOKELY? PRESENT.

Biko and Stokely are my sons—my heart. When Biko was born, he redefined for me what love is, and with Stokely, I was taught the definition of love's depth. Daily, the two of them teach me about life. Relative to my program of research, I learn through how others respond to them and how Biko and

Stokely are subject to being defined as objects by folks who feel the need to control their Black bodies. This sounds harsh, I know, but it's real.

Before going in, I think it's important to note that, by all accounts, Biko and Stokely are good boys. They are responsible, respectful, kind, generous, and cooperative. Mikki and I are blessed to be able to honestly say that this is who they are. It is equally important to underscore that the two are *boys*, young people figuring their way through the world. They are raised to be all of the best characteristics one might ascribe to the best of people, but they get to this through trial and error and are given the room to make mistakes, to own those mistakes, and to build better versions of themselves toward being good men.

Neither Biko nor Stokely apologize for who they are. They have been trained to understand that this world is as much theirs as it is anyone's. Not in a Western, dominance sense but in a gifted-by-God, responsible sense.

Along with their phenotypic expressions, Biko and Stokely elicit sharp responsess to who they are because of their personalities. This is typical for precocious Black boys within the American context.

To be clear, Biko and Stokely are different. Biko is seven years older than his brother and, though he has a temper, he is characteristically nonchalant in his resistance to authority. If asked to do something that he thinks need not be done, Biko simply won't do it. There isn't a lot of demonstration or talk about it. He says what he thinks matter-of-factly and proceeds. Stokely, on the other hand, is quite unapologetic in his challenge of authority through question and correction. He is confident and sure of himself, and he is undaunted.

As might be expected, teachers are the authority that Biko and Stokely press against the most. Fortunately, the boys' teachers have been well taught and are well-meaning and invested in their young students, mostly. Still, as uneventful as the early learning environment was for both boys—they attended the same early learning place—the traditional construct that is Western schooling prevailed and demanded intervention. And this, for both boys, first happened when they were three.

For Biko, it was a super nice white woman who was a nanny before assuming a lead-teacher role in the classroom. She was cheery and friendly and liked Biko just fine. Toward the middle of the school year, there was a parent-teacher conference. Until then, things were better than fine. Biko was acknowledged as being "well spoken" and "bright," and aside from reports of not wanting to nap, not following directions once or twice, and wanting snacks from school rather than from home, it was all good.

Then Mikki and I came in for a sit-down. With programming oversight from a prominent graduate school of education in the area, Biko's scores were very high. This was good—expected, but good. Then Ms. Teacher explained that "the problem with Biko is . . . ," and there was a discussion about how

Biko would not conform. He was not "obedient." This language gave me pause. I was tolerant with "well spoken" and "bright," but "problem with" and "obedient" weren't couched quite right.

I began with, "Let me help you with your language. Given consistent reports throughout the term and scores that complement high intellectual performance . . . " Mikki grabbed my leg tight under the table as the woman began turning beet-red and started a bit of pre-cry. I kept on but toned it down, explaining that all that was really necessary was to talk *to* Biko and not *at* him. Things were up and down from there, until they went permanently down when Ms. Teacher told me weeks later how "articulate" and "good with words" I was. I came as close as I could to ignoring her for the next several months, and then the family was saved by Ms. Melton, Ms. Upshaw and Ms. Murphy, Biko's bomb pre-K teaching team.

For Stokely, it was a well-meaning white man. He was always sure to talk to me when I dropped Stokes off at school. He would comment on my sneakers, bring up sports or anything he thought was good small talk. I knew that I'd developed a bit of a reputation at the school, so I tried to be friendly. But I don't like small talk and am not really a morning person. And when I drop the boy off, that is my time with him to tell him he is great and to remind him that he is going to body the day ahead.

Every day after school, we were told that Stokely "had a great day." He was doing well with sight words, got along with friends, and was a good listener. The thing about Stokely is that he would score at the genius level if we had him tested, for real. His vocabulary far exceeded that of other children in his class and years senior because of how verbal everyone in the family is, especially his big brother. Stokely's grasp of concepts and comparative analysis would often leave the adults in his social group laughing because of how aware and analytical he was. Anyone could see Stokely's giftedness, anyone.

When it was time to talk with Mr. Teacher about Stokely's progress in the class, it was just me. Mikki wasn't going to disturb herself with the negativity we anticipated was going to be dropped on us. The conversation began with how we shouldn't be concerned with the low marks and Stokely's progress because he "still had time" to get where he needed to be. "Ain't *this* a blip," I thought to myself. Mr. Teacher was softening me up for disturbing news that, in fact, was not disturbing because the indicators were wrong. It was asserted that Stokely was not doing well with sight words, that he could not connect the simplest of concepts, and I thought they were going to tell me he didn't know his own name when I asked Mr. Teacher to stop.

"You are telling me a lot of things that are wrong with Stokely and his learning," I interrupted. "Given the obvious gifts that Stokely has with communication, is there anything positive you might be able to offer?" Mr. Teacher explained that Stokely did a great job "separating" when I left him in the morning. Mikki handled whatever remaining meetings after that, and we were saved, again, when Ms. Melton and the crew entered for Stokely's pre-K year.

In rereading what I've put here, I can understand if the scenarios present as not a big deal—perhaps taken, simply, as a father who really digs his kids (I do) or who is seeing something that is not really there. One might say, "Your kids are not geniuses; they're just as regular as the next kid."

My response: "Absolutely, my kids are geniuses (it will do no good to argue this)," and most importantly they are absolutely just as regular as the next kid. All kids, all boys, Black boys and certainly my Black boys, are geniuses. It is just a matter of how. To be bound to assessments that sort and generalize for the purpose of most anything except affirming the little ones as of value is wrong. Following Ms. and Mr. Teacher in dampening the genius of our little ones, however well-meaning they might be, is also wrong.

The Biko and Stokely stories are a big deal. They are instances where little Black boys were positioned as being behind the jump. We were told that Biko and Stokely needed to catch up when we knew they were, in fact, ahead. Biko and Stokely were simplified because of experiences with and expectations of Black boys as less than. Even in the most positive spaces with the most positive people around, they were unseen, missing.

It is important to complicate Black boys into sight. As the great developmental psychologist Margaret Beale Spencer once told me, "Let little Black boys be boys," let them be full-fledged, regular people.

It should be clear that complicating Black men and Black boys is not typically done, bluntly, because we don't know how to do it. As discussed, we've been trained to slip into narrow definitions of self. Deconstructing those spaces, however, making them wider, is important because in the elaboration, not in the reduction, of identities there is the opportunity to find health, strength, and authentic fit. In looking at the salient examples in finding fit for Black boys and men, specifically, there is the opportunity to advance general behavioral theory and practice.

Chapter 11

Between Shakespeare and Showing Up

William Marcel Hayes

It is a peculiar sensation, this double-consciousness, this sense of always looking at one's self through the eyes of others, of measuring one's soul by the
tape of a world that looks on in amused contempt and pity. One ever feels his
two-ness,—an American, a Negro; two souls, two thoughts, two unreconciled
strivings; two warring ideals in one dark body, whose dogged strength alone
keeps it from being torn asunder.—W. E. B. Du Bois, *The Souls of Black Folk*

In a recent training on racial literacy, I was prompted to think about my earliest racial memory. The prompt was designed not only to allow participants
to recall the events of their first memory of this kind but also to articulate
the way the memory made them feel. As an educator who sees the trauma
inflicted on children by systems of white supremacy and oppression daily, I
found it difficult to recall my first racial memory, primarily because it wasn't
rooted in a perceivably traumatic experience. It was interesting that I went to
my own preconscious interpretation of the prompts intended to elicit a traumatic negative memory despite no explicit directions to do so.

I then realized it was also never suggested that our first racial memories
needed to exist in the context and presence of whiteness or difference. Yet
my brain scanned only for a racial memory earmarked in that way. I shared
the story below:

I was in first grade. I was one of a few Black children in a predominantly white
school. As a six-year-old, my experience had been positive and offered little
need for me to interrogate my Blackness as a result of negative interactions
with whiteness. I do not recall ever saying I wanted to be white or desiring to be

white, nor did I ever feel ashamed of being Black. I navigated divergent worlds
between home and school aware of the differences but seemingly unbothered by
a need to consider them. On this particular day, we were engaging in a coloring
activity where we were given the opportunity to color cartoon-like images of
people. My teacher, a Black middle-aged woman, circled around the classroom
and stood over me as I colored in the characters with the peach crayon, like my
other classmates. Without questioning or probing, she handed me the brown
crayon and said, "Why don't you color with this one." I accepted the crayon and
proceeded to color the characters in the coloring book. I even went as far as to
add a black high-top to match my own.

I have little memory of how I felt at that moment. Understanding the events
from back then has come in my adult years, after fitting awareness and language to make meaning of the experience. This is typical.

Young children often make sense of the world around them through the
characters they create on paper and the events they share through stories.
Images and the way children portray characters serve to fill the gap between
emotions and words, particularly when young people don't have a vocabulary
matured to the point of explaining the nuances of their feelings or the details
of an event.

For many years my work in schooling has been rooted in supporting students in developing a positive racial identity while combating the negative
impacts of trauma and poverty. I connect this imperative of my work to the
step I took on that day of "characterizing" myself. That thinking-back event
provided an opportunity to explore the ways in which individuals go through
a process of identity orchestration as prompted by outside interrogation of
observable presentations of self. For me, it was that high-top faded self.

My first-grade reflection is an example of how, even at a young age, I was
learning to frame identity and to make connections based on the interplay
between my perception of self and the world around me. I was "storying"
myself, creating an image of me by interpreting the choices and consequences
of such a person—high-top fade and all.

I like Shakespeare. One of my favorite pieces of his is from *As You Like
It*: "All the world's a stage, And all the men and women merely players;
They have their exits and their entrances; And one man in his time plays
many parts."

The passage has me thinking through play to the multiple stages of development and the dynamic nature of the human condition. We do, in fact,
"play" many parts. Central questions are which parts are true representations of our most authentic self, and how do we go about discovering and

developing these true identities that make up an authentic self/character for the "world's stage"?

In reflecting on my own childhood, I realize that much of our identity orchestration is captured through the objective interpretation of characters. So much of how we view ourselves is impacted by what we observe in those around us as they navigate the *stages* on which they might have us play. Like an audience member, we watch to see how the story unfolds for each of the characters, but not without agency. The characters we most readily connect with serve as our own personal proxies to see and interpret how they might present as compared to others and how they/we advance from scene to scene—context to context.

We also carefully watch to see how other characters respond to and talk about our chosen identity protagonist and how the plot advances as a result of the intersections between their thoughts, words, and actions. Intriguing psychology, to be sure. As we observe and figure, we make meaning of the events, making assumptions about our own experiences, and orchestrate identities in line with goodness of fit.

We do this in a space that we define as mentally and emotionally safe for us to explore and expand. How we choose to express our immediate feelings and understandings directly correlates with our level of comfort on and in the stage of identity development that we find ourselves. Every observation becomes a rehearsal for what we might expect of our own identity journey.

It appears that prior to going through the internationalization and integration necessary for identity dilemma articulation—where a person defines for themselves (at least) two worlds to be negotiated—individuals navigate a process of characterizing outsiders, figuring the consequences of demonstrating varying expressions of a specific identity marker (characteristic) for the "character." Perceptions and interpretations remain deeply rooted in the degree to which we attribute the consequences a character experiences to the identity marker or some unpredictable outside force.

For example, in the traditional socialization of boys and girls, young children learn social advantages with the overt expression of stereotypically gendered characteristics. Accordingly, many times students suppress identities that do not advantage the self with social acceptance and feelings of belongingness. This iterative process of identity dilemma articulation occurs at various points in our life as we expand our view of the world and of ourselves within it.

Unfortunately, this process is limited by the number of characters and plot sequences a child is able to view at a particular time and the attached generalizations they make about their potential outcomes across a variety of contexts.

For this reason, many educators advocate for an increase in experiential learning, exposure, and enrichment for children of color with limited access and opportunity around them. This push to expand context creates added prompts that increase identity possibility. In the same way we recognize that new learning requires a solid schema on which to build, so too does the process of an effective and exhaustive analysis of one's own identity potential. This expansion of the worldview through multiple observations gives children an opportunity to imagine and to re-imagine who they are and who they can be in the world. The internal process of interpreting the multiple outcomes for those who share similar identity markers serves to complicate their thinking and to increase perceived possibilities for themselves. It stands to reason that if our children's understanding of the world around them is limited to stereotypical images of themselves on television, the limited revisionist history they receive in schools, or the cyclical reproduction of characters in their most proximal community, then so too is their identity potential.

Growing up I was acutely aware of how expectations and the social norms of those around me provided an inflexible cue for the ways in which I was meant to think, speak, and act. Perhaps it was because I had navigated so many drastically different social contexts before I was twelve years old.

I was born in South Carolina, while my mother was in college, and was raised in the first few years by my grandmother, mother, and three teenage aunts. After I attended Head Start in South Carolina, my mother moved our family to Virginia. From there we went to live with my aunt in Long Island, New York, where I was one of only a few Black children in a predominantly middle-class neighborhood and school. This school and community of relative privilege provided me an early opportunity to learn an instrument, join Cub Scouts, study Shakespeare, and travel out of the country before grade four.

We returned to South Carolina during my fourth-grade year, after my mother lost employment. It was in the middle of my practicing for the lead in Hamlet. I was immediately forced to reconsider and renegotiate a new context: poverty. And I was subject to all the childhood cognitive dissonance that could occur from having multiple worlds and identities taken and/or shattered. The identity and rules I operated by previously didn't fit, and I struggled until I learned to operate within the new context. I suppressed previous interests, identities, and expressions that no longer served me while developing and elevating new ones. This isn't to suggest something inherently wrong or uncommon about this type of identity processing, rather to offer perspective by which to understand, particularly when context and affiliated identity negotiations are rooted in survival and then in the individual's opportunity to thrive.

During this transition I also encountered a reckoning with the ways in which the combination of identity and context impact social expectations of how an individual is to show up in the world. I wasn't just Black anymore. I was poor. And Black. And a boy. And southern. The identity dilemma that ensued was brutal. I wasn't street smart enough to be poor. I did not speak as Black people were supposed to speak. I wasn't tough like the other boys. I didn't possess the deference and humility of a Black boy in the South when faced with discrimination and whiteness. And until I learned the rules of how these identities were supposed to show up in this context, I suffered the consequences.

Additionally, I struggled because so many of the characters around me were meeting those stereotypical expectations and offered little opportunity for me to observe how someone who looked like me could navigate a different expression of identities. Seeing no safety to conduct experiments of expression on my own, I didn't. I simply elevated the appropriate expressions of who I was supposed to be at the time.

When I was growing up in the South, young children operated by certain cultural expectations and beliefs. For example, children should always give respect and deference to anyone older, regardless of relationship. When adults spoke, you listened, and there was an expectation of how you were to respond to adults in both tone and word. You never called an adult by their first name, and when they asked you a question you always responded ending with "ma'am" or "sir."

In the move back to South Carolina, I was largely unaware of the nuances of southern socialization. I got in trouble in class one day, and my teacher pulled me outside for correction. She finished her admonishment asking, "Do you understand me?" I replied, "Yes." She responded sharply, "Yes what?" Not quite getting it, I replied, "Yes, I understand." She instructed, "You mean, yes, ma'am." I fell in line, parroting her, "Yes, ma'am." In that moment I was reminded of my identity as a child and immediately reinforced the expectation of the way my identity was supposed to be expressed whenever an adult was around.

I took that lesson and many more like it as a reminder of how my identity and its expression must take context into account. I was fooled into demonstrating a certain identity that was misfit to me. And I wasn't the only one. Long conversations with friends over the years has proven as much.

Our lives become a series of interactions and experiences that reflect back to us the value and position of our identities in specific spaces as well as the relative safety of expressing those identities. As we grow older and develop our capacity to make meaning, we are able to look at previous incidents and make new meaning from the intersectionality of our identities, the social context of that time, and how we are allowed to show up.

For example, for the better part of my life I continued to speak to adults older than me using "ma'am" and "sir" with the understanding that I was young and adults always deserved that type of respect. I didn't look further into the behavior and saw no detrimental cost to my identity expression as a result of responding the "southern way." It wasn't until I learned about internalized racial oppression and the ways in which white supremacy has promoted the belief that Black people are inferior that I began to notice that my grandmother and many of her peers, when speaking to white people younger than them, responded as I had to all people who were older, with "ma'am" and "sir."

Here I was forced into an interesting and often frustrating process whereby an individual gets new information that expands their schema, demanding they reinterpret past identities with a new lens. I have taken this journey through my childhood several times over. On each account I took note of my limited understanding of self at the time and the rules I thought I understood about how I could show up.

It is this type of reflexivity that further complicates the journey through an unadulterated presentation of self, maintaining fidelity to core identities, no matter the social cost. One must simultaneously grapple with their decision to show up in different ways in the past and how it will impact the ways in which they decide to show up in the future.

In working with children, I often see myself in them. Having worked in a variety of schools, serving students in grades pre-K through twelve, I match many of the identity processes I assumed as a child to what I see kids going through daily. They navigate and negotiate an ongoing internal interrogation of who they are and who they want to be relative to the world around them. They are often compromised by a limited worldview and an underdeveloped, underappreciated self-efficacy. As a result, many students battle between aspiration and expectation. They find themselves, as I was, limited by their own experience in the world until that world is expanded and they recognize and accept multiple identities.

Young people look into the world and search for characters that match their most salient identity markers and develop a belief about what they can expect of their own lives. Even while they might aspire to something different in themselves and the world around them, their aspirations are limited by what they can see and expect of similar characters. Their motivation is often impacted by the degree to which they feel confident they can bridge the gap between their current presentation of self and their aspirational self. Perceived expectations of self, based primarily on the consequence of observable characters with similar identity markers, either positively or negatively influence their continued motivation to bridge current and aspirational selves.

History has proven that marginalized groups must learn to navigate the inherent risk in their own identity expression, in being themselves without apology. While some identities are more salient—race and gender—others provide the individual with a choice point in considering the degree to which they express the ideals, interests, and values of their identity. These identities may include but are not limited to socioeconomic status, education, sexuality, religious beliefs, and political affiliations. They are further complicated by the time and space in which an individual must be present. The perceived threat associated with expression promotes a sort of private experimental design process in which the individual observes pieces of their identities that they readily see in those around them. We unconsciously collect multiple data points, document patterns of response, and make a determination about the relative safety and potential consequences of the unadulterated presentation of self. In schools across the United States, you can see this play out as students navigate between home, neighborhood, and school with new complexities to consider as time passes.

One of the safest ways to run such an internal experiment is to do so in the presence of others in a social network that makes identity exploration safe. A challenge arises for many people, young and old alike, when social networks do not reflect back to the individual the presence of those identities integral to who they are at the time. It is in the absence of characters with explicitly or implicitly recognizable identity markers that individuals must depend on their own self-efficacy and understanding to make a determination about how they will show up.

In my experience in the first grade, I recognize my ability to articulate and to reflect my own represented identity on the page with drawings and coloring as limited by a social network that did not reflect important pieces of who I was. This holds true for individuals who lack the opportunity to explore various portions of their identity due to lack of exposure, opportunity, and experiences with social groups that affirm and make safe the expression and interrogation of their multiple complex identities. This process is further compromised when the individual has internalized a monolithic, "appropriate," "acceptable," and "safe" expression of their identities.

For many years educators have pushed the importance of hiring a diverse educator workforce. Aside from the obvious academic impact of a highly qualified teacher, having a teaching staff that reflects the students they serve provides students with "mirrors and windows." Students are able to see their identities reflected back to them as a source of affirmation, and they are able to see their futures through the person in front of them. Educators, much like parents, family members, and peer groups, represent the first social network where individuals recognize and interrogate the presence and development of their multiple identities. These groups either provide a safe space to do so or signal to the individual that it is unsafe to explore particular portions of who they are.

I have come to realize that much of my own identity exploration was done first and foremost with people who looked like me. Likewise, for many Black and Brown children, the signal of the appropriate expression of their identity is first presented to them by people who look like them. Our first under-standing of our personal identities occurs through the socialization process facilitated by those in closest proximity to us. We learn to speak, move, and exist in ways that reflect the values and expectations presented to us by those around us. However, those in closest proximity are often not those who are most culturally connected. Accordingly, there is the additional identity work of "code-switching."

As we think about the expression of development and identity in conjunc-tion with social norms, it is important to consider how time and space influ-ence relative comfort in expressing one's identity. For example, within our schools we see a growing number of students expressing their identities in ways never imagined by generations before them. Girls and boys are push-ing back on previously accepted gender norms as students move fluidly and unapologetically across sexual identifications. In many ways, schools are now serving as generational mediators between students and guardians, who are often flustered by the ways in which their students are enacting their identity orchestration.

In recent years researchers have begun to explore how intersectionality influences not only the ways in which individuals view the world but even more the ways in which intersectional expressions of identity impact the way the world responds to them. This experience is highly dynamic and influ-enced by the social context and location of the experience.

Most Black men and boys can attest to raced and gendered feelings they get in various spaces depending on the ways in which people in those spaces project biases and expectations or assert their privilege and power. This situ-ational navigation of confirming or resisting stereotypes—burden of proof—represents an unconscious choice point for the individual to decide how they show up in response to the social cues they are receiving.

The first time I consciously saw myself as a character in a story, I was a master chameleon, oftentimes bending to the expectations of others with no real regard for who I truly wanted to be in the moment. An event occurred during a discussion in one of my graduate school courses. An article we were reviewing focused on boys of color and their unique needs as a result of being "at risk." The term *at risk* has continued to be an identity marker ascribed to Black boys that I've always resisted for many reasons better explained in a chapter of their own. The piece was filled with a number of deficit-based statistics and theories about the negative outcomes of boys of color growing up in poverty.

Prior to class, I read the articles and navigated the process of seeing myself as a character in the readings. This character wasn't someone I aspired to be but was instead a character that I once was. A white woman classmate commented after the reading, "I feel so bad for these poor boys in single-parent homes. It's like they don't even have a chance." I was met for the first time with an experience where someone else articulated a predictable negative consequence for a character in whom I saw myself. She was commenting on me.

In that moment, feeling both triggered and obligated to reply, I mustered up some articulate synthesis of her deficit thinking and the countless counternarratives available to suggest the possibility of a positive outcome for students regardless of the context in which they live. I highlighted my presence at the same table as her as valid and sufficient evidence for her to believe that Black boys in single-parent homes do have a chance and deserve far more than her pity.

While my visible persona remained cool, beneath the surface there was a crisis of conscience occurring. My heart and mind raced with questions. Did she not look at the boy, see me, and think to herself that I was an example of how great that boy could become? Or did she look at the boy, look at me, and consider me an exception to the rules of how his story would end? Or did she look at me and not even see the boy? Had I hidden that boy from her view, from the world? Was I a sellout? Who was I to these people around me? And most importantly, who was I to myself? I hold these questions as central in my current presentation of self, always. I consider the questions, Which identities am I allowing to show up? Which identities am I keeping from showing up? Which identities have I forgotten?

I have struggled with the construct of exceptionalism professionally and among family. While I hope to be an example for many, it has often been the case that my own ability to accomplish my dreams was not enough to convince those around me of their own self-efficacy. I recall a conversation with one of my former high school students. He was an amazing kid that lived life on an identity pendulum. Depending on the events that were transpiring in his life, you never knew what you were going to get. He grew up in one of the toughest parts of the city, but you could look at him and tell he wasn't a tough guy. What he lacked in brute strength and size he made up for in quick wit and a sharp delivery. He was a smart student with A+ potential but C+ motivation and belief in himself.

He, much like my teenage self, could tell that he was different but struggled to see a future beyond the perceived expectation of people that looked like him and lived where he lived. He was like so many young people I work with, trapped in a constant echo chamber that reinforced his own limited expectations of how he must show up in the world to survive, and in not knowing all that was possible for him.

In a sit-down conversation with him, I asked rather casually what college he was going to, confident this kid could and would thrive on any college campus. He responded, laughing, "Man, I'm not going to college. Do you know where I'm from?" I was shocked. He foreclosed on the idea despite having all the academic chops and financial need to ensure a full scholarship somewhere after high school. I continued talking to him, noting several parallels between my life and his and how I was able to go off to college and to see the world. He replied, "That's great, but I'm not like you. You're different." Just like that, I was reminded that similar is not the same. And despite the obvious overlap of several identity markers, the ways in which he perceived his own ability to step safely outside of a stereotypical box impacted the degree to which he could accept the outcome of a similar character as possible for himself.

Children of color, and more specifically those growing up in poverty, experience a unique set of barriers in their iterative journey through identity development, articulation, and presentation. Not only must they navigate the internal struggles natural to all young children going through the stages of development; they must do so while navigating the struggles associated with how the world responds to the expression of their most salient identity markers. Additionally, these young people are bound by the limits of a worldview that too often presents to them a singular, static set of characters with shared identity markers. The echo chambers of media, self-talk, and peer socialization are ever present in this process of development and significantly inhibit a child's ability to safely explore who they are and who they want to be.

Children of color growing up in poverty are not often afforded the mental and emotional "safe space" to freely imagine, explore, or experiment. The consequences of showing up in the wrong way while navigating systemic racism and oppression make their world a chronically stressful space and threat to one or more of their identity markers. It has been a commonly held belief that in the face of a threat, our bodies and brains enact one of three responses: fight, flight, or freeze. More recently theorists have introduced the concept of "fawn" as a fourth stress response, in which the individual lets go of their own beliefs and identities in exchange for who and what the stressor in their life wishes them to be. I would argue that young people must navigate these threats and stress responses across identity orchestration.

At several points throughout the academic year, I encourage teachers and leaders in my school to remind themselves of why they do this work. My answer, though often accompanied by different examples over the years, remains the same. I do this work to be for children what I needed someone to be for me. Growing up I needed someone to be a tangible example of who I was and all that I could become. I needed someone to stretch my imagination beyond the limits of my own understanding. I needed someone to hold space for me to be vulnerable, to take risks, and to make mistakes without the full weight of the consequences I feared. I needed someone to affirm and to love all the pieces of my identity and to teach me to do the same. I needed someone to encourage me to show up as I wanted to and not simply as the world expected me to. I needed to be seen so that I could see myself.

Chapter 12

High-Stakes Orchestration

Understanding Expressions of Identity and Appeals to Belonging in the College Personal Statement

Gregory Davis

Acceptance into a top-tier program for undergraduate and graduate training at America's top universities is the dream of many young adults. In essence, admission is the first step on a road toward higher status, better opportunity, and a more meaningful life. The application process for these programs, however, can be something of a nightmare. Although many see a clear image of the benefits of college admission, few of us really understand the *process* of college admissions (Ishop, 2008; Warren, 2013). Applications to undergraduate and graduate programs are incredibly varied, and what exactly schools do with applicants' completed portfolios is largely a mystery (Jones, S., 2013; Samraj & Monk, 2008). One aspect of the application that is difficult to explicate fully is the personal statement—the autobiographical essay that describes an applicant's life course and desire to attend a specific university or program.

Here we review the literature regarding personal statements and the psychology of identity, centering on the intersection of the personal statement and the Black lived experience. In the first part, I will set the scene, highlighting the personal statement as both the university's tool for recruitment and selection as well as the applicant's prime opportunity to discuss themself as an ideal student. Here, I will discuss the personal statement as an example of high-stakes writing, where the impact of the statement on the reader has major repercussions on the writer. Since the personal statement has such high stakes, writing it can be difficult, especially for applicants who have had limited access to the college application process. I finish Part I of this writing by delving into the research and rhetoric on the difficulty of writing the personal statement, especially for first-generation and otherwise marginalized applicants.

Next, I will recap the literature on personal statement writing specifically. Although nearly every scholar has to write one or more personal statements in their lifetime, there is a paucity of research on the subject (Brown, 2005; Murphy, Klieger, Borneman, & Kuncel, 2009; Warren, 2013). The literature that does exist focuses on the rhetorical aspects of the personal statement. This includes the ways successful applicants craft personal statements to appeal most to schools and express optimal fit. Applicants must also leverage diversity—the interest in bringing different experiences and backgrounds to the university campus and classroom culture—in their application writings. In Part II of this essay, I will review this literature and describe the salient aspects of the personal statement.

Last, I will discuss how the personal statement intersects with narrative identity and identity articulation in Part III. Essentially, the personal statement requires applicants to leverage their identities to make an appeal to belong to an elite group. This process involves the strategic deployment of the life narrative, a version of the autobiography limited by both linguistic and political constraints. Here, I will discuss impression formation, life narrative, and identity articulation with a special emphasis on adolescents and young adults—the majority of personal statement writers. In addition, I will delve deep into Rice's (2008; 2013) forms of identity orchestration and how applicants can employ them in personal statements. I will then tie this research into the discoveries about the personal statement, leading me to pose some questions for future research.

A vital aspect of this work is to involve the autobiographical and to reflect on my own experiences of drafting and submitting personal statements. I've had the opportunity to do so three times—as a high school senior applying to the all-male HBCU Morehouse College, as a graduating senior applying to law school at UCLA, and as an outgoing JD applying for my PhD at the University of Michigan and Harvard University. Throughout these application processes, I have considered and deployed all that I discuss from the literature without knowing it. Hence, I will bookend each part of this chapter with a personal reflection on my applications, incorporating the personal with the scholarly.

For applicants, and especially Black students who apply to America's top college and university programs, the personal statement is a high-stakes opportunity to orchestrate one's identity to succeed in major life tasks. Here, I reveal how the quality of these statements often turns on the authenticity and poignancy of the account. For young Black applicants, these two aspects of the personal statement can be paradoxical, coaxing the writer into a stance that may contradict an authentic account of their history, ultimately encouraging them to underplay their courageous acts of normalcy and relate the more dramatic aspects of their life. We conclude with a larger discussion of high-stakes orchestration and appeals for belonging, situating the personal statement as an opportunity for identity depletion or replenishment.

PART I: THE PERSONAL STATEMENT—ITS USE BY THE APPLICANT AND THE SCHOOL

Traditionally, the common attributes of an application to an American college or university are an informational questionnaire, academic transcripts from prior schools attended, score reports for required standardized tests, letters of recommendation from known associates, and one or more personal essays (Carbado & Harris, 2008). Some programs—particularly graduate programs—also require a sample of academic writing, but for many applications, the personal statement serves as a proxy (Ishop, 2008; Samraj & Monk, 2008). All these requirements allow admissions officers to compare (directly and indirectly) the applicant's achievements and potential to the expected levels of the incoming class or cohort (Carbado & Harris, 2008).

The personal statement is normally a short piece of writing—between one and five pages—that introduces the student to the application reader and describes why the applicant would be a good candidate for admission (Brown, 2005; Ishop, 2008). Applicants usually respond to a prompt provided by the college or university and mold their application essays specifically to the prompt's wording while still being general enough to use one essay for multiple applications (Ishop, 2008). Indeed, personal statements can become so general that their quality rarely predicts successful completion of graduate programs (Murphy, Klieger, Borneman, & Kuncel, 2009). Rather, the personal statement ensures only that the college or university can individualize applicants and review them on metrics other than test scores and demographics, although the statements are used for more depending on the discipline (Carbado & Harris, 2008; Samraj & Monk, 2008).

In addition, the personal statement provides the applicant with an opportunity that they do not have elsewhere in the application. Although each application requirement satisfies some aspect of the college's needs (GPA and test scores to directly compare other applicants, letters of recommendation to assess the applicant's reputation), the personal statement serves a special role: allowing applicants to introduce themselves and appeal for admission in their own voice (Brown, 2005; Vossler, 2007; Warren, 2013). Moreover, the personal statement allows applicants to reveal in their own words why they chose to apply to a specific college or university and the extent of that intentionality (Goldstein, 2011; Jones, J. M., 2013; Murphy, Klieger, Borneman, & Kuncel, 2009). In other words, "the personal statement serves as the only place in the application where applicants can personalize their application package and present themselves as both unique individuals and competent candidates" (Ding, 2007, p. 388).

Personal statements also give the college or university the opportunity to convey desired values and institutional foci to the applicant (Ishop, 2008; Jones, S., 2013; Samraj & Monk, 2008). Within the wording of a personal statement prompt, applicants can decipher the college's specific focus and the perspective it wishes to elicit in its applicants (Jones, S., 2013). Interviews, a requirement of some graduate programs and few undergraduate ones, allow for similar assessments for both the college and the applicant but are much less common and much more arduous for those involved (Albanese, Snow, Skochelak, Huggett, & Farrell, 2003). In some ways, the personal statement's wording and emphasis can tell an applicant as much about the college or university as the statement tells the college about the applicant.

Those who study the personal statement find significance in the applicant's sharing. In her dissertation research, Ishop (2008) discusses at length the institutional use of the personal statement. Selective institutions, she insists, sort initial applicants by quantitative measures (GPA, test score) and then use qualitative assets like the personal statement to choose among applicants likely to do well. The statement provides access to three essential questions a college will have about an applicant: "[their] capacity to perform, [the] effect of education on the individual, and [their] potential to contribute" (p. 3). Thus, the personal statement does not just give the life story of the applicant; it also positions the applicant as a potential contributor to the academic and social experience of the college or university (Ishop, 2008; Samraj & Monk, 2008; Warren, 2013).

Perhaps because of this dynamic, personal statements pose a considerable threat to the admissions goals of many college and university applicants (Brown, 2004; Warren, 2013). At the time of application, most students' grades and test scores are set, the content of the letters of recommendation static, and extracurricular activities completed. The personal statement, therefore, is one of the only application components done at the time of application that is completely in the applicant's hands (Brown, 2005; Ding, 2007; Goldstein, 2011). In some circles—most notably middle-class communities with parental resources dedicated to college preparation—personal statement writing becomes a communal effort with applicants, parents, and admissions counselors directly participating in personal statement drafting (Goldstein, 2011; Warren, 2013). For the most part, however, students stand alone in the creation of their personal statements, as the name implies (Jones, S., 2013; Warren, 2013).

My own experience writing my college personal statement was a solo, though supervised, effort. Though neither of my parents attended college, my older sister had her master's degree and valued education more than anyone I've ever known. Coming from Detroit, college served as an escape and life-line away from the life trajectories society prescribed for us.

My first drafts of my college personal statement were nearly unreadable. My sister—who by this time worked in graduate admissions at the University of Michigan–Ann Arbor, threw out most of my writing and reminded me to "be exactly what they're looking for, but unique at the same time." Taking this cryptic advice, I eventually crafted a six-hundred-word piece that I thought fit the goal. Reviewing my now fifteen-year-old statement and thinking on the findings mentioned above, this passage stands out:

> In my studies, I have learned to set goals, prepare for the future, and maintain drive. My mentorships have given me role models to look up to, providing me with a sense of pride and blessing I hadn't obtained prior. During the school year, I maintain my interest by participating in activities and taking courses geared towards science while also mixing in my other interests. I am a founding member of my school's Men of Vision organization, which is made up of a group of dedicated and aware Black males that reach out to the community through various programs. In the last year, I have helped to organize Dental Panel 2004 and Legal Panel 2005, in which African American professionals from the before mentioned occupations come in to talk to serious minded students on a Saturday morning. The great turnouts to both events provided many with invaluable information to aid them in the future. In my academics, I have taken a wide range of honors sciences, including natural science, biology, chemistry, physics, psychology, and calculus. This array of courses has helped me ascertain a grasp of my post-high school education.

Here, I honed in on my high school experience and how it prepared me for college. Without knowing it, I addressed Ishop's (2008) three essential personal statement questions, mentioned above. My capacity to perform showed in my diverse honors curriculum. Education impacted me via a sense of maturity and drive. Last, my organizing and leadership easily translated to the college environment (or so I hoped).

With my personal statement, I got my sole chance to orient admissions committees on who I felt I was and what I felt I could do. As I will discuss in the next part, while my self-presentation was unique, my language and rhetoric were not. These aspects followed rules meant to make me accessible and empathetic to admissions officers and thus were not a true expression of my voice.

PART II: WRITING THE PERSONAL STATEMENT—POSITIONING AN APPLICANT UNDER RHETORICAL RESTRAINTS

A winning statement must not only be well written but also give due deference to the often nebulous aspects of the essay—its usefulness to society and to the college or program specifically and how to best use the rhetorical limitations and freedoms of the forum to appeal for admission (Chiu, 2013; Ishop, 2008; Jones, J. M., 2013). Here we will review the literature on both of these aspects, in turn revealing hidden parts of the statement and areas that may perniciously harm Black applicants or those who have limited knowledge of the application process.

The Difficulties of Writing the Personal Statement

This dual purpose of the personal statement—an introductory writing by the applicant and an appeal to the college that the applicant will contribute to the university's goals—creates confusion on the part of the applicant as to what exactly they should focus on. Worse yet, the personal statement incentivizes students to engineer and fit their statements to what they think colleges want to hear. This process creates angst and frustration for the applicant, and those without the resources or wherewithal to understand these hidden agendas before submitting an application often fail to secure an acceptance (Chiu, 2013; Ishop, 2008; Stevens, 2014; Vossler, 2007; Warren, 2013). Because of this, many have argued about the use of the personal statement (Solana, 2005; Stevens, 2014), with at least two works having advocated for abolishing the personal statement altogether (Goldman, 2014; Murphy, Klieger, Borneman, & Kuncel, 2009).

In addition, personal statements burden students differently, from both a sociolegal and psychological perspective (Carbado & Harris, 2008; Warren, 2013). Vidall's (2007) work interrogates student writing, college admissions, and the life stories of those with disabilities. In her case studies, Vidall finds that minority students walk a fine line in discussing their identities in personal statements. On one hand, students with disabilities—not unlike many applicants from other underrepresented groups—"cannot assume that [their] readers have substantial or even basic understandings of [their] topic, disability" (p. 616). This challenge brings questions (and the accompanying anxiety) about the normativity of disclosure as well as the optimal technique of disclosure, putting a unique pressure on these applicants and not the majority.

On the other hand, applicants with disabilities use various rhetorical techniques to turn the personal statement to their advantage. These writers simultaneously rebuke and counter stereotypes about their respective ability by employing powerful narratives and illustrating a strong and stable identity, but also produce pity and/or admiration for their struggles and resulting resiliency (Vidall, 2007). These writers often do not point fingers at societal, institutional, or governmental processes for causing or contributing to their disability but instead internalize and individualize their life experience to simultaneously support and supplant the reader's impression of the struggles inherent in being a person with a disability.

Another work looks at race, reader expectations and biases, and the personal statement. In their theoretical essay, Carbado and Harris (2008) interrogate the personal statement in the context of a post–affirmative action admissions scheme. Focusing on the anti–affirmative action proposals passed in states like California and Michigan, the authors cite the personal statement as an assessment tool that reveals white privilege and materially hampers applicants of color.

Specifically, Carbado and Harris posit that personal statements that demand that applicants describe their self-journey without mention of race bolster the essays of white applicants and handicap the writings of students of color. These racial minority students—to the authors—see their life courses affected by their racial experiences, making their writings "unintelligible" to the admissions official (p. 1161). This pressure on the writer and reader to be colorblind creates a new and unfair preference in the admissions context, particularly knowing that racial categorization and stigmatization are often implicit. The personal statement, in these contexts, limits and contrives the expression of applicants of color, providing an avenue in which white applicants may have an advantage in the admissions context.

A more recent development in personal statement politics—and a move that brings Carbado and Harris's (2008) concerns more to the fore—is the diversity statement. Many colleges and universities ask for diversity statements in addition to a personal statement. These tasks specifically ask applicants to describe their views on collegiate diversity and on how they will bring diversity to the incoming class. Kirkland and Hansen's (2011) piece, "'How Do I Bring Diversity?' Race and Class in the College Admissions Essay" specifically looks at the diversity statement as an area replete with pitfalls for applicants of color and for those without a clear understanding of what admissions officials want from such statements.

Using a sophisticated propensity score matching statistical model, Kirkland and Hansen analyzed how students discussed diversity and positioned themselves in relation to it in their college essays (Kirkland & Hansen, 2011). To the applicants the authors studied, diversity meant not just race and ethnicity but also "gender, religion, class, sexual orientation, disability, opinions, music and food (nearly always mentioned as a pair), culture, internationalism, small town sensibility, and individual uniqueness" (p. 116).

Minority students, the authors discovered, focused on traditional barometers of diversity to discuss how they bring diversity to the class, while white students focused more on how everyone is diverse—and the need to focus on individual differences. Even after matching applicants, the authors still found that Black students were least able to discuss diversity as anything other than race and ethnicity and that colleges and universities subsequently marked these applicants as "diverse" (p. 128). Overall, Kirkland and Hansen found that the diversity essay existed mostly for students to individualize—an explicit goal of diversity-oriented admissions as expressed by many colleges and universities as well as the Supreme Court.

From this literature, we now know that applicants and admissions officers look specifically to the personal statement to make the most direct argument for the applicant's admission. We also know that hopeful students have uncovered many of the hidden aspects of the personal statement that colleges and universities seek but rarely ask for. Unfortunately, in addition to the knowledge gap on how to best tackle the personal statement across status levels, the burden of the personal statement is not equal across applicant groups. Black applicants in particular may be at a disadvantage due to (1) a difficulty in consolidating their identity with that of a scholar and (2) a contrived and limited rhetorical framework from which to draw a statement.

I first encountered the diversity statement when applying to law school. Being both Black and bisexual, I had a rich history of discrimination, subordination, perseverance, and success to pull from in making a connection between me and any law school's diversity initiatives. I couldn't mention my race, however, for my (ultimately successful) application to UCLA School of Law. The state prohibited UCLA from considering race in any admissions context. Yet, they still asked us to write about how we contributed to diversity.

This is the exact conundrum that Carbado and Harris (2008) discuss. I knew I couldn't just say, "I'm Black. Let me in," for my statement, but the edict to withhold race made crafting the statement infinitely harder. I attended a historically Black college—could I talk about that? What about my participation as a Summer Research Opportunity Program research intern—an opportunity specially designed to get future minority scholars into research? How could I talk about any of my lived experiences without mentioning race? For better or worse, and due to forces entirely outside of my control, being Black affected every facet of my life.

In the end, I was forced to discuss something else entirely: my height. At six foot, nine inches, I was almost always the tallest person in the room, and in some ways my height affected my daily life as much as my race. But since I didn't play sports or volunteer as a high-shelf-reacher at my local grocery store, I had little clue how to tie my height into the demands of the diversity statement. I eventually settled on drawing out an extended metaphor relating my height to my sense of perspective, concluding my diversity statement with the following:

> In everything that I am and that I do, I have been described as grand. I am well aware that I stand out in a crowd. I like and take full advantage of this aspect that makes me so different from others. So far, I have been able to acquire skills that have allowed me to flourish as an effective leader, to use my height as a means to network and start conversation, and to treat others with dignity by respecting what makes them different. I may lose every game of hide-and-seek, but I sincerely hope to use my difference to win in everything I endeavor.

Upon rereading my law school diversity statement, the first word I associate with it is *corny*. It did the trick, however. During my second year of law school, I bumped into an admissions officer for the school. After craning her neck to look me in the face, she asked me if I wrote the diversity statement about being tall. When I confirmed her suspicion, she thanked me for writing the piece, informing me that the school sent my essay to aspiring applicants, citing it as an excellent example of what they were looking for. Apparently, I overcame the burden of hiding my Black identity by leaning in to another trait that made me stand out at a place like UCLA. Without knowing it, I somehow made the diversity statement work for me.

RHETORICAL FRAMES AND STRUCTURES WITHIN THE PERSONAL STATEMENT

Given this, there is still some question about how exactly other students make the personal statement work for them. After all, "the true nature of the college essay is not an invitation to write for someone who really wants to know a student better. It is, rather, a high-stakes competitive writing task that can make the difference between college acceptance or rejection" (Warren, 2013, p. 44). Accordingly, writers of personal statements must turn what appears to be an informational essay into a persuasive argument without explicating the rhetorical mechanics (Ding, 2007).

Again, Ishop's (2008) research is helpful; by investigating what students write about and how it fits into the college's hidden goals, the author mapped admissions essays onto a small set of appeals. These included direct recollections engendering schools to believe the applicant developed "(a) perseverance, (b) willingness to take risks, (c) educational and personal growth, (d) maturity, [and] (e) leadership and service" (p. 81). While these attributes are certainly important to admissions officials, exactly when and how to infuse them into applicants' personal statements remains a mystery to many applicants, particularly those of color and first-generation students.

Vossler's (2007) master's thesis work—focusing on personal statements in the field of library science—discussed at length the use of the personal statement to indicate institutional fit. Discussing Brown's (2004) paradox, wherein the personal statement must individualize the writer in the reader's eye and simultaneously position the applicant as a perfect fit in the desired program or school, Vossler remarked on the inherent challenge of the personal statement: "The real challenge facing applicants lies in figuring out what kind of applicant each program desires, and how to emphasize the[ir] personal qualities most in keeping with each program's agenda" (Vossler, 2007, p. 8). In the library sciences, successful applicants revealed themselves as emerging professionals with "already-developed ideas about [library science], and how they will fit into the profession" (p. 56).

The best rhetorical approach for the personal statement changes according to the program or specialization the applicant applies to, however. In their study, Samraj and Monk (2008) reviewed personal statements in three graduate program fields: electrical engineering, business administration, and linguistics. For each, the researchers found that a unique focus in the personal statement facilitated acceptance into the different programs. Successful applicants to each program focused on different selves—the self as researcher (electrical engineering), the self as a future success who was missing key education (MBA), or the self as an experienced scholar ready for advanced work (linguistics). Further, the authors found that each discipline expressed the respective goals in their application materials, helping to "explain" the differences (p. 207).

My applications for law school—written hastily between studying for the LSAT and trying to squeeze every ounce out of my senior year of college— use multiple rhetorical angles to appeal to admission committees. Although my grades were good and my LSAT score above the ninetieth percentile, I was a psychology major who took few courses in English, political science, or philosophy. Like many college seniors facing the realities of the "real world," I applied to law school mostly due to a lack of vocational imagination and compliments from others that I "loved to argue."

Thus, my personal statement had to do a lot of heavy lifting. In order to justify my sudden interest in law, I wrote a narrative from my high school days, when I went to Washington, DC, to protest in defense of the University of Michigan, which was fighting for its right to maintain its affirmative action programs. I wrote about a burgeoning sense of justice I felt since that day, appealing directly to law schools' perspective of students as fighters and world changers:

As the gathering of pro-affirmative action protesters moved downhill from the Supreme Courthouse to the Lincoln Memorial, I could only take in the sights momentarily. There were people arguing right in front of each other's faces in every direction. I walked onto the Memorial in silence.

At the Memorial, I realized what I was truly missing. I needed to have that cause—that fight—that would spur me to yell, waive, and dispute for what I believed in. My life would have more meaning in fighting for my beliefs.

After that day, I recommitted myself to finding my cause over the course of high school and college. In that time, I have gotten into many arguments, and fought bitterly against friends and superiors alike for my beliefs on all subjects. I found overtime that my cause was people—the basic fight for people and their freedoms. My work on African-American identity and with queer interest groups over the last four years has only strengthened my resolve to keep fighting for my values and for those multitudes that have yet to find their voices.

Because I had little concrete evidence that I would make a good law student (no pre-law honors society, no mock trial tournaments, no summer internship with the local district attorney), I used more amorphous rhetorical frames to couch myself in the law school context. I needed to wrap up the grander narrative of my life where the most logical next step was law school—and hopefully with a scholarship. With my personal statement, I attempted that maneuver within the bounds of a few pages and a single anecdote.

PART III: NARRATIVE IDENTITY AND THE PERSONAL STATEMENT—HIGH-STAKES IDENTITY ORCHESTRATION

Narrative Identity Development at the Time of Application

Personal statements are just one example of an appeal to belong to a group. Like joining a country club or co-op, many people apply to college out of the desire for upward social mobility and/or the material benefits of exclusive membership. Importantly, the desire to be a part of groups and organizations is not just material, or even social. The need for affiliation, acceptance, and belonging is a deep psychological motivation, propelling us to be social animals (Leary, 2010).

We are naturally inclined to affiliate, and belonging to high-status groups or institutions like colleges and universities compels applicants to make special appeals showing themselves as "responsible, trustworthy, loyal, cooperative, and dedicated individual[s] who support the goals and norms of the relationship or group" (Leary, 2010, p. 873). The personal statement directly tests this ability by inviting the applicant to engage in self-disclosure—itself a common tool of affiliation—to ingratiate, self-promote, or exemplify the writer to the reader's mind. Others (perhaps disproportionately applicants of color and those from poorer backgrounds) use this space to "convey impressions of neediness or helplessness (supplication) to enhance their relational value to [application readers]" (p. 871). Regardless of what technique the applicant uses, we can best describe the personal statement as an appeal to belong, an important endeavor in any life.

Perhaps not coincidentally, the majority of applicants write personal statements as adolescents or young adults. This also happens to be a time when individuals develop the "life narrative," or the ability to articulate an internalized story delineating the institutions, events, and themes in one's life that coalesced to create the fully realized self (McAdams, 2001, p. 101). In other words, the life narrative explains, "Who am I, how did I become who I am, and when did I become it?"

The answers to these questions are in essence the core of the personal statement. Applicants use this space to discuss their "self-defining memories," or those that are "emotional, personally important, [and] central to the life story" (McLean & Fournier, 2008). This is an active and engaged project of the writer, "employ[ing] stories to . . . influence others as a tool of persuasion or rhetoric" (Singer, 2004, p. 442). Accordingly, it is important to understand this process in order to study the personal statement and the way an applicant develops their essay.

Furthermore, the life narrative derives out of an established cultural and social world (Harris, 1989). Group membership, position within hierarchies, and social standing can all direct and limit what type(s) of life narratives are acceptable and appreciated (Leary, 2010; Singer, 2004). In the American context, valuing bootstrap meritocracy supports life narratives rooted in individualism, internally realized motivations, and an unending drive toward success (Alim, 2014). Across different genders, races, sexual orientations, (dis)abilities, and economic statuses, the best life narrative for acceptance and affiliation with an elite group may fall along these lines. This is true regardless of whether it feels most authentic for the writer.

Applicants also use the personal statement to impart their personality on the reader (Ding, 2007; Hatch, Hill, & Hayes, 1993; McAdams et al., 2004). Early research shows that personal writing is a vital tool in deploying personality. Hatch, Hill, and Hayes (1993) detail the power of personal writing on the reader's perception of the writer: "The rhetorical task, then, is to convince admissions officers that the writer is the kind of student they would want to admit to the university. This task represents a particular kind of rhetorical situation, one in which the writer is consciously trying to persuade the reader that he or she has certain personality traits" (p. 571). From their study, the authors concluded that rhetorical moves dictated the reader's impression of the personal statement writer. Of course, this effect could be for better (e.g., the writer's acknowledgment of the contributions of others, giving the impression of being modest and mature) or worse (e.g., the writer's use of pretentious language, giving the impression that the writer is arrogant or phony).

In linking the work of writers to the psychology of "impression formation" (p. 570), the authors show that when multiple readers read a sample personal statement, they come to the same conclusions about the writer's personality traits at rates much higher than chance. What's more, these assessments correlated to behavior; personal statement readers who viewed the writer's personality positively (likable, down-to-earth, etc.) or negatively (naïve, dull, etc.) were more likely to vote for or against admission, respectively (p. 579). From this, the authors advocated for writers to employ certain rhetorical moves to boost positive personality perceptions in their personal statements. From this work and the work of others, it is evident that the personal statement serves particular needs of both the college and the applicant.

Identity Orchestration within the Personal Statement

Rice (2008) studies identity orchestration and individuals' ability to discuss their life narratives while simultaneously reconstructing identities. In *Balance*, Rice delineates four articulations of identity orchestration, using focus group data from a cohort of Black male youth to ground his theory. Discussing the double-consciousness-like "twoness that is created by a dilemma related to 'Black identity' and 'success'" (p. 56) that sometimes stymie Black articulations of self, Rice places special emphasis on Black men's ability to navigate high-stakes and high-pressure situations of identity articulation and still develop well-rounded senses of self.

One of the articulations of identity Rice (2013) discusses, he calls acute identity expression (AIE). Unlike other of Rice's articulations, where discomfort or frustration with displaying identity is evident in the narrative, AIE focuses on the individual's need to seek recognition or visibility, hyperarticulating their strengths and underplaying their weaknesses. This mode of deploying and articulating one's identity seems to map perfectly onto the personal statement, where applicants have to present a hyperstylized version of themselves to appeal to the reader's idea of a successful and worthy candidate. Displaying resiliency, perseverance, and success despite low odds are examples of AIE used in personal statements (Alim, 2014; Brown, 2005).

Identity, narrative, and applied linguistics play a large part in the personal statement and happen to be intricately connected. We need language to understand our identities, and we seek to communicate those identities to others (Harris, 1989; Hyland, 2010). Both the communicator and the communicated actively construct and interpret the expressed identity, making the use of linguistics and rhetoric critical to the endeavor (Hatch, Hill, & Hayes, 1993; Hyland, 2010; McAdams et al., 2004). Thus, the rhetorical and institutional boundaries of the personal statement help shape how applicants' senses of self meld into the written personal statement.

As I prepared to leave law school, I made the wise decision to apply for my PhD. On the surface, this was a good idea. I responded positively to the theoretical and scholarly sides of the law—spending hours in the library and reading copious law review articles. My response to the application of the law—the trial advocacy training, business law courses, and high-pressure internships at august firms—was the exact opposite. Accordingly, continuing on and getting a doctorate degree made sense.

Deeper down, going to grad school again was a terribly misguided notion. My journey in law school was mostly a disaster. I was burned out from the first day and never really got my bearings. Consequently, my grades were middling, I failed to secure a job, and I had little confidence I would pass the bar exam. Instead of facing my defeats head on and forging ahead with my chosen profession, I retreated to the reset button that was more school.

My personal statement couldn't convey any of this doubt. I knew from my two prior application experiences that I would have to present myself not as defeated and doubtful but instead as decisive and determined. I relied on acute identity expression to paint myself as successful, multitalented, and knowing exactly what I wanted to do and how. Although none of this was true at the time, I knew that the readers of my application would need reasons to root for me and open their doors to me once more. I began my doctoral personal statement with a pithy account of my entire collegiate experience:

> Since beginning college more than seven years ago, I have always tried to serve the students around me. I have served as a tutor, a mentor, a guide, or simply a silent ear to countless peers—both friends and strangers. Largely, I have done this without pay, but have also been lucky enough to be paid to help students navigate the sometimes-treacherous path through college. While doing this work—at both the historically Black Morehouse College and the large, publicly funded university that is UCLA—I have had much exposure to students of color and those from disadvantaged backgrounds like myself. From this, I uniquely understand how vitally important it is to create diverse environments that foster the best of each student and not just create a superficial image of various colors. In my doctoral studies, I hope to create powerful research from this work and influence policy changes that will help every student.

Here, I defined myself as essentially a teacher and a guide—someone with a purpose and a track record of success. I essentially reconstructed my experiences as not peppered with personal failures but filled with teachable moments I imparted to others. The rest of the statement focuses solely on the things I did well academically and within the community both at Morehouse College and UCLA. With a completely unfounded confidence, I closed the personal statement like this:

> Thinking back on these discrete, though paralleled experiences, I have realized that I have the skills and knowledge necessary to increase and perfect the diversity efforts of colleges and universities so that students of color, LGBT students, and other students from underrepresented backgrounds do not feel marginalized or alone. I feel that my graduate study will allow me to promulgate research that will make diversity a salient and impactful goal of schools and leave students of color proud to attend (and graduate) college. Through my research and my community work, I have strived only to make college and graduate school more inviting for students. As a PhD doctoral student, I can propel that previous work and touch the lives of countless students.

In hindsight, I'm incredulous that I wrote so confidently while I was in the midst of personal and academic turmoil. I'm not surprised, however. By that time, I had spent many years crafting my life narrative. In my mind, my life was converging to one central path—that of an academic and public servant. I used AIE to present myself in the optimal light, ready and able to succeed at the next level. I have no doubt that thousands of other doctoral applicants did the same as they wrote their personal statements.

CONCLUSION

Throughout this piece, I've discussed the personal statement as a high-stakes document. With it, the applicant has some level of control over how readers view them. Critical mistakes in writing the personal statement lead the reader to conclude that the applicant is unprepared, unsure, or possibly unbalanced. Applicants have for decades had great difficulty writing these statements. They must put themselves in the role of the reader and guess at what they want to hear while simultaneously staying true to themselves. The introduction of the diversity statement—a new hurdle to clear for applicants who may feel they don't belong or aren't truly wanted—only makes things more difficult. Nevertheless, applicants have developed rhetorical frames to express themselves as themselves while appealing to the sensibilities of people they will likely never encounter. This is no small feat, particularly for Black applicants facing legacies of exclusion and stereotyping.

REFERENCES

Albanese, M. A., Snow, M. H., Skochelak, S. E., Huggett, K. N., & Farrell, P. M. (2003, March). Assessing personal qualities in medical school admissions. *Academic Medicine, 78*(3), 313–21.

Alim, J. A. (2014, December 14). *Experts divided over impact of absent father-themed college admission essays.* Retrieved from Diverse: Issues in Higher Education. diverseeducation.com/article/68501/.

Brown, R. M. (2004, July). Self-composed: Rhetoric in psychology personal statements. *Written Communication, 21*(3), 242–60.

Brown, R. M. (2005). *The rhetoric of self-promotion in personal statements.* PhD dissertation, University of Texas at Austin, Austin, TX.

Carbado, D. W., & Harris, C. I. (2008, October). The new racial preferences. *California Law Review, 96*(5), 1139–214.

Chiu, Y.-L. T. (2013). *Academic literacies study of personal statements for higher education: Students' and academics' interpretations and assumptions across institutional contexts.* PhD dissertation, Kings College London, Department of Education and Professional Studies, London, UK.

Ding, H. (2007). Genre analysis of personal statements: Analysis of moves in application essays to medical and dental schools. *English for Specific Purposes, 26*, 368–92.

Goldman, S. (2014, May). *Abolish the personal statement.* Minding the Campus. Retrieved December 12, 2014. http://www.mindingthecampus.com/2014/05/abolish_the_personal_statement/.

Goldstein, D. S. (2011). Feeding the pipeline: Helping students of color write college entrance essays for the university 2.0. *The International HETL Review, 1.* https://www.hetl.org/feature-articles/feeding-the-pipeline/.

Harris, J. (1989). Constructing and reconstructing the self in the writing class. *Journal of Teaching Writing, 8*(1), 21–29.

Hatch, J. A., Hill, C. A., & Hayes, J. R. (1993, October). When the messenger is the message: Readers' impressions of writers' personalities. *Written Communication, 10*(4), 569–98.

Hyland, K. (2010). Community and individuality: Performing identity in applied linguistics. *Written Communication, 27*(2), 159–88.

Ishop, K. B. (2008). *The college application essay: Just tell me what to write and I'll write it.* PhD dissertation, University of Texas at Austin, Austin, TX.

Jones, J. M. (2013). *Evaluating intentionality: A psychometric rubric for statements of purpose.* EdD dissertation, Grand Canyon University, Phoenix, AZ.

Jones, S. (2013, August). "Ensure that you stand out from the crowd": A corpus-based analysis of personal statements according to applicants' school type. *Comparative Education Review, 57*(3), 397–423.

Kirkland, A., & Hansen, B. B. (2011). "How do I bring diversity?" Race and class in the college admissions essay. *Law & Society Review, 45*(1), 103–38.

Leary, M. R. (2010). Affiliation, acceptance, and belonging: The pursuit of interpersonal connection. In S. T. Fiske, D. T. Gilbert, & G. Lindzey (Eds.), *Handbook of Social Psychology* (5th ed., Vol. 2, pp. 864–97). Hoboken, NJ: Wiley.

McAdams, D. P. (2001). The psychology of life stories. *Review of General Psychology, 5*(2), 100–22.

McAdams, D. P., Anyidoho, N. A., Brown, C., Huang, Y. T., Kaplan, B., & Machado, M. A. (2004, August). Traits and stories: Links between dispositional and narrative features of personality. *Journal of Personality, 74*(2), 762–84.

McLean, K. C., & Fournier, M. A. (2008). The content and processes of autobiographical reasoning in narrative identity. *Journal of Research in Personality, 42*, 527–45.

Murphy, S. C., Klieger, D. M., Borneman, M. J., & Kuncel, N. R. (2009). The predictive power of personal statements in admissions: A meta-analysis and cautionary tale. *College & University, 84*(4), 83–86, 88.

Rice, D. W. (2008). *Balance: Advancing identity theory by engaging the Black male adolescent.* Plymouth, UK: Lexington Books.

Rice, D. W. (2013). Rakim, Ice Cube then *Watch the Throne*: Engaged visibility through identity orchestration and the language of hip-hop narratives. *The Journal of Popular Culture, 46*(1), 173–91.

Samraj, B., & Monk, L. (2008). The statement of purpose in graduate program applications: Genre structure and disciplinary variation. *English for Specific Purposes, 27*, 193–211.

Singer, J. A. (2004, June). Narrative identity and meaning making across the adult lifespan: An introduction. *Journal of Personality, 72*(3), 437–60.

Solana Jr., A. (2005, May 2). *A guide to the law school application process for people of color and members of other historically underrepresented groups.* For People of Color.org. Retrieved December 12, 2014. http://www.aap.ucla.edu/mentoring/pdf/02_a_guide_to_law_school_application.pdf.

Stevens, M. (2014, November 13). *Stop obsessing over your college essay—admissions officers don't (But they do care what you think of their clever questions).* New Republic. Retrieved December 12, 2014. http://www.newrepublic.com/article/120249/colleges-admissions-essay-questions-and-what-they-actually-reveal.

Vidall, A. (2007, July). Performing the rhetorical freak show: Disability, student writing, and college admissions. *College English, 69*(6), 615–41.

Vossler, J. J. (2007). *Must it be perfect? An analysis of statements of purpose submitted to UNC SILS, 2003–2007.* Master's paper, University of North Carolina at Chapel Hill, School of Information and Library Science, Chapel Hill, NC.

Warren, J. (2013, fall). The rhetoric of college application essays: Removing obstacles for low income and minority students. *American Secondary Education, 42*(1), 43–56.

Chapter 13

Black Boys, "Church," and Supplementary Education, General Considerations

David Wall Rice, Brenda Wall,
and William Marcel Hayes

FRAMING

Black men and boys face a unique predicament with respect to academic achievement within the American context. Historically, Black communities have valued high achievement in spite of the daunting challenges of segregation and its limited allocation of educational resources. Within current mass culture, however, a deficit model has emerged to account for academic disengagement and has helped to redefine Black American youth, Black men and boys in particular, as underachievers. The "traditional" educational system has been statistically successful in distancing young Black boys from academics by the time they reach the fourth grade and completely severing the academic relationship for a disproportionate number of young, Black American students before their completion of the twelfth grade (Gordon, Gordon, & Nembhard, 1994; Gordon, 1999; Kunjufu, 2004). Accordingly, "school house" education in America struggles with the implications of underpreparedness, disengagement, and rejection for Black American boys and men, who experience a drop in academic success concurrently with soaring rates of association with correctional facilities. The normed understanding of these youth through a lens of pathology contaminates engagement that may highlight paths toward strong academic performance—a characteristic attached to high achievement and multiple successes.

Black men and boys are too often positioned as less than the "norm," a subordination that is consistent with an educational approach that assumes the learner as the problem rather than a problematic system that has been demonstrated to lack the capacity to accommodate the needs of the learner. For example, in early elementary education, referrals for special education resource rooms, attention deficit hyperactive disorder, and learning disabilities come to characterize Black boys far more readily than an identification of giftedness, creativity, or leadership. The prevailing educational focus supports the child who can accommodate an orientation toward curriculum/ content focus. Conversely, children who require focus on the learner in order to achieve are labelled as of lower aptitude and achievement and perceived as having behavioral inadequacy. Such perceptions yield ongoing marginalization of young children and an overly simplistic view of Black American boys as pathologically hyperactive, aggressive, and academically unmotivated. Failure characterizes classroom experience in terms of the outcome of the teaching model with little attention to addressing the failure of the model itself. It is not surprising, then, that models that successfully promote affirmative development and achievement equity among Black American men and boys are so poorly understood. This attention to success is even less prevalent when attempting to thread research involving this group through a behavioral eye that is strengths based.

There are at least two approaches that must be explored in order to understand how marginalized Black American boys can be recognized and nurtured as academically successful. One is to shift the paradigm, to articulate new strengths-based models. Efforts along these lines have been introduced to develop curricula that are successfully focused on students. Systems prime for replication in this regard are found in New York City's Harlem Children's Zone, the University of Maryland Baltimore County's Myerhoff Program, and Morehouse College's Oprah Winfrey Scholars Program. To varying degrees and within varying contexts, these arenas of learning integrate educational webs that are interdependent and student focused and that assume the best for each learner. The much-maligned Black boy/man has found tremendous academic success within these systems.

There is also the need to supplement traditional models. Compensating for a prevailing educational orientation offers avenues toward academic success that can be reinforced in traditional education—which may well be deficit based—by providing healthy cultural attachment and personality expressions that occur in strengths-based arenas. Academic reinforcement as well as the critical dimension of cultural and personal context are underexplored components of academic success for many Black boys who achieve and who are academically competitive. These nuanced framings and places of success are important to recognize because of the need to integrate and to exercise strengths within communities and among those who might not be aware of them or of how this dimensionality might be fit to a schooling context. An integral part of that achievement and academic culture, and a source of high investment and high expectation for many Black boys, is the Black church. We argue here, then, that the incorporation of religious faith and church programs is helpful in enhancing strong academic development for many Black boys and that they are models of the best types of supplementary education.

Where supplementary education is understood as those contexts beyond traditional schooling where a person learns, it is interesting that the church is frequently an afterthought in considering places and models for the effective generation and reinforcement of tacit and explicit knowledge. The church, at least in theory, absent the politics that frequently frame it, exemplifies supplementary education well because of its ability to make learning and knowledge important and applicable. This is particularly evident through the integration of a socioemotional connection that incorporates safety, love, and space for the figuring of psychological balance.

BACKGROUND

The exploration of behaviors that are psychologically and socially rewarding is pertinent to understanding achievement of Black men and boys within a complex reality. In a historical and contemporaneous context, there are places where academic success has been normalized for Black American boys. As is the case for most people, achievement for Black American men and boys is often interwoven into community, which includes anchoring in religious life, belief, and ritual. Whether the Black church is a part of the community continuum of liberation and praxis or whether it is seen as a current support for social pressures that affect children and their families, educational engagement within the church helps children to become more viable and confident in their life experience. Structured education programs within the church are found in autonomous schools associated with the institution, traditional Sunday school, youth church, teen summits and youth workshops, Bible study, and summer vacation Bible school. With this depth of educational dedication and active involvement, it is not a reach to suggest that the church holds significance among those who are a part of the religious body. The purpose here is to discover how supplementary education, which occurs in the church setting—be it structured or more amorphous, but just as impactful as sermon content, high church community expectation, moral imperatives, and the like—functions in support of the learner's success beyond the church walls.

THE PROBLEM

At least three causal variables have been identified as compromising academic achievement for Black men and boys: hostile or unsupportive environments associated with residual racism, absence of adequate socialization to the attitudinal and behavioral demands of the academy, and limited exposure to models of academic excellence and exemplars of scholarly practice (Bridglall, 2004). Another causal variable that is often overlooked is the disconnection between the learner's identity and purpose and the community and larger society. We contend that an activity-based religious environment can neutralize these obstacles to academic achievement with exposure to appropriate guidance; moral and technical support; examples and models of relevant learning behaviors; high-performance learning communities; and inspiration, motivation, and exhortation for identity and purpose in personal and collective achievement. This activity-based perspective is an important orientation to have within one's educational repertoire because of its ability to allow for integration into multiple designs for education, including traditional learning environments.

In a content-focused learning environment, educators and researchers may attend to the mechanics of learning. They may even introduce content that is culturally inclusive as a way of motivating the learner, or perhaps require cultural diversity training for teachers who work with different communities and their children. A learner-focused approach, however, provides enhanced opportunity for knowledge acquisition by integrating into the education process the value of the child and what the child brings to the institution of learning. Learning is more evident when the culture is highly valued and reinforced. It then becomes easier to suggest purpose in larger society as a natural and necessary outcome. When there is an emotional and social connection to learning, there is success. Alternatively, with the absence of an emotional and social connection, there is distancing from the learning experience. Signs such as acting-out behaviors, apathy, and rebellion often surface, interfere with learning, and can undermine the formal learning process. The church as supplementary education allows for an example of an integrated socioemotional connectedness to knowledge that can serve as a template in attending to meaningful academic achievement and intellective competence.

The language we use to understand achievement is bound in the affirmative development of academic abilities (Gordon, 2001) and the positioning of learners toward intellective competence. The church, then, can be explored as an example of supplementary academic experience and support apart from the religious belief system. Thus, we consider religion here not just in terms of doctrine or belief systems but also as a holistic individual support that allows for practice toward effective human learning and an associated orchestrated psychological balance (Rice, 2008).

In situating the potential of practiced faith toward high academic achievement for Black males, we look at the relationship between the cultural significance and role of the church and education.

AN OVERVIEW

Supplementary education is the formal and informal learning and development opportunities provided for students outside of school. Gordon, Bridglall, and Meroe (2004) discuss this reframing of education as the hidden curriculum for high academic achievement, stipulating that the whole person is engaged and is taught best through experiences and alternatives made richer by that which is shared within the four walls of the schoolhouse. Paths toward supplementary education, then, are generally presented as traditional, nontraditional, curricular, and extracurricular and are frequently understood as travel, tutoring, summer camps, basketball leagues, and interactions with other high-achieving students and family members (Bennett, 2001; Cohen, 2003). Even when considering afterschool programming and ideas of supplementary education stoked by the No Child Left Behind Act of 2001 and the proliferation of for-profit education services, a circumscribed view of the construct is still apparent. It is not presented as comprehensive in scope as its architects would have us understand. And often, as a result of this limited view, the wealthy and families who appreciate capitals associated with achievement are thought to have an advantage in supplementary education that is similar to advantages held in traditional modes of education.

In operating from this quasitraditional academic model, disparities between the socioeconomic statuses of minority and nonminority students persist. This contributes to a perceived inequity of opportunities available to white students, even in a comprehensive education paradigm that demonstrates a capacity to be ever more inclusive. Employing a postpositivist worldview that reinforces errant generalizations about Black males, rather than a constructivist or pragmatic effort that explores alternative and enhanced understandings, compromises the completeness of educational opportunity and paths toward high academic achievement. This perceived lack of opportunity then affects the aspirations of many ethnically diverse students (French, Eisenberg, Vaughan, Purwono, & Suryanti, 2008; Levin & Taylor, 1998).

In the face of such complex social, economic, and academic realities, marginalized students and their families must look to all positive environments, activities, and examples that promote healthy principles leading to academic excellence. Bridglall (2004) outlines a variety of implicit supplementary educational experiences: parenting, nutrition, family talk, parental enjoyment, decision making, reading along with children, socialization and acculturation, social networks, travel, and environmental support (Wolf, 1966, 1995) and explicit supplementary education opportunities including academic development, tutorials, advocacy, redemption, standardized test preparation, one-to-one tutoring, Saturday academies, specialized services, sociocultural opportunities, and student-centered social groups.

For many marginalized families, the most conspicuous of supplementary education arenas, places of worship, have evolved into multifaceted support systems that extend beyond religious service to include day care, youth services, and even stand-alone schools, making them a logical source for integration into present circumstances. Sociocultural and socioeconomic presses and pulls often make "church" a natural fit in the family's search for value, balance, and replenishment. This oasis of worship, of course, is also available for middle-and upper-middle-class families that are often understood as less marginalized but who may face the same compromises associated with the achievement gap. These compromises include fear of disapproval or rejection by peers, such as fears of being labeled as acting white (Fordham & Ogbu, 1986); hostile or unsupportive environments associated with residual racism (Aronson et al., 1999); absence of adequate socialization to the attitudinal and behavioral demands of the academy (Ogbu, 2003); and limited contact with and exposure to models of academic excellence and exemplars of scholarly practice (Gordon, 2001). Solutions to these compromises could come in realizing and maximizing the fundamentals of practiced faith toward the end of high academic achievement.

In exploring practiced faith through the lens of the Black church, there are easy nods to the expectation of high academic achievement echoed in the Black church's role in establishing many of the nation's historically Black colleges and universities. The Black church is a natural fit to a social, emotional, and personal connection within community and the larger society because of its role as a catalyst throughout the civil rights movement. The church's primary responsibility has been to develop and sustain the fulfillment of individual spiritual needs through religious emphasis. However, it is not possible to meet such a need without addressing the totality of the community. Thus, the church institution has expanded into the arena of social justice with the related programs of health, economic empowerment, and education to address broader societal needs.

Cohen (2003) stipulates essential components of supplemental education. Among them are a strong tutor/parent/teacher connection, experienced providers, proven methods of instruction, customized instruction, and a positive learning environment. Accordingly, places of worship present as readymade centers of supplementary education; however, they remain under-identified for their potential and role within the development of academic achievement. Further, religious practice and "church" activity are particularly salient among ethnic and racial minorities (Bennett, 2001; Levin & Taylor, 1998; Riggins, McNeal, & Herndon, 2008), largely because religious involvement is a source of developmental enrichment accessible across socioeconomic and sociocultural boundaries (Charters, Taylor, Jackson, & Lincoln, 2008; French et al., 2008; Levin & Taylor, 1998; Unruh, 2004).

Unruh (2004) cites religious service programs and religious activity in general as crucial educational and social spaces that can provide extensive behavioral influence. Acts of spiritual discipline such as prayer, reading, knowing and incorporating books of worship into daily living, and overall self and community development are common across doctrines and support the idea of religious practice as relevant to supplementary education. Through these activities, those being educated can be not only inspired but also supported in developing religious identity and religious expressions (French et al., 2008; Levin & Taylor, 1998; Simpson, Newman, & Fuqua, 2007).

Through its major principles and precepts, the Black church has proven a particularly strong model for supplementary education, implicitly and explicitly. Knowledge of scripture, self-discipline, and community uplift are general principles that help to advance the idea of how high academic achievement among Black Americans is culturally significant when framed by practice or principles that are familiar—church principles that shade into academic imperatives required for curriculum mastery.

In attending to the particulars of Black men and high academic achievement, the Nation of Islam also provides worthwhile consideration. Widely recognized as one of the most successful groups in uplifting oppressed Black males and noted for transforming the lives of the most broken, the Nation has held a commonly respected position in the Black community around the development of strong, dedicated, disciplined men—characteristics that fit neatly into effective supplementary educational programming. While there are several factors that have helped the organization to achieve these goals, we note the pervasive focus on the development of the self as cornerstone. And this development of self is rooted in the use of knowledge to improve personal conditions as well as the oppressive conditions within the community.

Though spiritual in thrust, the outcome is an example of the priming of intellective competence. Places of worship have the ability not only to orient and practice toward great accomplishment but also to allow for authentic expressions of self without reprisal and with an attending to the basic need of psychological safety.

A SAFE SPACE

At an early age, students become aware of factors that foreshadow potential difficulties in attaining success, such as rejection and disrespect, poor role models, lack of mentors, low grades, and past disappointments. In the face of unfavorable odds, minority males may experience a negative perception of future possible selves. Such a dismal outlook has implications for future academic disengagement. Oyserman and Fryberg (2006) discuss the "interface between possible selves and content of racial/ethnic identity" and contend that understandings around this intersection "would allow for the development of effective interventions to reduce the achievement gap and decrease risk of other negative outcomes contained in stereotypes" (p. 23). It is reasonable, then, to posit that a boy's performance in school is enhanced by the presence of role models who provide a positive image of men who have benefited from education and by a support system that develops and promotes high achievement. Supplementary education designed to build self-efficacy and positive identity development tends to incorporate an academic identity and a possible self that portends high academic achievement and overall success. It begins with a present self that is accepted, respected, and protected. This sheltering experience for youth occurs actively in the institutional church.

One appeal and special strength of a religious space is the acceptance of any individual who desires to be included. This availability to all is a quality that builds a foundation for individual growth and trust within the group and beyond. Boykin and Ellison (1995) consider an optimal educational environment as one that positions a mainstream world bending to facilitate the needs of the individual. This in turn aids in maintaining a consistent level of psychological balance, or identity stasis (Rice, 2008), for the student. Boykin's concept stands on the premise of a school system that builds on the assets that a child brings to the classroom. For adolescents these assets might include not only those general aspects that are culturally developed but also a culturally informed racial identity. In a place where a school system is unable (or unwilling) to do so, a religious body can take on the task. Accordingly, a religious body able to accept an individual for who they are, and one that is able to understand the person beyond stereotype, has the potential to provide Black boys and others with a place to negotiate their own identity toward balance without fear of being treated as less than or of being devalued.

Faith focuses on the development of the individual, the recognition of one's inner strength, and the ability to achieve despite seemingly insurmountable odds (Kohlberg, 1974). The presumption is that as one grows in religious commitment and understanding, one grows in one's ability to face challenges and to reach individual goals. The process builds on developed values and is expressed through ritual and activity governed by said values. Using Erickson's ego-identity construct, Flum and Blustein (2000) highlight the importance of agentic behavior in the development of an identity that is "flexible, autonomous, and self-defined" (Lapan, 2004, p. 55). These types of learners typically achieve at higher levels and are more fulfilled by their work. It is this achievement that promotes students to a valued place in society or a lack thereof that relegates them to society's margins. However, it is the healthy development of a positive self-constructed identity that potentially prepares students to define their role in society and to navigate the systems of success.

The understanding of self and its relationship to society as a whole has the potential to minimize the anxiety associated with navigating these systems. Supplementary education that supports this development typically seeks to integrate the active exploration, goal formation, and internalization of positive values. Religious institutions provide the necessary entities to support such development. This is evinced in shared community rituals that serve to strengthen the group by supporting identity development and opportunities for individual growth and achievement. Such programs build on Rappaport's (1981) model of empowerment, which seeks to "enhance the possibilities for people to control their own lives" (p. 15). The assumption is that students already possess the ability and capacity necessary to succeed academically but encounter impeding factors to that success during the transitional years of life, such as during high school.

In the face of obstacles or periods of storm and stress, the individual who affiliates with church has a group of people and a faith base that serve as a support system and guiding force. The focus is shifted from the challenges of life to the individual's potential to overcome those challenges as a result of a higher power and their own belief. Therefore, their faith becomes an element of motivation and a protective factor in facing academic challenge and low self-efficacy. This choice of faith and potential becomes increasingly defined apart from, but not without the influence of, corporate nurture. And this ability to self-nurture results in an increase in the sense of agency and a personal ability to overcome and to achieve despite adversity.

The strength embedded in this kind of supplementary education might paradoxically seem to be one of its greatest experimental flaws: it is built on faith. Yet, faith is one of the primary tenets of religion that is completely within the individual's control and therefore is one of the few areas in life where the person has choice and power. As the individual exercises their power, the hope is that the beginnings of empowerment lead to success in other areas, academic success among them.

Affiliation with a religious body or institution has the potential to provide students with an image of themselves not subject to the failures of their present circumstances. In these institutions, individuals find hope and examples of triumph and success. For students whose lives are surrounded by the negative images of disappointment and despair, religious text provides students with a counternarrative. Perry (2003) defines a counternarrative as "one that stands in opposition to the dominant society's notions about the intellectual capacity of Black Americans, the role of learning in their lives, the meaning and purpose of school, and their intellect" (p. 49).

Equally important to this process is the socioemotional support that students receive as members of a church, mosque, or assembly. Psychoanalytic theorist Erik Erikson reports that "we deal with a process 'located' in the core of the individual and yet also in the core of his communal culture. . . . Identity formation employs a process of simultaneous reflection and observation. . . . This process is, luckily, and necessarily, for the most part unconscious except where inner conditions and outer life circumstances combine to aggravate a painful or elated, 'identity-consciousness'" (Tatum, 1997, p. 19).

At a basic, practical level, the religious institution has the potential to redefine the individual's environment. Many religious institutions develop youth and special interest groups that provide individuals with the opportunity to reflect and to observe while building a social network of likeminded people. For students without traditional family support or safe environments, the religious body to which they belong can offer a space to fill that void. Many individuals are drawn to religious institutions as a place of refuge and an emotional safe haven. Rather than exposing the deficits in personal capital, the "church" has the practical ability to close perceivable gaps with the surplus of human, social, and financial capital it possesses. The spiritual equivalent is the restoration of the individual to a place of psychological and/ or spiritual balance.

The church, then, is a place where health, political, cultural, and social capital can be exercised in ways that make scholastic education work. This attending to capital and the "working" of it is greatly influenced by a strong home and resources (Gordon & Bridglall, 2007). As framed, for many minorities—Black Americans in particular—the church represents a common component of the home and an active resource, particularly as it relates to Black males and social capital.

Social capital is most easily understood in terms of social networks, social norms, cultural styles, and values (Bourdieu, 1986). The social capital that is provided through religion can be used to bolster those areas of disconnect that might compromise academic success. Specifically, the type of interconnectedness provided by the community of the church offers ongoing opportunities to address issues of hostile or unsupportive environments, inadequate socialization to the demands of the academy, and limited exposure to models of academic excellence.

"Practicing" religion can also act to diffuse the impact of components of mass culture that might distract from multiple types of achievement, including academics. For example, when the "cool pose" (Majors & Billson, 1993) makes academic achievement appear undesirable, practiced faith can help to integrate protective factors where needed (Guth, Green, Kellstedt, & Smidt, 1995). This safety net for those most at risk—Black males—is a function of religion's ability to involve members in volunteering, charitable contributions, and other acts of mercy and social concern, thus aiding in the development of socialization complementary to academic success and additional positive, affirming expressions of self and potential selves.

The social capital that religion can provide also has a potential bidirectional relationship with cultural themes that can positively influence academic achievement. Boykin's triple quandary provides a framework that proposes social realms within which the Black American transacts in achieving an identity (Boykin, 1986; Boykin & Ellison, 1995). The theoretical construct emphasizes an African cultural ethos and interrelated dimensions of spirituality, harmony, movement, verve, affect, communalism, expressive individualism, oral tradition, and social time perspective. The sophistication of the social capital that governs the Black boy's orientation to these social realms within the church and school context has the ability to reinforce self in ways that suggest academic achievement as interwoven into a community-related self, positioning academic achievement as an assumed responsibility. Jones (2003) extends this consideration of cultural capital as a function of social capital in a very specific argument with African-rooted themes considering time, rhythm, improvisation, orality, and spirituality. These themes are large parts of the Black church and allow the institution to possess sophisticated cultural capital that translates to social capital in other settings.

RELIGION AND EDUCATION: A STRAIGHT LINE

Glanville, Sikkink, and Hernández (2008) look at the relationship between religious involvement and education outcomes, specifically evaluating the mechanism(s) behind religiosity's positive influence on academic achievement. With findings that extend the social and cultural capital argument, their research suggests that religious expression influences academic motivation and achievement by promoting intergenerational, normative, and lasting networks with higher educational resources and by engaging young students in extracurricular activities. This religious participation is shown to be a positive and effective mechanism in which academic motivation can be cultivated and education can be supplemented from a holistic perspective. Religious influence has been seen in both non-Western cultural groups and in varied religious groups (Charters et al., 2008; French et al., 2008). Religious participation has also been shown to influence academic performance indirectly by influencing parenting practices that promote high academic performance (Park & Bonner, 2008).

Of course, parents and adult mentors play significant roles in most religious settings. Parents are often the main reason children attend church, especially during formative years when children are socialized. Many families determine church attendance and participation in certain rituals as part of the family norm. Therefore, children actively engage in order to uphold family standards no matter the extent to which they appreciate participation. Mentors within a church, including the pastor and lay leaders, are also pillars of support. They are often disciplinarians and role models who contribute to the child's maturation experience. These associations help to determine the degree to which religious involvement heightens the educational expectations for young people to succeed academically (Regnerus, 2000).

At base, heightened expectations extend from the support systems received within religious institutions. These expectations often present themselves in the overt reinforcement of academic achievements. For example, when a student achieves honor roll, maintains perfect attendance, or is accepted into college, it is not uncommon to receive recognition from the church with special certificates, scholarships, or ceremonial celebration. This, as might be expected, is designed primarily to encourage students and their families and to reinforce the religious body's support of the child while also setting the bar of achievement for other church youth. Seeing the academic achievements of others encourages and sustains success because of the high expectations set for them. Furthermore, Black males are motivated by an understanding that their accomplishments will be recognized and honored, a response not always guaranteed in an academic setting.

The encouragement felt by students participating in religious practices often surpasses the encouragement teachers and other administrators might normally give in a school setting. Rauner (2000) recounts the perspective of a sixteen-year-old boy on the effects of church on his academic success: "At school, you receive encouragement, but there is a lot of negativity. . . . At Church you know somebody will pick you up if you need it and there is always a hand on your back, and you always feel it there" (p. 118). Such a statement separates the general reinforcement a student might receive in a well-meaning academic setting from encouragement they receive within the context of a religious body. The difference hinges on a community that aspires with the Black male student, particularly considering a universal context that is understood as frequently unsupportive, whether intentionally or unintentionally. Community investment in the religious setting differentiates the support and positions it as more meaningful and potentially more motivational. Because students feel as if they are not alone in their academic pursuits, they are more likely to reach out for help instead of risking academic failure. Also, when students do not perform well academically, they are likely reprimanded by the same community that is there for times of encouragement. These expectations are adopted and sustained beyond one's academic family and schooling, within the entire religious community, therefore increasing the magnitude and frequency of the message and meaning of academic achievement being delivered.

In addition to external expectations, young people are likely to develop intrinsic motivations for academic success because of their religious involvement. Youth who are involved with religious activities such as Bible studies and other youth groups have reported greater feelings of hope, love, and purpose in their lives than youth who are not religiously involved (Markstrom, 1999). These orientations can translate into academic motivation. As students anchor their lives in purpose (that is presumably informed by hope and love), they are likely moved to fulfill that purpose through steps to success, academic and other.

Certainly, academic achievement is foundational in how many young people begin to understand how to position their futures. The hope that students feel as a result of their religious affiliations can aid in perseverance through academic pitfalls. The love young people describe in Markstrom's (1999) study can also aid students in feeling comfortable enough in vulnerable spaces to extend beyond these pitfalls. As Markstrom points out, because of the love given to the students, they are open to pursuing academics as a central theme of their lives. When students are intrinsically motivated, they are much more likely to succeed than if they only feel outside pressures for achievement. The love, hope, and sense of purpose many religious institutions provide help in achieving a balance between religious affiliations being external motivators and the development of a sense of internal motivation to succeed because of contextual support.

Another tangible effect of religious involvement is the decrease in risky behaviors by adolescents who are active in their religious institutions (Good & Willoughby, 2006). Religiously affiliated teens are less likely than non-religious teens to engage in behaviors such as using drugs and alcohol and having unprotected sex (Regnerus & Elder, 2003). Of course, negative behaviors increase the likelihood that students will compromise their academic performance, and students who avoid self-destructive behaviors are more inclined to be academically focused and successful.

Arguably, it is not the strength of an individual's beliefs that lead to the positive effects described but rather the act of performing religious rituals that are the true supplementary education aids. Good and Willoughby (2006) find that young people involved with religious institutions experience more positive effects than nonreligious youth regardless of the strength of their beliefs. The seemingly mundane act of attending a service requires an individual to make it a priority. The assumption of this religious "exercise" is not unlike prioritizing studying and other scholastically relevant activities to ensure academic success. The activity of religious involvement often translates into practices like planned study and completion of assignments that lead to academic success.

Historically, the Black church has played a pivotal role in literacy among Black people. Religious readings are, of course, integral to religious doctrine, and this explains much of their importance across faiths (Harvey, 1995; Ambrose, 2006). For many Black people in the United States, there is also the fact that the Bible was the primary text used to become literate during slavery and the years following.

The experiences shared in a struggle to self-educate and to liberate from slavery through reading passages of the Bible are symbolic of the high value of education for Black people within a church context. For many during this time period, education was viewed as a great equalizer and a direct correlate with the tenets of freedom. These ideologies coupled with scriptures help to lay the framework for a religion that emphasizes the simultaneous development of the mind, body, and spirit.

Fundamentally, the recital and memorization of scripture demands focus and discipline. The exercise is introduced early on to children in church. Even before children can read, the importance of scripture is evident to them. In Sunday school, vacation Bible school, and other church events, children begin learning Bible verses and Bible stories. Both memory and recitation are introduced along with reading and listening skill development. The child must devote time and energy to memorizing text and to an understanding, at least cursory, of its meaning. As the child grows older, understanding of the readings is enhanced and the themed messages can be generalized to life events and contexts. The rehearsal and eventual integration of scripture serve to develop an internal mediator for decisions and lessons learned. Here the young person learns to consider a "goodness of fit" that allows for the refinement of intellective competence, or the integration of what is learned into common, novel, and specialized problems.

Church readings supplement formal school expectations around skills such as reading, writing, critical thinking, and proper verbal communication, as well as the acculturation of achievement in these areas. These lessons are often enhanced at home through conversations about scripture and among peers by consolidating identity around the faith and peace of Jesus. The fundamental principles located at the very foundation of scripture reading are therefore reinforced in multiple arenas of the child's life.

In addition to enhanced language skills that emerge from the role of religious text in the church, direct benefits from the moral and religious principles that are taught in the church also reinforce the Black American male learner. For the student who is at risk for disproportionate rates of behavioral referrals in the school setting, poor self-control is a factor that can sabotage the academic environment. The concept of self-control and self-denial involve denying impulsive inclinations and instead exhibiting an attitude of humility and strength (Edwards, 1745/2004). Again returning to the roots of the Black church in slavery, self-denial and sacrifice were ever present, as seen in other religions as well. In fact it was these biblical principles that often sustained slaves during their constant fight against the brutal system of slavery. A large motivating factor for denial of self and sacrifice was belief in God's faithfulness to his people and the journey toward becoming more "like Christ" (Edwards, 1745/2004).

Forms of self-denial vary, including fasting and placing the needs of others before self. In this context, these principles can be presented as strong avenues for supplementary education. Older students involved in the Black church are often pointed to scriptures discussing controlling one's self to gain reward at a later time, whether in heaven or on earth. By living out these principles, students learn to achieve balance in their lives through discipline that results from self-control. Students are not driven by their internal desire to succumb to temptation but learn to discover ways to control those impulses. Hence, self-denial is understood as modeling the divine but also yields personal benefits including attaining control and order that can inform academic success.

Ironically, the denial of self might seem, at first pass, poorly fit to a person-centered goal of educational achievement and success. However, the process is advanced in that the individual's personal goal of educational achievement is shared within the religious body, is supported by religious text and ideologies, and is connected to the principle of community uplift. Educational objectives are not individualized; they are an integral part of the advancement of the community and its beliefs, an act of commitment toward the advancement of others. It can also be argued that educational achievement in itself is an act of self-denial. It takes discipline to study rather than play, to attend to rather than to ignore or daydream. Even pursuing higher education or any level of education beyond a state-required level of attendance takes self-motivation and a degree of self-denial that delays instant gratification in pursuit of long-term goals.

The principle of community uplift is the way in which the Black church can affirm identity and purpose through teaching students about problems in the world while providing them with opportunities to work to solve those problems. The learner's identity and purpose within the community and the larger society is interconnected. In the traditional classroom, students are repeatedly exposed to problems in the world stemming from economic instability, energy depletion, war, homelessness, racism, and poverty. School affords a theoretical exploration of injustices in the world. However, the church provides these students with the opportunity and means to conceptualize both problems and solutions.

Furthermore, Black churches are in a position to support Black males and family struggles within the institution. The programs supported by churches have the potential to alleviate some of the stress associated with meeting fundamental needs where there are limited resources. Children who might otherwise have to negotiate school without sufficient food, shelter, or clothing may be supported in these areas. Churches are able to leverage their collective capital to uplift the individuals within the community, thereby building a cyclical relationship of uplift among its members.

ENHANCED IDENTITY AND
IDENTITY ORCHESTRATION

Psychologically, religion's utility as a supplementary education tool is best understood when the idea of unity of self is taken into consideration. The ability to maintain a clear and authentic self across social contexts is paramount to adaptive functioning. In terms of cognitive structure, lacking integration of self-aspects is linked to maladaptive functioning (Constantino, Wilson, Horowitz, & Pinel, 2006). Self-aspects are comprised of semantic, episodic, and autobiographical memories from a particular context (e.g., school, home, church). The memories in each self-aspect contain specific contextual demands, role expectations, self-evaluations, and evaluations from others. Role expectations in different social situations in our complex society become so diverse and "mutually exclusive" that successful integration of these self-aspects can create stress and may seem impossible to achieve. What becomes of extreme importance for adaptive functioning is the degree to which schema in one self-aspect parallel with other self-aspects.

In order for a student to be successful in the school environment, the culture, norms, and expectations of school must be internalized and integrated into the self-system. For many Black students, this internalization may require more psychic energy due to the opposition of culture that exists between the culture of the American educational system and the unique culture of the home and neighborhood context of Black American students. Because of the more numerous and diverse roles that a child takes on at home and in the neighborhood, the behaviors enacted in these contexts are more likely to be integrated into the self-system. Children are apt to adapt to the school environment when there are similarities between the different situational contexts they must navigate. Religion with its core principles and positive reinforcement creates a context that integrates the demands and cultural nuances of schooling with other seemingly unrelated selves.

Religious practice through both principles and positive interaction enhances the likelihood of academic success for Black boys and developing men. The principles of knowledge of scripture, self-denial, and community uplift represent concepts that parallel ideas and behaviors rewarded in the educational context. The same skills required to memorize scripture are utilized in studying and memorizing academic concepts. Because a young child has had a familiar experience at church and home and has received positive feedback from these social environments, when the child encounters similar tasks in school, they are more likely to feel efficacious in completing the task. Their competency will result in positive feedback from teachers, which will positively reinforce academic success. Again, because the church and school context require many of the same skills, it becomes easier for the child to adapt to the school environment. Rather, no taxing psychic energy is needed to address the stressful experience of an unfamiliar and possibly hostile situational context. This means that cognitive energy can be focused elsewhere, such as on academic excellence.

Religion and education's cultural similarities are not limited to the similar skill set required in both. As discussed, cultural church norms are often the same behaviors that are positively reinforced in schools. Respect for authority, self-discipline, and respect for order are all behaviors prioritized in both the church and in the educational context. Many academically successful children are first introduced to these concepts at church. As these children mature, these concepts are recognized as pivotal in successful classroom performance. Accordingly, children are able to generalize the cultural lessons learned in the church to the classroom context and feel more comfortable enacting these behaviors in school because of familiarity with them.

CONCLUSION

Gordon (2008) comprehensively delineates critical approaches in considering the education of Black males. He highlights four categories of issues in seeking a conceptual basis to improve achievement in this specialized group: (1) normal biological variations and vulnerabilities, (2) paradoxical conditions of socialization, (3) contradictions in the intent of the political economy, and (4) natural patterns of subaltern cultural resistance. While we trust that the treatment of "church" addresses all of these categories to some degree, the paradoxical conditions of socialization and natural patterns of subaltern cultural resistance most cleanly help to summarize the importance of church as a particularly effective form of supplementary education for Black males.

Paradoxical conditions of socialization suggest foundational cognitive dissonance among Black boys because of a disconnection that becomes more pronounced when they must learn from people whose distrust in them increases as they mature, and when they must learn content and values of those who represent both their oppressors and their suspecters (Gordon, 2008). Contextualizing this socialization through tools from church socialization helps to minimize this gap and helps in supplanting distrusting agents with mentors and modeling of love and support. With a church lens, there is also an opportunity to integrate educational themes and information into personal points of liberation and community uplift that usurp normed values contradictory to achievements and successes among Black men and boys.

And lastly, the healthy church provides profound engagement that values Black males in ways that allow for a full realization of self and connected purpose. Traditionally, this is the opposite of how they are considered. As a result Black boys assume "natural patterns of resistance to exploitation" (Gordon, 2008) and push against structures, often in academic spaces, that oppress. Again, a church lens offers the opportunity to influence those "pushes" in ways that help Black boys to leverage beyond systems of marginalization and oppression. This is done through contextualizing the larger world for the Black boy to operate and negotiate within this context. To be clear, we are not suggesting the church as a panacea. The institution is of society and as such can reflect pieces of the contextual ills that we have articulated as particularly destructive to Black Americans in general and Black boys and developing men specifically. Nonetheless, the complexity of church experiences and its core principles and precepts can connect well to the complex needs of the Black men and boys created by the American educational system—in ways that address the failures of an educational system and that nurture the successes, achievements, and potentials of Black American boys and men in school and beyond.

REFERENCES

Ambrose, S. D. (Ed.) (2006). *Religion and psychology: New research.* New York: NovaScience.

Aronson, J., Lustina, M. J., Good, C., Keough, K., Steele, C. M., & Brown, J. (1999). When White men can't do math: Necessary and sufficient factors in stereotype threat. *Journal of Experimental Social Psychology, 35*(1), 29–46.

Bennett, C. (2001). Genres of research in multicultural education. *Review of Educational Research, 71*(2), 171–217.

Bourdieu, P. (1986). The forms of capital. In J. Richardson (Ed.), *Handbook of theory and research for the sociology of education* (pp. 241–260). Westport, CT: Greenwood.

Boykin, A. W. (1986). The triple quandary and the schooling of Afro-American children. In U. Neisser (Ed.), *The school achievement of minority children: New perspectives* (pp. 57–92). Hillsdale, NJ: Lawrence Erlbaum.

Boykin, A. W., & Ellison, C. M. (1995). The multiple ecologies of Black youth social-izations: An Afrographic analysis. In R. L. Taylor (Ed.), *African-American youth: Their social and economic status in the United States* (pp. 93–128). Westport, CT: Praeger.

Bridglall, B. L. (2004). Mentoring and its role in developing intellective competen-cies. *Inquiry and Praxis, 7,* 1–4.

Charters, L. M., Taylor, R. J., Jackson, J. S., & Lincoln, K. D. (2008). Religious coping among African-Americans, Caribbean Blacks and Non-Hispanic Whites. *Journal of Community Psychology, 36*(3), 371–86.

Cohen, J. H. (2003). Supplemental education: Six essential components. *Principal, 82*(5), 34–37.

Constantino, M. J., Wilson, K. R., Horowitz, L. M., & Pinel, E. C. (2006). The direct and stress-buffering effects of self-organization on psychological adjustment. *Journal of Social and Clinical Psychology, 25*(3), 333–60.

Edwards, J. (2004). *A treatise concerning religious affections.* Whitefish, MT: Kessinger. (Originally published 1745.)

Flum, H., & Blustein, D. L. (2000). Reinvigorating the study of vocational explora-tion: A framework for research. *Journal of Vocational Behavior, 56*(3), 380–404.

Fordham, S., & Ogbu, J. U. (1986). Black students' school success: Coping with the "burden of 'acting white.'" *The Urban Review, 18*(3), 176–206.

French, D. C., Eisenberg, N., Vaughan, J., Purwono, U., & Suryanti, T. A. (2008). Religious involvement and the social competence and adjustment of Indonesian Muslim adolescents. *Developmental Psychology, 44*(2), 597–611.

Glanville, J. L., Sikkink, D., & Hernández, E. I. (2008). Religious involvement and educational outcomes: The role of social capital and extracurricular participation. *Sociological Quarterly, 49*(1), 105–37.

Good, M., & Willoughby, T. (2006). The role of spirituality versus religiosity in ado-lescent psychological adjustment. *Journal of Youth and Adolescence, 35*(1), 41–45.

Gordon, E. T., Gordon, E. W., & Nembhard, J. G. G. (1994). Social science literature concerning African American men. *Journal of Negro Education, 63*(4), 508–31.

Gordon, E. W. (1999). *Education and justice: A view from the back of the bus*. New York: Teachers College Press.

Gordon, E. W. (2001). Affirmative development of academic abilities. *Pedagogical Inquiry and Praxis, 2*, 1–4.

Gordon, E. W. (2008). *Towards the education of young Black males*. Manuscript in preparation.

Gordon, E. W., & Bridglall, B. L. (2007). *Affirmative development: Cultivating academic ability*. Lanham, MD: Rowman & Littlefield.

Gordon, E. W., Bridglall, B. L., & Meroe, A. S. (2004). *Supplementary education: The hidden curriculum of high academic achievement*. Lanham, MD: Rowman & Littlefield.

Guth, J. L., Green, J. C., Kellstedt, L. A., & Smidt, C. E. (1995). Faith and the environment: Religious beliefs and attitudes on environmental policy. *American Journal of Political Science, 39*(2), 364–82.

Harvey, P. (1995). *Selfless mind: Personality, consciousness, and nirvana in early Buddhism*. London: Routledge.

Jones, J. M. (2003). TRIOS: A psychological theory of the African legacy in American culture. In C. Daiute & M. Fine (Eds.), *Youth perspectives on violence and injustice* (pp. 217–242). Malden, MA: Wiley-Blackwell.

Kohlberg, L. (1974). Education, moral development, and faith. *Journal of Moral Education, 4*(1), 5–16.

Kunjufu, K. (2004). *Countering the conspiracy to destroy Black boys*. Sauk Village, IL: African American Images.

Lapan, R. T. (2004). *Career development across the K–16 years: Bridging the present to satisfying and successful futures*. Alexandria, VA: American Counseling Association.

Levin, J. S., & Taylor, R. J. (1998). Panel analyses of religious involvement and well-being in African-Americans: Contemporaneous vs. longitudinal effects. *Journal for the Scientific Study of Religion, 37*(4), 695–709.

Majors, R., & Billson, J. M. (1993). *Cool pose: The dilemmas of Black manhood in America*. New York: Touchstone.

Markstrom, C. A. (1999). Religious involvement and adolescent psychosocial development. *Journal of Adolescence, 22*(2), 205–21.

Ogbu, J. U. (2003). *Black American students in an affluent suburb: A study of academic disengagement*. Mahwah, NJ: Lawrence Erlbaum.

Oyserman, D., & Fryberg, S. (2006). The possible selves of diverse adolescents: Content and function across gender, race and national origin. In C. Dunkel & J. Kerpelman (Eds.), *Possible selves: Theory, research, and applications* (pp. 17–39). Huntington, NY: Nova.

Park, H. S., & Bonner, P. (2008). Family religious involvement, parenting practices and academic performance in adolescents. *School Psychology International, 29*(3), 348–62.

Perry, T. (2003). Achieving in post–civil rights America: The outline of a theory. In T. Perry, C. Steele, & A. G. Hilliard III (Eds.), *Young, gifted, and Black: Promoting high achievement among African-American students* (pp. 87–108). Boston: Beacon Press.

Rappaport, J. (1981). In praise of paradox: A social policy of empowerment over prevention. *American Journal of Community Psychology, 9*(1), 1–25.

Rauner, D. M. (2000). *"They still pick me up when I fall": The role of caring in youth development and community life.* New York: Columbia University Press.

Regnerus, M. D. (2000). Shaping schooling success: Religious socialization and educational outcomes in metropolitan public schools. *Journal for the Scientific Study of Religion, 39*(3), 363–70.

Regnerus, M. D., & Elder, G. H. (2003). Staying on track in school: Religious influences in high-and low-risk settings. *Journal for the Scientific Study of Religion, 42*(4), 633–649.

Rice, D. W. (2008). *Balance: Advancing identity theory by engaging the Black male adolescent.* Lanham, MD: Rowman & Littlefield.

Riggins, R. K., McNeal, C., & Herndon, M. K. (2008). The role of spirituality among African-American college males attending a historically black university. *College Student Journal, 42*(1), 70–81.

Simpson, D. B., Newman, J. L., & Fuqua, D. R. (2007). Spirituality and personality: Accumulating evidence. *Journal of Psychology and Christianity, 26*(1), 33–44.

Tatum, B. D. (1997). *"Why are all the Black kids sitting together in the cafeteria?" And other conversations about race.* New York: Basic Books.

Unruh, H. R. (2004). Religious elements of church-based social service programs: Types, variables, and integrative strategies. *Review of Religious Research, 45*(4), 317–35.

Wolf, R. M. (1966). The measurement of environments. In A. Anastasi (Ed.), *Testing problems in perspective* (pp. 491–503). Washington, DC: American Council on Education.

Wolf, R. M. (1995). The measurement of environments: A follow-up study. *Journal of Negro Education, 64*(3), 354–59.

Chapter 14

Seeing the Unseen

The Role of Identity in Empathy Modulation

Kristin Moody

Group membership is one of the most powerful influences on behavior and a defining element of individual self. As identity evolves through context, understanding, and experience, individuals construct a whole self that exists in relation to and because of the people and the world around them. Individual identities are unique, and every identity is comprised of subscriptions to innumerable groups that create the amalgam of values, ideals, and beliefs that comprise a whole self. Some motivational theorists posit that all behavior is the manifestation of identity: humans act in ways that are compelled by their identity markers, thereby making visible the interrelated set of dynamic memberships in various collective identity groups through their choices and actions.[1] Automatic and often subconscious "assignment" of self and others to identity groups modulates choice making in a number of processes, including those related to affective engagement and empathy.[2]

bell hooks maintains, "Dominator culture has tried to keep us all afraid, to make us choose safety instead of risk, sameness instead of diversity. Moving through that fear, finding out what connects us, reveling in our differences; this is the process that brings us closer, that gives us a world of shared values, of meaningful community."[3] That we are *socialized* to reject empathy, rather than innately driven by physiological instinct, is a premise supported by researchers across the sciences.

Empathy is a function that many animals, including humans, are born with the capacity to employ at will. It is a resource worthy of analysis because it is required to successfully navigate many of the social processes in which people participate, and although it is biologically accessible to most neuro-typical humans to some degree, it is largely modulated by identity constructs. Through an assessment of group membership of self and others, individuals choose to employ empathy where there is a match and modulate degrees of empathy where there is not.[4]

We are often told that humans are, by nature, self-centered and competitive, operating instinctively at the expense of those around us. However, a study of empathy across a range of sciences from neuroscience to social psychology shows that humans are organized as social animals, and most neuro-typical humans are biologically engineered to cooperate, live in peace, work toward equity and justice, and connect empathetically with others in service of these goals.[5] The desire to connect and to affectively synchronize is one that is not only instinctual but has transformative potential for conflict resolution, collective goal attainment, self-actualization, and a host of other positive outcomes from medicine to finance. This examination reviews how empathy functions in humans and specifically looks at the role identity plays in modulation of empathy as it relates to the dehumanization of outgroup members.

DEFINING EMPATHY

The impact of empathetic engagement has been illustrated across myriad sectors: emotional intelligence frameworks are correlated with influential leadership in management studies,[6] empathy is highly correlated with increased positive health outcomes for patients in the medical field,[7] empathetic connection is the foundation for conflict resolution in peace studies and mediation,[8] and student outcomes have been transformed after teacher participation in empathy interventions in education.[9]

Dr. Susan Moore, a physician, died at the age of fifty-two from COVID-19. Just days before her death, she shared her experience as a Black woman who felt an absence of professional respect and personal empathy as a patient of white doctors.[10] Her experience is echoed by countless Black patients in America, whose pain, frustrations, and concerns in medical settings have led to disparities in patient outcomes. Practice and research conclusively show these disparities can be mitigated by empathy-based training and strategies, and empathy interventions are implemented across medical schools and training programs to close disparities in patient outcomes across race, gender, and socioeconomic status.[11,12,13] When utilized as a formal structure that leverages physiology in measurable ways, empathy has proven power to literally save lives.

The concept of empathy is complex, with a range of frameworks and competing definitions across the various fields in which it is explored. Concepts like sympathy, which is most commonly interchanged with empathy; cognitive empathy, wherein one intellectually grasps the perspective of another without fully engaging their emotional state; emotional contagion, wherein one adopts the emotional state of another without engaging the source of that state (or intentionally engaging the other); or mimicry and synchronization, which are phenomena in which physiological states like yawning, crying, or laughing are adopted across individuals involuntarily—are all examples of related concepts that are conflated with empathetic engagement.[14] Although the biological processes that facilitate empathy utilize many of the same biological processes that facilitate these phenomena, they are wholly different experiences that foster different outcomes.

The concept of empathy, used in this analysis, is informed by the social sciences and aligns with the research included herein: an individual chooses (consciously or subconsciously) to focus attention on the other over the self; the empathizer accurately interprets the other's emotional state and ideas; and the empathizer shares in that state with apposite emotional parity, reacting with appropriate concern and/or action.[15] If the experience shifts to self—my similar experience, my perception (judgment) of your experience, my distraction by my own emotional reaction to your emotional state—the experience ceases to be empathic. Likewise, if the experience is stripped of shared emotional states and a reaction that accurately conveys parity, it ceases to be empathetic. For example, cognitive empathy does not include affective elements and does not introduce the full range of neurobiological elements that empathy leverages. Sympathy does not require accurate emotional interpretation or parity: it is a state of personal distress over another's negative emotional state that shifts the focus to self. Emotional contagion requires no understanding of the ideas or the origin of an emotion, and there is no decision to engage: it is an involuntary experience. Likewise, whether mimicry is voluntary or involuntary, a crowd can laugh together without sharing feeling or understanding. There is powerful connection in the shared experience of empathy that engages neurological processes that sympathy, mimicry, emotional contagion, and related phenomena do not require.

> Thus hatred becomes a device by which an individual seeks to protect himself against moral disintegration. He does to other human beings what he could not ordinarily do to them without losing his self-respect.—Howard Thurman

THE POWER TO UNSEE

Empathy grants enormous power through its potential to improve outcomes, access another's internal emotional state, and create shared experience. But perhaps most powerful is the impact of the rejection of empathy for another. Through the decision to withhold or deny empathy to another, people do more than create affective distance: they foster the capacity to unsee someone. This phenomenon has been explored in a study of macaque monkeys. In one study, monkeys are allowed to choose to give their partners juice or an unpleasant puff of air to the eye.[16] Most chose to give their partners juice, even though making a more prosocial choice for their partner wasn't externally rewarded. What joy the "benevolent" monkeys may have derived in assigning their partners juice or "malevolent" monkeys may have derived in assigning their partners an air puff can only be hypothesized. However, the majority of monkeys who more often chose to give their partners juice then chose to engage in meaningful eye contact when the juice was delivered, connecting empathetically to their partners' positive experiences. The malevolent monkeys more often chose to look away when their partners received the eye puff, suggesting that the reward for choosing the juice could be found in the shared joy of watching the partner receive the more pleasant treatment, whereas the discomfort of seeing the air puff administered, for whatever reason the monkeys chose it for their partners, was something they would rather unsee.

The most interesting trend in empathetic bonds from this study is about unseeing. Sometimes, researchers randomly assigned air puffs and juice to partners, and before the air puff was delivered, an alarm sounded. Monkeys that tended to make more benevolent choices for their partners would rapidly blink at the sound, empathetically responding to the air puff *their partner* was about to receive. But the monkeys who more often made malevolent choices for their partners, who chose air puffs over juice, who again and again chose to unsee their partner as they experienced the outcome of the decision they had made for them, fought the urge to blink. In fact, at hearing the warning that the air puff was about to be administered to their partner's eye, the malevolent monkeys strained to *not blink* so strenuously as to fight the empathetic physiology that they statistically under-responded to the stimuli.[17] The decision to look away as partner monkeys receive an air puff to the eye and fight the urge to instinctively blink is the act of unseeing others.

There are hundreds or more similar studies with rats and monkeys and even ferrets doing all manner of other empathetic things—stopping electrical shocks from being administered to cagemates, providing packmates with extra food, redistributing Ensure across a group rather than saving it for themselves: again and again, animals are sharing, freeing, and caring for other animals with no external rewards and an unusual host of competing incentives to distract them. These studies support the supposition that social animals are biologically wired for empathy and the affective connection fostered is its own greatest reward. It is only when animals reject prosocial behavior that they avert their eyes, refuse to make contact, and reject the touch or look of packmates or other members of the study. In these same studies, participants fight instincts to look, turn their heads toward a cage mate, or move in the direction of a reward that will force them to encounter a participant they wronged—whenever study participants have rejected empathy, they render those they rejected invisible.[18] They unsee them, ignore them, pretend they aren't there. This is a phenomenon that transcends species.

Empathy, in some cases, happens with automaticity. If the conditions are appropriate for empathy, an individual may be in a setting wherein focused attention is on another, there is no competing task or distraction for attention, and the empathetic connection is made spontaneously. This is the case when one feels empathy for a character on television or becomes enrapt in an overheard conversation. More often, though, empathy requires active choice. If the affective synchronicity is initiated by a conscious decision (I choose to engage), the empathizer has determined both that the other is someone with whom a connection can be made and that the results of that connection will be worthwhile. But for many, empathy is rejected before any information is shared based solely on a hypothesis of the other's group memberships. In these cases, the rejection of identity not only halts an emotional connection; it facilitates the power to unsee others and render them less human.

Anticipated Exhaustion and Dehumanization

Anticipated exhaustion is the theory that people will avoid the costs of affective engagement when they hypothesize their empathetic connection will literally be more exhausting than what they are willing to offer or sustain. Anticipated exhaustion is commonly reported by "experts": those in professional roles that require them to be of service to others who are persistently in need of their expertise.[19] Experts might be medical professionals, those who provide care for the elderly, even customer service professionals. By maintaining emotional distance, people in these roles believe they are preserving their emotional health because their role requires sustained engagement with people who have higher emotional demands. Although the research is mixed on whether emotional distance actually prevents or compels burnout across professions, some anticipate the emotional toll of engaging with every patient, client, or customer in service of their job would be unsustainable and emotionally unhealthy and cite this rationale for a conscious decision to reject empathetic connection.

Anticipated exhaustion is also the rationale for rejecting empathy for members of "extreme" outgroups. Members of "extreme" outgroups are those who are likely to be stigmatized by a majority based on some aspect of their identity—people living with addiction, homelessness, incarceration, or persistent states of need. These people are often "unseen" by those outside of their identity group based on the projected "cost" of engagement. Emotional parity and appropriate reaction (which may entail helping behaviors) are defining aspects of empathy, and the anticipated exhaustion compels the conscious decision of outgroup members to reject empathy.[20] This could look like physical avoidance, emotional unavailability, or the phenomenon of unseeing: when people are able to look through or ignore others in plain sight and proximity, having made a decision to reject empathetic engagement. This unseeing is demonstrated through the physical act of crossing the street to avoid someone who may be perceived as homeless or in need before the encounter or not engaging in advocacy for the rights of incarcerated people because of the perception of the persistence they need.

One of the most dangerous by-products of anticipated exhaustion is the misperception of the cost. It is not the cost of withheld empathy for the other or the absence of helping behaviors that are the greatest threat to those whose emotional needs are perceived as exhausting. Rather, the decision to withhold empathy compels a process of subconscious internal emotional reconciliation to justify the act: the human mind manufactures dehumanization and/or infrahumanization of those from whom empathy was withheld to prevent emotional turmoil for those who reject empathy. Perceiving the full range of human characteristics of another, such as complex emotions, pain, and morality, compels compassion and impedes immoral behavior.[21] As social animals, the rejection of empathy for another requires us to consider another as less human in order to preserve our own self-perception of morality. Infrahumanization is the experience of assigning others less complex or deep human qualities—an oversimplification to justify the rejection. Infrahumanization supports emotional coping and alleviates guilt for groups responsible for injustices committed against other groups: by considering those harmed less emotionally complex and as having less fully developed lives, the atrocity of injustices can be assuaged in the actors.[22] This is the process of refusing to look when the study mate gets the air puff to the eye, straining not to blink when physiology compels us to respond in solidarity to the discomfort of another.

What is most dangerous about this, from the perspective of identity, is how dehumanization of others occurs wholly in appraisals of identity of self and then others, often without participation of the other to affirm the identity. We are not required to dehumanize others to do them harm, only to withhold empathetic connection, and we require no facts about the other's identity to make the choice to withhold. The entire transaction is predicated on a hypothesis about the identity of the other not matching that of the self, that the labor of emotional connection with the other will be too intense due to group membership disparities. As we become emotionally burdened by social media, divisiveness in communities, hostile workplaces, and difficult conversations, the choice to emotionally disengage as a strategy for self-preservation can feel tempting. The perception of those around us as outgroup members from whom we can abstain from forming emotional connections may lead to an inability to bridge divides, increase division, and create socially acceptable understanding that outgroup members are somehow less human.

Modulation of Empathy in Outgroups

The process of identity assessment continues once the decision has been made to engage with another, whether it was made consciously or not. Once the projected cost of empathy has been deemed acceptable, identity of the self and perceived identity of the other continues to modulate empathy.[23] The shorthand for group membership—ingroup and outgroup—belies an over-simplified bifurcation that is untrue for the dynamic identity formation process that continually evolves in a complex milieu. Given the array of group memberships that may contextualize an individual identity, it is common for one aspect of an identity to be more prominent in a given situation and a wholly different aspect to dominate in a different setting.

Likewise, no group membership comes with cleanly delineated parameters: some shared experiences that may be included within race, gender, socioeconomic, and cultural identities are not common to all who subscribe to the group and may not have to be true for one to identify as a group member. However, group membership does compel action in service of other ingroup members and discourage connection to outgroup members in empathetic engagement. All it takes is the suggestion that someone is an ingroup member, and the affective connection process takes place in a completely different way with different neurology and outcomes.[24]

Studies on the relationship between group membership and emotional recognition have suggested that affective cues, like body language, facial micro-expressions, and vocal intonation are more reliably and rapidly understood by members of ingroups.[25] Group membership is a slippery slope: groups can be defined in myriad ways, ranging from racial identity to the high school from which one graduated. Given the limitless ways that ingroup status can be defined, the cause of improved empathetic understanding isn't in the shared experience ingroup status might suggest. It is not necessarily because we are of the same religion that I am better able to interpret your facial expressions or because we are of the same income level that you recognize my body language. Rather, research shows that a suggestion that someone is of the same ingroup compels a focus of attention and willingness to affectively engage that allows for empathetic connection that is disallowed between outgroup members.

In a study of emotional recognition across racial groups, participants across two racial identities were given pictures from within and outside of their racial group to evaluate. They were consistently more rapidly and accurately able to interpret the emotional states of those in the same racial group.[26] In a follow-up study, participants were given pictures of people who were all from within the same racial group but told that half who had been randomly selected were actually from outside their racial group.

Again, they were consistently more rapidly and accurately able to interpret the emotional states of those they were told were in their racial group than those they were told were outside their racial group.[27] This concept has been replicated across other identity groups in several other studies. Hurricane Katrina survivors were given vignettes of other survivors to review. They more accurately interpreted more complex emotional states, assigning secondary emotions like grief, mourning, remorse, and sorrow, only to those survivors identified as coming from the same racial group. In fact, participants infrahumanized those survivors identified as outgroup members, accurately interpreting primary emotions but depersonalizing their experiences and misinterpreting secondary emotional cues.[28]

These studies demonstrate the power of motivation to holistically empathize with ingroup members and how important that motivation is to affective synchronization. The Hurricane Katrina study also shows correlation between interpretation of secondary emotions and motivation for helping behaviors. Without access to the full range of others' complex emotions, participants were not compelled to help survivors, which led to a consistent correlation between the suggestion that a survivor was an ingroup member and a participant's motivation to engage in service to survivors.[29] Only full empathy could motivate acts of service, and it could only be accessed when participants were told they were seeing members of their ingroup.

The neurology of these empathetic connections may reveal why ingroup members empathize in ways that interpret a fuller range of understanding, whereas outgroup members infrahumanize. Functional MRIs are used in studies to examine where brains are active in the process of empathetic engagement. These images show that images of ingroup members engaged in an activity are processed in different places of the brain and with different levels of intensity than those of outgroup members. Like the studies on racial identity, it takes only the suggestion that someone is an ingroup or outgroup member to modulate where and how the brain processes that person's experience. The actual identity is irrelevant. We modulate our evaluation of another's entire experience using a completely different part of our brains, depending on whether we see them as "one of us."

Participants in one study were asked to look at pictures of people pricked by a needle. When they viewed pictures of people they were told were

members of outgroups, they showed lesser engagement on the fMRI and processed the pain in the intellectual centers of their brains. When they viewed
pictures of people they were told were ingroup members pricked by the
needle in the same way, the experience lit in their brains more brightly and
in the part of their brains that would engage if they were pricked by a needle
themselves.[30] In another study, participants viewed videos of patients infected
with a blood-borne illness: participants were told some had contracted the
illness through transfusion and others had contracted the illness through intra-
venous drug use. The empathetic activity, such as interpretation of emotional
state of the patients, intensity of emotional effect on the participant watching the patient in pain, and general affective arousal was moderated by the
participants' preexisting attitudes about how the patients had contracted the
illness. The fMRI revealed that the participants processed their interpretation
of the patients' experiences in different places in their brains depending on
if they believed the patients were ingroup members, with group membership
determined by how patients acquired the disease.[31]

THE POTENTIAL FOR IDENTITY

The dehumanization and infrahumanization of groups of people enable
humans to accept disparate outcomes, uphold inequitable systems, and
sustain immoralities against those positioned as outgroup members while
keeping self-perception intact. The safety of outgroups is that we can detach
ourselves from their outcomes and still be righteous. The modern mechanisms of communication—text-based messaging, social media—further strip
interaction of affective elements and provide socially acceptable means of
emotional dissociation. The systems of communication we have come to rely
on, coupled with misinformation about the nature of humans as self-centered
animals, positions us to expect and even seek emotional disengagement.
When difficult and complex conversations are initiated in these platforms,
stripped of facial expression, vocal intonation, physical mimicry, and all of
the physiological processes that compel emotional connection and parity,
there is no possibility for empathy. Prevailing beliefs that emotional distance
provides self-preservation and limiting beliefs about the power of empathy
all deepen divisions, advancing the infrahumanization between people with
different group memberships.

The cost of ingroup connection is outgroup empathy modulation. Wherein
outgroup status compels infrahumanization, we are bought in to what bell
hooks calls the "lie of dominator culture," the concept that diversity and distinctive identities prevent people from coming together across group identities to "a world of shared values, of meaningful community."[32]

This is hardly a call for people to join hands and break into song. This is a reckoning that the belief in the necessity of sameness as a condition for empathy is the lie identity scholars are positioned to correct. The construction of an authentic and meaningful sense of self is an amalgam of experiences, values, and contexts that is unique to each individual in its formulation but is composed of shared experiences, values, and contexts that comprise vast, diverse groups. It is in the vastness of these groups that the capacity of empathy can be leveraged and the narrow definition of an ingroup can be corrected.

NOTES

1. Eccles, J. (2009). Who am I and what am I going to do with my life? Personal and collective identities as motivators of action. *Educational Psychologist, 44*(2), 78–89.

2. Zaki, J. (2014). Empathy: A motivated account. *Psychological Bulletin, 140*(6), 1608.

3. hooks, b. (2003). *Teaching community: A pedagogy of hope* (Vol. 36). Psychology Press.

4. Weisz, E., & Zaki, J. (2018). Motivated empathy: A social neuroscience perspective. *Current Opinion in Psychology, 24*, 67–71.

5. De Waal, F. (2010). *The age of empathy: Nature's lessons for a kinder society.* Broadway Books.

6. Brown, F. W., & Moshavi, D. (2005). Transformational leadership and emotional intelligence: A potential pathway for an increased understanding of interpersonal influence. *Journal of Organizational Behavior: The International Journal of Industrial, Occupational and Organizational Psychology and Behavior, 26*(7), 867–71.

7. Hojat, M. (2007). *Empathy in patient care: Antecedents, development, measurement, and outcomes.* Springer Science & Business Media.

8. Holmes, M., & Yarhi-Milo, K. (2017). The psychological logic of peace summits: How empathy shapes outcomes of diplomatic negotiations. *International Studies Quarterly, 61*(1), 107–22.

9. Okonofua, J. A., Paunesku, D., & Walton, G. M. (2016). Brief intervention to encourage empathic discipline cuts suspension rates in half among adolescents. *Proceedings of the National Academy of Sciences, 113*(19), 5221–26.

10. Sykes, Stefan. (2020, December 28). Black physician's COVID-19 death demonstrates bias of U.S. healthcare system, peers say. NBC News. https://www.nbcnews.com/news/us-news/black-physician-s-covid-19-death-demonstrates-bias-u-s-n1252290.

11. Drwecki, B. B., Moore, C. F., Ward, S. E., & Prkachin, K. M. (2011). Reducing racial disparities in pain treatment: The role of empathy and perspective-taking. *Pain, 152*(5), 1001–6.

12. Roberts, B. W., Trzeciak, C. J., Puri, N. K., Mazzarelli, A. J., & Trzeciak, S. (2020). Racial and socioeconomic disparities in patient experience of clinician empathy: A protocol for systematic review and meta-analysis. *BMJ Open, 10*(6), e034247.

13. Burgess, D., Van Ryn, M., Dovidio, J., & Saha, S. (2007). Reducing racial bias among health care providers: Lessons from social-cognitive psychology. *Journal of General Internal Medicine, 22*(6), 882–87.

14. Decety, J., & Ickes, W. J. (Eds.). (2011). *The social neuroscience of empathy.* Social Neuroscience.

15. Decety, J., & Ickes, W. J. (Eds.). (2011). *The social neuroscience of empathy.* Social Neuroscience.

16. Ballesta, S., & Duhamel, J. R. (2015). Rudimentary empathy in macaques' social decision-making. *Proceedings of the National Academy of Sciences, 112*(50), 15516–21.

17. Ballesta, S., & Duhamel, J. R. (2015). Rudimentary empathy in macaques' social decision-making. *Proceedings of the National Academy of Sciences, 112*(50), 15516–21.

18. De Waal, F. (2010). *The age of empathy: Nature's lessons for a kinder society.* Broadway Books.

19. Zaki, J. (2014). Empathy: A motivated account. *Psychological Bulletin, 140*(6), 1608.

20. Cameron, C. D., Harris, L. T., & Payne, B. K. (2016). The emotional cost of humanity: Anticipated exhaustion motivates dehumanization of stigmatized targets. *Social Psychological and Personality Science, 7*(2), 105–12.

21. Bandura, A. (1990). Selective activation and disengagement of moral control. *Journal of Social Issues, 46*(1), 27–46.

22. Cameron, C. D., Harris, L. T., & Payne, B. K. (2016). The emotional cost of humanity: Anticipated exhaustion motivates dehumanization of stigmatized targets. *Social Psychological and Personality Science, 7*(2), 105–12.

23. Zaki, J. (2014). Empathy: A motivated account. *Psychological Bulletin, 140*(6), 1608.

24. Weisz, E., & Zaki, J. (2018). Motivated empathy: A social neuroscience perspective. *Current Opinion in Psychology, 24*, 67–71.

25. Echols, S., & Correll, J. (2012). It's more than skin deep: Empathy and helping behavior across social groups. *Empathy: From Bench to Bedside*, 55–71.

26. Chiao, J. Y., Iidaka, T., Gordon, H. L., Nogawa, J., Bar, M., Aminoff, E., . . . & Ambady, N. (2008). Cultural specificity in amygdala response to fear faces. *Journal of Cognitive Neuroscience, 20*(12), 2167–74.

27. Young, S. G., & Hugenberg, K. (2010). Mere social categorization modulates identification of facial expressions of emotion. *Journal of Personality and Social Psychology, 99*(6), 964.

28. Cuddy, A. J., Rock, M. S., & Norton, M. I. (2007). Aid in the aftermath of Hurricane Katrina: Inferences of secondary emotions and intergroup helping. *Group Processes & Intergroup Relations, 10*(1), 107–18.

29. Cuddy, A. J., Rock, M. S., & Norton, M. I. (2007). Aid in the aftermath of Hurricane Katrina: Inferences of secondary emotions and intergroup helping. *Group Processes & Intergroup Relations, 10*(1), 107–18.

30. Singer, T. (2006). The neuronal basis and ontogeny of empathy and mind reading: Review of literature and implications for future research. *Neuroscience & Biobehavioral Reviews, 30*(6), 855–63.

31. Echols, S., & Correll, J. (2012). It's more than skin deep: Empathy and helping behavior across social groups. *Empathy: From Bench to Bedside*, 55–71.

32. hooks, b. (2003). *Teaching community: A pedagogy of hope* (Vol. 36). Psychology Press.

Chapter 15

LeBron James, Personalized Goal Complexity, and Identity Orchestration

Jason M. Jones

Goals are contextual and a natural part of who we are since we position our lives around what we aim to obtain (see Emmons, 1999). In terms of psychological balance, arguably, the pursuit of balance is everlasting. For Black men and boys, American sociocultural realities present salient experiences for us to attend to our work to be and achieve, complicating our goal pursuits. Given broad considerations of goals in human functioning, there is a narrow understanding of how people negotiate goals with the additional complexity that race places on the self-system. When striving for psychological balance, or for situational and personal goals, Black men and boys can encounter misinterpretation that often renders them invisible because of their maleness and the biopsychological and cultural-historical realities of race. This essay considers this additional complexity of goal pursuit by framing as example elements of the career and lived experiences of LeBron James, a notable basketball player.

National Basketball Association (NBA) players who are Black are often understood through stereotypes. This is in line with how Black athletes are understood within the United States and more broadly. Historically, their framing by media and a league of networks positions their race and masculinity, behavior, attitudes, and performance as attached to thin understandings of hip-hop and street culture (Cunningham, 2009; Andrews & Silk, 2010; Wenner, 2010). There is a lack of context and related understanding, at least in part, because those telling the stories and interpreting the lived experiences of these men are white journalists writing for a mainstream audience that does not, in large part, have the same lived experiences as the Black NBA player (Blackistone, 2012). Therefore, there is the opportunity and need to reframe these players more accurately, more wholly.

Centering on goals, a shared psychological construct, helps to provide greater access into the who, how, and why of these players. And their notoriety, because of their participation in such a popular sport, gives even more visibility to the normalcy of Black men.

PERSONALIZED GOAL COMPLEXITY AND PSYCHOLOGICAL BALANCE

Personalized goals, or the goal-directed nature that occurs in human behavior, are located in personality in the area of characteristic adaptations (McAdams & Pals, 2006). While dispositional traits focus on the broader outline of human personality and psychological individuality, characteristic adaptations—more specifically, our goals—represent our unique pursuits in daily life (McAdams, 2009). Personalized goals demonstrate future-orientated pursuits of what we are trying to obtain through different life domains and further represent culturally defined life contexts (Little, 1983; McCrae & Costa, 2008). In personality research, personalized goals have multiple conceptualizations, including personal strivings (Emmons, 1986), personal projects (Little, 1983), life tasks (Cantor et al., 1987), developmental goals (Heckhausen, 1999), and personal goals (Nurmi, 1992; Salmela-Aro & Nurmi, 1997).

When striving for psychological balance, the self holds significance in how Black men and boys strive for identity construction (Rice, 2008; 2013). Through this process, personal goals are layered within the multiple self-aspects that make up the complex self (Linville, 1987). Although the self is a complex system of multiple identities and self-aspects, personalized goals represent those multiple behavioral, cognitive, and affective (see Emmons, 1999) life pursuits toward psychological balance and a state of equilibrium (see Rice, 2013). Further, personal goals represent human functioning as the person makes sense of the world through identity orchestrations (identity dilemma articulation, burden of proof, unadulterated presentation of self, and acute identity expression) and anticipated futures (see McAdams & Pals, 2006; Rice, 2008; 2013).

Thinking on the significance of personalized goals through identity orchestration has led to the novel construct of personalized goal complexity. This construct attends to individual differences and human individuality in human personality and describes the adaptive arrangement and contextualization of personalized goals within the social ecology of the everyday and through life course pursuits. Personalized goal complexity contends that with human personality each person has a complex goal system resulting from situations, role demands, developmental tasks, challenges, and similar expressions related to human functioning. Furthermore, personalized goal complexity contends that the process of personality development unfolding within the American context further complicates the goal system. For the purposes of the present analysis, this context demands that the individual adapt goals to the contours of racism. Accordingly, the adaptation and arrangement of goals occur, to varying degrees, based on racial group membership. The significance of race in the task of goal adaptation is consistent with explanations offered by other scholars about the psychological significance of racism and personality, including Boykin's (1986) triple quandary theory, Jones's (1991) theory of Black personality, Harrell's (1999) Manichean psychology, Winston's (2012) theory of race self-complexity, and Rice's (2008; 2013) identity orchestration theory.

LEBRON JAMES: BEYOND THE BALLPLAYER

From his years at St. Vincent–St. Mary High School to his *decision* to "take [his] talents to south beach" and subsequent championship wins in 2012 and 2013 (Miami), 2016 (Cleveland), and 2020 (Los Angeles), the career of LeBron James has been replete with critical controversy and substantial goal achievement. In his first NBA season in 2003, James accentuated a unique drive for the game of basketball attended to with special focus as a high school straight-to-the-league player with a demonstrative drive to master, enjoy, and learn through the game as a team player. From that first year, James became a beloved and respected NBA player with a palpable tenacity to win and to humbly illustrate his great skill. James's professional accolades include 2003 rookie of the year, three all-star MVPs, four NBA finals MVPs, and a fifteen-time All-NBA honoree (NBA, 2021).

When looking beyond his ability to play basketball, the lived experience of LeBron James is important to consider relative to goals, understanding that they are largely informed by if not translated through his skill as a player. Further, James's public-facing persona affords a unique opportunity to examine choices and career-related pursuits as a representation of the adaptive arrangement of goal pursuits that extend toward psychological balance.

THE DECISION

A defining moment in LeBron James's career occurred on July 8, 2010. With a televised special airing on ESPN (see Abbot, 2010), James, an unrestricted free agent, publicly made the decision to leave the Cleveland Cavaliers after seven seasons to play for Miami. This public display was unprecedented at the professional level, going against typical player-owner dynamics to pursue future goals (Ratchford, 2012). Jim Gray, interviewing James, asked him, "What was the major factor, the major reason in your decision?" James answered,

> I think the major factor and the major reason in my decision was the best opportunity for me to win and to win now and to win into the future also.
>
> And winning is a huge thing for me. Jim, you know, ever since I was a rookie or even in high school, we always talked, that was the number one thing for me: Help my teammates get better and just wanting to win. And I've done some great things in my seven years, and I want to continue to do that.

To many critics, James's "spectacle" in announcing his decision was in lock-step with rugged individualism, calculated competition, and profit-driven values (Ratchford, 2012, p. 56). However, through a goal-related, personality-grounded lens, one could understand the decision, absent the lights and cameras, of James's goal for the "best opportunity for me to win and to win now." With the drama that came with the decision, James illustrates a hyperarticulated self-affirmation through an acute identity expression (Rice, 2013) to "win . . . win now" and "win into the future," which is a recognition of his strengths and positioning them toward goal achievement while simultaneously wanting to "get better" and "continue to do [great things]."

Later in the interview, James explained his intention to move forward as a team player and what the game of basketball meant to him when it came to playing alongside future teammates Dwayne Wade and Chris Bosh. The interviewer asked of a potential issue: being on a team with other players that match James's ability, meaning that the three would now "*share the spotlight and the limelight.*" James responded,

> For me it's not about sharing. You know, it's about everybody having their own spotlight and then just doing what's best for the team. You know, at this point D. Wade, he's the unselfish guy here.
>
> To be able to have Chris Bosh and then LeBron James, to welcome us to his team, it's not about an individual here. Because if that was the case, D Wade wouldn't have asked us to join him, or we wouldn't have asked him if it was

okay to come down there. It's not about individuals. It's about a team, and that's what this game is about.

Here, James expresses a sense of communion and his personal goal of being a team player while situating an unadulterated presentation of self (McAdams, 2001; Rice, 2008; 2013). He explained looking forward to playing alongside his teammates in collaboration rather than fighting with other Black men for a single prize, as might have been surmised from the interviewer's presentation of a possible dilemma. James, with his response, challenges the assumptive question, responding and reframing with an answer that assumes collaborative strength and cohesion between three accomplished Black men relative to a common goal.

With his decision, James made a definitive statement about what the next step in his career meant to him, certainly knowing it would not come without consequence. In his narrative James demonstrates identity dilemma articulation (Rice, 2008; 2013), positioning his choice in opposition to what others, especially fans in Cleveland, wanted for him. He explained,

> This is a very emotional time for me. I know it's emotional for the fans and also for the area. And if it was a perfect world, I would have loved to stay, because I've done so many great things for that team, they've done so many great things for me. But I feel like it's time to change.
>
> Jim Gray: What do you think will be the fans' reaction back there, and will you still live in Akron?
>
> LeBron James: I'm not sure. You know, they can have mixed emotions, of course, but it's going to be a lot of emotions not understanding why. And then you're going to have the real friends who love me for who I am. For me being from Akron, Ohio, and loving Akron, Ohio, it's always home for me. I'm still going to live there, always be home. And Akron, Ohio is always home for me and that area.

Explaining possible reactions to his choice as mixed proved a soft prediction by James. Following his decision, many criticized him with negative descriptors like "arrogant," "selfish," and "traitor" (Banagan, 2011, p. 157). Furthermore, the Cavaliers owner termed the once-beloved leader of Cleveland basketball as a "coward narcissist" (Ratchford, 2012, p. 53). While trusting his "real friends" would love him for who he was, James, as a Black man, arguably recognizes the potential for unique criticism given the dynamics of race and how a personal goal for himself, his loved ones, and his chosen attachment and dedication to basketball would be subject to ridicule given the emotion and personality "ownership" by fans of sport intersecting with what psychologist James Jones (2003) calls the universal context of racism.

In recalling a conversation with his mother in making his decision, James suggests a deeper goal to minimize psychological strain when having to adapt to the contours of expectation when Black men have to choose between their best interests and others' (Rice, 2013). James spoke to the importance of his mother's advice in the decision he made:

> And one thing my mother told me when I was going through this process and what ultimately helped me make my decision is you have to do what's best for you and what's going to make you happy at the end of the day, because no one can live with the consequences or anything that comes with your decision besides you.

This description of negotiated adaptation further represents identity orchestration in resisting alignment with the expectations placed on him by those not invested in his person but rather in his persona. In the account James illustrates a sense of psychological growth as he explains his personal goal to do "what's best" to make himself happy versus serving happiness to a corporate other. Thus, his decision and his drive to "win" demonstrate a complexity beyond his career, representing a coping to minimize psychological strain by attending to self and personalized goal pursuits (Emmons, 1999).

A RETURN TO CLEVELAND

After playing four seasons with the Miami Heat and earning two championships, an essay was published by *Sports Illustrated* online in which LeBron James charted a return home (James & Jenkins, 2014), explaining the importance of Akron, Ohio, to him:

> Before anyone ever cared where I would play basketball, I was a kid from Northeast Ohio. It's where I walked. It's where I ran. It's where I cried. It's where I bled. It holds a special place in my heart. People there have seen me grow up. I sometimes feel like I'm their son. Their passion can be overwhelming. But it drives me. I want to give them hope when I can. I want to inspire them when I can. My relationship with Northeast Ohio is bigger than basketball. I didn't realize that four years ago. I do now.

With the goal of winning secured in Miami, James articulated a new personal goal: to give "hope" and to "inspire." He presents Miami as for "winning" a championship, Cleveland for *being* a champion and being "bigger than basketball" with community.

In explaining his return to Cleveland, James recounted the "tough" challenge he endured with his televised decision four years prior:

> Remember when I was sitting up there at the Boys & Girls Club in 2010? I was thinking, This is really tough. I could feel it. I was leaving something I had spent a long time creating. If I had to do it all over again, I'd obviously do things differently, but I'd still have left. Miami, for me, has been almost like college for other kids. These past four years helped raise me into who I am. I became a better player and a better man. I learned from a franchise that had been where I wanted to go. I will always think of Miami as my second home. Without the experiences I had there, I wouldn't be able to do what I'm doing today.

In considering psychological balance (Rice, 2013), James underscores the importance of coping through his decision to leave Cleveland. However, he articulates psychological growth and maturity as he frames his communal personal goal, a representation and acknowledgment of boy-to-man that typically goes unexamined and/or misrepresented in the stereotypical consideration of Black men. In his narrative he also removes the conflict and dissociation that presents itself when opposing goals do not align (Emmons, 1999).

In presenting his new goal, James is compelled toward explanation and the framing of his own *being* and *doing* with the need to write "this essay because I want an opportunity to explain myself uninterrupted." Again, James offers an unadulterated presentation of self (Rice, 2008; 2013) while also positioning a new goal and aspiration(s). This is all done very much on his own terms with his choosing not to have a "press conference or a party" because "after this, it's time to get to work." This declaration and activity is linked to obtaining the goal(s) described (James & Jenkins, 2014):

> When I left Cleveland, I was on a mission. I was seeking championships, and we won two. But Miami already knew that feeling. Our city hasn't had that feeling in a long, long, long time. My goal is still to win as many titles as possible, no question. But what's most important for me is bringing one trophy back to Northeast Ohio.
>
> I always believed that I'd return to Cleveland and finish my career there. I just didn't know when. After the season, free agency wasn't even a thought. But I have two boys and my wife, Savannah, is pregnant with a girl. I started thinking about what it would be like to raise my family in my hometown. I looked at other teams, but I wasn't going to leave Miami for anywhere except Cleveland. The more time passed, the more it felt right. This is what makes me happy.

James stacks onto his "decision" to "win as many titles as possible" with layers this many years after the ESPN "show." He does this with the assumption of burden of proof, centering family and a dedication to Cleveland that is set to disprove a stereotypical belief about him that was attached to the agency he employed in leaving Cleveland for Miami. With this we see James's identity orchestration and goals manifest in his description of the game and associated values that bridge work with family and community, further demonstrating how his goals hold communion in his self-system with who he loves:

> I'm not promising a championship. I know how hard that is to deliver. We're not ready right now. No way. Of course, I want to win next year, but I'm realistic. It will be a long process, much longer than it was in 2010. My patience will get tested. I know that. I'm going into a situation with a young team and a new coach. I will be the old head. But I get a thrill out of bringing a group together and helping them reach a place they didn't know they could go. I see myself as a mentor now and I'm excited to lead some of these talented young guys.

> But this is not about the roster or the organization. I feel my calling here goes above basketball. I have a responsibility to lead, in more ways than one, and I take that very seriously. My presence can make a difference in Miami, but I think it can mean more where I'm from. I want kids in Northeast Ohio, like the hundreds of Akron third-graders I sponsor through my foundation, to realize that there's no better place to grow up. Maybe some of them will come home after college and start a family or open a business. That would make me smile. Our community, which has struggled so much, needs all the talent it can get.

> In Northeast Ohio, nothing is given. Everything is earned. You work for what you have.

> I'm ready to accept the challenge. I'm coming home.

Again, illustrating maturity and psychological growth, James assumes a new goal/role as mentor and leader, grounding this identity in "responsibility . . . above basketball," representing as a father, husband, and adult man going back to the community that gave him so much.

Ultimately, then, we see that identity orchestration is helpful in the novel consideration of LeBron James and a typical pursuit of psychological balance across atypical circumstances, even for a superstar athlete. Through select narratives dealing with his departure from and return to home, there is also an advance of the personalized goal complexity construct. These psychological devices add to a deeper and more whole understanding of LeBron James, and, by extension, Black boys and men who are too often made invisible by blaring stereotypes.

REFERENCES

Abbot, H. (2010). *LeBron James' decision: The transcript.* Entertainment and Sports Programming Network.

Andrews, D. L., & Silk, M. L. (2010). Basketball's ghettocentric logic. *American Behaviorist Scientist, 53*(11), 1626–44.

Banagan, R. (2011). The decision, a case study: LeBron James, ESPN and questions about us sports journalism losing its way. *Media International Australia, 140*(1), 157–67.

Blackistone, K. B. (2012). The whitening of sports media and the coloring of Black athletes' images. *Wake Forest Journal of Law and Policy, 2*, 215–25.

Boykin, A. W. (1986). The triple quandary and the schooling of Afro-American children. In U. Neisser (Ed.), *The school achievement of minority children* (pp. 51–92). Lawrence Erlbaum.

Cantor, N., Norem, J. K., Niedenthal, P. M., Langston, C. A., & Brower, A. M. (1987). Lifetasks, self-concept ideals and cognitive strategies in a life transition. *Journal of Personality and Social Psychology, 53*, 1178–91.

Cunningham, P. L. (2009). Please don't fine me again!: Black athletic defiance in the NBA and NFL. *Journal of Sport & Social Issues, 33*(1), 39–58.

Emmons, R. A. (1986). Personal strivings: An approach to personality and subjective well being. *Journal of Personality and Social Psychology, 51*, 1058–68.

Emmons, R. A. (1999). *The psychology of ultimate concerns: Motivation and spirituality in personality.* Guilford Press.

Harrell, C. J. P. (1999). *Manichean psychology: Racism and the minds of people of African descent.* Howard University Press.

Heckhausen, J. (1999). *Developmental regulation in adulthood. Age-normative and sociostructural constraints as adaptive challenges.* Cambridge University Press.

James, L., & Jenkins, L. (2014, July 11). LeBron: I'm coming back to Cleveland. *Sports Illustrated.*

Jones, J. M. (1991). The politics of personality: Being Black in America. In R. L. Jones (Ed.), *Black psychology* (pp. 441–68). Cobb and Henry.

Jones, J. M. (2003). TRIOS: A psychological theory of the African legacy in American culture. *Journal of Social Issues, 59*(1), 217–42.

Linville, P. W. (1987). Self-complexity as a cognitive buffer against stress-related illness and depression. *Journal of Personality and Social Psychology, 52*(4), 663–76.

Little, B. R. (1983). Personal projects: A rationale and method for investigation. *Environment and Behavior, 15*, 273–309.

McAdams, D. P. (2001). *Coding autobiographical episodes for themes of agency and communion.* Unpublished manuscript, Foley Center for the Study of Lives, Northwestern University.

McAdams, D. P. (2009). *The person: An introduction to the science of personality psychology.* John Wiley & Sons.

McAdams, D. P., & Pals, J. L. (2006). A new big five: Fundamental principles for a integrative science of personality. *American Psychologist, 61*, 204–17.

McCrae, R. R., & Costa, P. T. Jr., (2008). *A five-factor theory of personality*. In L. A. Pervin & O. P. John (Eds.), *Handbook of personality: Theory and research* (3rd ed., pp. 1–58). Guilford Press.

National Basketball Association. (2021). *Los Angeles Lakers #6 Forward LeBron James.* 2021 NBA Media Ventures.

Nurmi, J. E. (1992). Age differences in adult life goals, concerns, and their temporal extension: A life course approach to future-oriented motivation. *International Journal of Behavioral Development, 15*, 487–508.

Ratchford, J. L. (2012). "Black fists and fool's gold: The 1960s Black athletic revolt reconsidered": The LeBron James decision and self-determination in post-racial America. *The Black Scholar, 42*(1), 49–59.

Rice, D. W. (2008). *Balance: Advancing identity theory by engaging the Black male.* Rowman & Littlefield.

Rice, D. W. (2013). Rakim, Ice Cube then *Watch the Throne*: Engaged visibility through identity orchestration and the language of hip☐hop narratives. *The Journal of Popular Culture, 46*(1), 173–91.

Salmela-Aro, K., & Nurmi, J.-E. (1997). Goal contents, well-being and life context during transition to university—A longitudinal study. *International Journal of Behavioral Development, 20*, 471–91.

Wenner, L. A. (2010). Sport, communication, and the culture consumption: On language and identity. *American Behavioral Scientist, 53*(11), 1571–73.

Winston, C. E. (2012). Human personality: Race self complexity and symbolic meaning of persons living race in American society and culture. In A. U. Branco and J. Valsiner (Eds.), *Cultural psychology of human values* (163–94). Information Age.

PART IV

Making Meaning

Chapter 16

The Black Athletic Aesthetic

Fast Thoughts on Sport, Art, and the Self as Freedom Work

David Wall Rice

In considering the 1936 Olympic Games in Berlin and the courage to stand against the juggernaut of white supremacy that existed in Germany at the time, my mind raced and set on the work of Jean-Michele Basquiat. I thought on his sketches of "the Negro Athlete" that he centered in many of his pieces, and then on the specific representations of Joe Louis, and then of Basquiat's 1984 *Big Snow* where Jesse Owens's name is tagged just under a brown face, as is Berlin 1936 and the Olympic rings.

Like many, I knew of Owens but not of the other seventeen Black Olympians who traveled to Germany to put in work against national racism abroad. This was done while also representing a United States that demonstrated as just as racist toward the Black bodies whose physicality literally built the nation and who were now sent overseas to build a reputation for the country in sport.

Deborah Riley Draper, with her book *Olympic Pride, American Prejudice* (2016), helps us by providing glimpses into the selves of the full set of the eighteen Black American heroes with rich time on the SS *Manhattan*, the ship that takes the thoughtful, anxious, and practicing bunch from New York City to Berlin. Interestingly, the New York Ship Building Corporation that built the *Manhattan* was based in Camden, New Jersey, home to boxer Jersey Joe Walcott, whose name is also on Basquiat's *Big Snow* piece.

On board the SS *Manhattan*, there is a point at which Ralph Metcalfe, regarded as the world's fastest human in 1934 and 1935, looks to put a bit of a battery in the back of his fellow sportsmen and women, explaining, ultimately, "All we should do is focus on our event, to think about our race, or our jump, our match. Represent yourselves and your school and country."

That call for representation hit different, as the kids say. It shows the same type of representation that the neoexpressionist Basquiat started us with, and this representation is his extension of the Black aesthetic that originated from the Black arts movement, an aesthetic that explicitly looks to the Black power of the Black nationalist movement and to representation as resistance. Architects of this aesthetic, of this expressionist movement, include Sonia Sanchez, Amiri Baraka, and Larry Neal, who says of the Black power that drives the work, "A main tenet is the necessity for Black people to define the world in their own terms."

Amiri Baraka, coeditor with Neal on the seminal anthology *Black Fire*, further explains the Black aesthetic as attached to a value system: "We use Blackness to represent the ultimate goodness, and the ultimate reality and the ultimate truth. So that to say, 'that's Black, or try to be Black, brother' is to raise yourself above the filth of easy accommodation in the white world" (Tufts University 1968).

That "ultimate goodness" and the expression of and striving for a self that is good and truthful is bound in self storytelling. This is identity work, self psychology. And because of the universal context of racism that persists for Black folk, it is fundamentally representation as resistance. The Black Olympians of the 1936 Olympics tell us this with their stories, and they are bound to folks like Muhammad Ali and Malcolm X.

But before stepping to these giants and the significance of their representationally resistant selves, it's important to scaffold a bit of a self primer. The self can be understood as individual, relational, and collective (2001). And these expressions of the self are adaptations to and affirmations relative to context. They are interculturally and intraculturally defined—think Du Bois's double-consciousness that portends a Black cultural and American cultural reality to be negotiated by Black folks.

So then, the individual self is "you" and how you differentiate your self-concept from others. The relational self is how you match to others, where your self-constructs are shared and personalized bonds of attachment are fomented. Examples are family, friends, or teammates, perhaps. And then the collective self is based on symbolic, perhaps impersonal bonds. It can be an idealized self that is seen in popular others or in representative members of the body politic.

Muhammad Ali and Malcolm X, through their self stories as we know them, illustrate the distinctiveness of the individual self, in their connecting—for the time they did connect—show the shared self-concepts of the relation selves, and the nationalism that they demonstrated through the Nation of Islam shows a collective self.

We find relational selves explicit in the Jim Brown–called Cleveland Summit (1967), where athletes from across sport supported Muhammad Ali and his refusal to go to Vietnam. It is also found in the 1968 Summer Olympics, where medalists Tommie Smith, John Carlos, and Peter Norman protested from a trilevel podium, for Smith and Carlos with Black power fists hoisted.

And in highlighting Olympic gold medalist Edwin Moses and his scientific approach to winning relays in his movie *Da Five Bloods*, Spike Lee offers connection to a possible collective self, one that Moses represents as archetypal excellence, an excellence that is representational resistance by default because of presumed stereotypes that are affixed to him as a Black man athlete. And, of course, if you went to Morehouse College, there is a relational self too because of how Moses and Spike represent a shared college self.

This type of flavor, or cultural continuity highlighted with the connected selves offered above, allows a natural pivot to an explanation of the Black athletic aesthetic. Nelson George (1999), with the examples of basketball players Marques Hayes and Darryl Dawkins (and I portend explicitly through the example of sports commentator and analyst Stuart Scott), explains of the Black athletic aesthetic that "not only did Black men change how the game was played, they changed how it was described."

To further this point of description, one might meditate on the Under Armour short film featuring the brilliant body articulation of Misty Copeland set to the poetry of Saul Williams (2017). The piece begins with Copeland dancing to Williams protesting that "the systemic structure they use to keep me in place is the stage I dance on. Black. And Woman." With this the two are locked to the fundamentals of the traditional Black aesthetic, to the contemporary Black athletic aesthetic and to the demands by both for Black people to define the world in their own terms.

So, this beautiful performance of identity through an unadulterated presentation of self is connected to the Black athletic aesthetic that we see today in the representation as resistance of contemporary athletes across sport. Among others, examples are Makur Maker in his taking his basketball talents to Howard University in 2020, football icon Deion Sanders becoming head football coach for Jackson State University that same year, former NBA player Mahmoud Abdul-Rauf refusing to stand for the national anthem, Colin Kaepernick doing the same years later in the NFL, Kenny Stills protesting the killing of Breonna Taylor, and the WNBA asserting "black lives matter" in American professional sports with their initial protests against the killings of Alton Sterling and Philando Castile in 2016.

Freedom work, indeed.

Chapter 17

Culture in the Age of the Revitalized Athlete Activist

Sport as a Microcosm of Society Post George Floyd

Chelsea Heyward

Decades beyond the civil rights movement of the 1960s, the cataclysmic summer of 2020 forced the revival of conscious conversations surrounding social justice and racial equality. Though rife with a slew of unjust Black deaths, including those of Ahmaud Arbery, Breonna Taylor, and George Floyd, America's revitalized reckoning with racism was preceded by two additionally heavy global pivot points. First, the emotionally straining death of basketball star Kobe Bryant, combined with the inception of a global pandemic spurred from the deadly COVID-19 virus, positioned Americans in an altered state of consciousness. With NBA player Rudy Gobert's contraction of the virus punctuating Americans' awareness of the pandemic and athletes across leagues speaking out against injustices as never before, the role of sport in shaping 2020 has been unprecedented and underevaluated. Appraising the role of athlete activism, post George Floyd, this work positions sport as a microcosm of society and presents a pedagogy from which to better understand how culture is formed, reformed, and preserved.

REDEFINING CULTURE THROUGH
ATHLETE ACTIVISM

The equality movement that metamorphosed in the summer of 2020 indicates there was never a complete resolve to the social injustices advocated against decades prior. Survivors of that work still grappled with its residual traumas when a white Minneapolis police officer casually knelt on the neck of a Black man for nine minutes and twenty-nine seconds, well beyond the cessation of visible signs of life. The viralized video of George Floyd's murder was shown to an audience of millions under stay-at-home orders due to the global COVID-19 pandemic. Unbound by extraneous obligations and compounded by the internet's limitless exposure, this whimsical disturbance to the fabric of tolerance sparked a resistance, resurrected four hundred years of stratified oppression, and illuminated a side of America most were unwilling to admit still existed. In this moment, athletes and sport played a pivotal role.

As diametrically incongruent beliefs clashed over the value of Black life, racism charted the mainstream media's agenda, becoming a space most of humanity was willing to sit in. Here, silence was perceived as complicity, as society acknowledged the ways in which racism ravaged communities of color and exacerbated generational wealth, health, and education disparities. With the intersecting identities of Black athletes enhanced by the internal desire and external demand to speak out, as well as the inadvertent accessibility quarantine allotted, the dormant athlete activist was resurrected. Thus, not mitigating the callous loss of George Floyd's life, this work acknowledges how a nine-minute and twenty-nine-second encounter changed American culture in ways still not entirely conceivable.

Before George Floyd's murder, only a handful of athletes publicly denounced injustice. During the civil rights era, athletes like Muhammad Ali, Tommie Smith, John Carlos, and Bill Russell began advocating for equality in various arenas (Kaufman, 2008; Kaufman and Wolff, 2010). Following that time, from the early 1980s to the late 2000s, athlete activism lie nearly dormant (Waller, Polite, & Spearman, 2012) as athletes intentionally avoided utilizing their platforms for social justice (Coombs & Cassilo, 2017; Gill, 2016; Kaufmann & Wolff, 2010; Schmittel & Sanderson, 2015). In the early 2010s, Black deaths such as those of Trayvon Martin, Mike Brown, Eric Garner, Alton Sterling, and Philando Castile forced athletes to publicly respond to injustice (Sanderson, Frederick, & Stocz, 2016; Schmittel and Sanderson, 2015; Marston, 2017). Yet still, the majority of athletes avoided the work needed to substantiate systemic change. Research suggests this avoidance was the result of various conflicting perceptions on racial tensions, racially driven attitudes and behaviors, fears for themselves and others' security, and the perceived stigma and value surrounding athletes' voices (Heyward, 2019). Thus, these underwhelming efforts previously defined athlete activism as a non-normative behavior (Kaufman, 2008).

Though initially rare, athlete activism is a social phenomenon that encapsulates crucial components for societal advancement. By definition, activism should include a commitment to policy reform (Marsh, 't Hart, & Tindall, 2010), and when applied effectively, athlete activism serves to elicit systemic change (Agyemang, DeLorme, & Singer, 2010; Gill, 2016) and can lead to nation building (Pelak, 2005). Professional athletes can also integrate communities (Babiak & Wolfe, 2009) and mobilize constituents on issues they would have remained ignorant of (Marsh, 't Hart, & Tindall, 2010). Ultimately, their involvement in systemic change is pivotal. After a series of seemingly disjointed events began reshaping this narrative, the summer of 2020 exhibited these efforts in application.

HOW 2020 PRIMED THE REVITALIZED ATHLETE ACTIVIST

Before understanding how athlete activism shapes culture, it is imperative to consider how the start of 2020 shaped athlete activists. Notably, a series of dynamic events mentally and emotionally readied the new athlete activist. The unfathomable death of Lakers legend Kobe Bryant was the first event of 2020 that showcased an athlete's ability to transcend their sport. As a thick, remorseless fog rested atop an unassuming Sunday morning in Los Angeles, Kobe's Sikorsky S-76B helicopter unforgivingly barreled into a Calabasas hillside. A result of low visibility brought about by the fog, the crash claimed the lives of Kobe, his thirteen-year-old daughter Gianna, and seven other passengers, including the pilot (ESPN, 2020). The weight of this event haunted headlines for weeks as acquaintances shared stories, public figures shed tears, and sports fans wrestled with his legacy (Davis, 2020). A celestial being in sports, Kobe's death dispatched emotional shockwaves across the globe, igniting conversations around the brevity of life and uniting millions through grief. That ability to empathize with strangers, en masse, over the loss of another stranger's life would be integral to the movement that erupted following George Floyd's murder.

As individuals grappled with the value of life post Kobe, a deadly virus threatened life all over the world. Beginning in China, a doctor attempted to warn health officials of the virus's danger in December 2019 (Buckley, 2020). But it was not until the virus reached sport in March 2020 that Americans more accurately assessed the threat. On March 11, minutes before game time, players from the NBA's Utah Jazz and Oklahoma City Thunder were hastily ushered off the court as fans were told to leave the arena. News eventually broke that Jazz center Rudy Gobert had tested positive for COVID-19 (Newman, 2020). In the following days, the NBA and other sports leagues postponed their season, companies sent workers home indefinitely, and various states closed nonessential businesses. COVID-19 had been a topic of conversation for weeks in America. But it would be sports that fast-tracked the unavoidable quarantine and, inversely, sports that forced conversations around reopening. This positioned athletes as trailblazers in pivotal moments, but before lifting quarantine, athlete activists would be further primed.

Americans were still mourning the loss of Kobe Bryant when another NBA legend presented the homebound audience with an outlet for release. Lacking clarity around quarantine's succession, the production crew overseeing a Michael Jordan docuseries accelerated its release from June 2020 to April 2020 (ESPN, 2020). This early release gave restless sports fans an escape from hard times. *The Last Dance*, a ten-part documentary focused on the 1997–1998 Chicago Bulls, provided audiences with a shared experience that was both the first sport-related event post COVID and one of the first and largest real-time collective experiences in almost two months (Chau, 2020). Finally, people, sports networks, and social media had positive, non-COVID, and sport-related content to converse about and curate. Reeling through times pre-COVID and the nostalgia of the 1990s, *The Last Dance* positioned sport as a pinnacle of hope and unification. The docuseries also unwittingly reintroduced the question of whether or not sports and politics should mix. Michael Jordan and supporters defended a 1998 comment he made advocating against commingling sports and politics. This moment marked one of the last times athlete activists remained the silent minority.

Though George Floyd's murder was the final catalyst igniting present-day athlete activism, two deaths preceding his stoked the nerve of intolerance within athlete and civilian activists. The first prominent death was that of Ahmaud Arbery, a twenty-five-year-old Black jogger who was unjustly hunted and killed by a white father-son duo, prompting the hashtag #RunWithMaud (Faussett, 2020). Though it took several months, and a lawyer leaking a video of the murder, for Ahmaud's case to garner national attention (Mervosh, 2020), the hashtag united Americans virtually as they honored Ahmaud on what would have been his twenty-sixth birthday. Supplementing the hashtag, supporters ran 2.23 miles, symbolizing February 23, the day of his murder.

Next, Breonna Taylor, a Black twenty-six-year-old woman, was fatally shot by police who entered her home on a no-knock warrant on March 13. Breonna's story also went reasonably unnoticed until May 21, when famed civil rights attorney Benjamin Crump agreed to represent the family and demanded national attention (Levenson, 2020). Four days later, the loss of George Floyd inserted itself into American history.

On May 25, a day shy of four months since Kobe's passing, a Minneapolis convenience store clerk called the police on George Floyd for allegedly attempting to spend a counterfeit twenty-dollar bill (Altman, 2020). When police arrived, they arrested Floyd. In trying to place him in the back of the police car, a struggle ensued (BBC, 2020). The tussle positioned Floyd on his stomach while multiple officers restrained him from behind. As one of the officers knelt on his neck, Floyd cried out in anguish more than twenty times that he could not breathe (BBC, 2020). For nine minutes and twenty-nine seconds, a corrected timeframe from the initially reported eight minutes and forty-six seconds, an officer pressed into George Floyd's neck. The abhorrent behavior continued almost two minutes beyond visible signs of life (Los Angeles Times, 2020). George Floyd was pronounced dead on the scene, and the whole incident, captured on video, began circulating on social media. As exposure increased, outrage reverberated globally, and protesters in over forty countries poured into the streets, demanding justice (NBC News, 2020).

Athletes were among the most prominent figures in protest, and by June 2020, athlete activists had been primed in several ways. First, a renowned athlete's death had instilled compassion and purpose in millions across the world. Second, a global pandemic quarantined most of humanity to their homes and increased internet use as individuals relied on broadband access for external exposure (Kang, Alba, & Satariano, 2020). The pandemic also halted sports globally at all levels for the first time in history (Suneson, 2020). Next, a sports juggernaut released a documentary that brought people together for the first time in months and reintroduced discussion around the appropriateness of mixing sport and politics. Lastly, several nationally publicized Black deaths unified Americans, including athlete activists, with the piercing cries to value Black life. The culmination of these moments thus revitalized the athlete activist with the goal of terminally addressing America's entanglement with racism. What later ensued is a case study for how sports are a microcosm of society and how athletes utilized their platforms to change American culture.

Once primed with empathy and exhausted by injustice, when athletes across leagues began advocating against racism and for a more equitable America, the amount of influence they held over society was evident. Interestingly, the celebrity adopted by athletes through sport remained as quarantine minimized distractions and maximized accessibility. Otherwise stated, the stoppage of sport removed the act yet preserved the actors, who ultimately capitalized on their power and position. Understanding athletes' increased influence, it is essential to note that racism in America did not become insufferable solely because athletes rebuked it. The increased push for systemic change resulted from a global intolerance for perpetuated attacks on the Black identity. But, aligning with psychology-based theories, the hierarchy of culture presented in this work models incidences of how sport is a microcosm of society and how cultural reform is accelerated through sport.

UNDERSTANDING THE HIERARCHY OF
CULTURE POST GEORGE FLOYD

Analyzing instances of athlete activism post George Floyd, this tiered yet fluid hierarchy of culture showcases how culture is formed, reformed, and preserved. Maintaining the definition of culture as the customs, arts, social institutions, and achievements of a particular nation, people, or other social groups (Oxford, 2020), four tiers, in particular, were identified. The first tier presented is language, where words mold narratives and shape belief systems. The second tier, the credence of the individual, recognizes how belief systems shape the identity of self. Moving up the hierarchy, multiple shared identities establish a third tier, the credence of the collective, which underscores how a collective consciousness solidifies a group's identity. Individual and collective flux illuminates the relationship between the credence of the individual and credence of the collective, which invokes both emotion and action as the identities of group and self seek equilibrium. Attempts at balance lead to the fourth and final tier, cultural culmination, where established identities cement position and legacy.

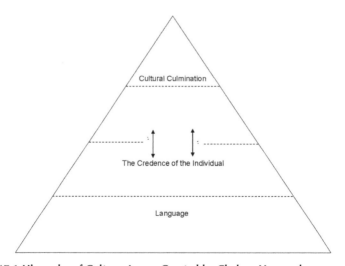

Figure 17.1 Hierarchy of Culture. Image Created by Chelsea Heyward.

LANGUAGE

As protests engulfed the news cycle following the murder of George Floyd, unprecedented public pressure was placed on organizations to speak out against injustice (Mull, 2020). Intolerant of vapid statements and empty PR pitches, employees demanded their organizations specifically condemn racism and police brutality in addition to taking tangible action (Mull, 2020). Organizations were listening. On June 4, a group of rogue front office employees convinced several disgruntled National Football League (NFL) athletes to release a video and publicly pressure the NFL to take a stronger stance against the condemnation of racism (NFL, 2020): "It's been 10 days since George Floyd was brutally murdered. How many times do we need to ask you to listen to your players? What will it take? For one of us to be murdered by police brutality? What if I was George Floyd?"

Explaining that they easily could have been some of the various victims who lost their lives to police brutality, the players went on to state their demands of the league: "We will not be silenced. We assert our right to peacefully protest. It shouldn't take this long to admit. So, on behalf of the National Football League, this is what we, the players, would like to hear you state: 'We, the National Football League, condemn racism and the systematic oppression of black people. We, the National Football League, admit wrong in silencing our players from peacefully protesting. We, the National Football League, believe Black lives matter.'"

Less than twenty-four hours later, the commissioner of the NFL, Roger Goodell, released a video response:

> It has been a difficult time in our country, in particular [for] Black people in our country. First, my condolences to the families of George Floyd, Breonna Taylor, Ahmaud Arbery and all the families that have endured police brutality. We, the National Football League, condemn racism and the systematic oppression of Black people. We, the National Football League, admit we were wrong for not listening to NFL players earlier and encourage all to speak out and peacefully protest. We, the National Football League, believe Black lives matter. I personally protest with you and want to be a part of the much-needed change in this country. Without Black players there would be no National Football League. And the protests around the country are emblematic of the centuries of silence, inequality, and oppression of Black players, coaches, fans, and staff. We are listening, I am listening, and I will be reaching out to players who have raised their voices, and others on how we can move forward together for a better and more united NFL family.

As an integral first step toward reform, athletes at the highest level demanded very specific language from an entity they felt had abandoned them in their fight against the systematic oppression of Black people. And, that entity responded. A stark difference from the 2016 approach the league adopted after quarterback Colin Kaepernick lost his job following his silent protest of police brutality (Mangan, 2019), this video symbolized both a shift in conversation and an emphasis on language. With over seven thousand languages shaping culture across the world (Ethnologue, 2020), language defines a person's social identity by providing a tool to express and rationalize their worldview (Kramsch & Widdowson, 1998). This tool constructs a person's cultural reality as they align themselves with or against groups (Kramsch & Widdowson, 1998). In addition to the NFL, more sports mobilized language as a tool for alignment and dissociation than ever before.

While several phrases continued to dominate the news cycle, one in particular contributed to framing narratives and strengthening belief systems for athlete activists. The phrase "black lives matter," popularized after the murder of Trayvon Martin in 2013, made its most influential mark in 2020. In addition to the Roger Goodell video, teams, leagues, and Black and non-Black athletes released statement after statement inclusive of the phrase "black lives matter." Athletes broke quarantine to join marches for justice across the country, chanting, "Black lives matter." Sequentially, as conversations emerged around restarting sports, athletes across leagues made it alarmingly clear they would not let sport position itself as a distraction from the country's social justice issues. Supporting their athletes, leagues instituted plans to weave social justice into their season. Following an emphasis on language, athletes affirming their beliefs and establishing their identities as unadulterated presentations of self was a catalyst for reform.

CREDENCE OF THE INDIVIDUAL

Prior to Goodell's public condemnation of racism and police brutality, New Orleans quarterback Drew Brees inserted his beliefs in a conversation that challenged his credence of the individual and helped opposing athletes and their allies fortify theirs. On June 2, when asked his thoughts on kneeling in the upcoming season, Brees responded, denouncing kneeling (Yahoo Sports, 2020):

> I will never agree with anybody disrespecting the flag of the United States of America or our country. Let me just tell you what I see or what I feel when the national anthem is played and when I look at the flag of the United States. I envision my two grandfathers who fought for this country, during World War II, one in the Army and one in the Marine Corp. Both risking their lives to protect our country and to try to make our country and this world a better place.

Though referring to the upcoming season, Brees's comments tapped in to a four-year-long argument surrounding Colin Kaepernick. Though Kaepernick explained that his kneeling symbolized an execration of police brutality, antagonists of his display erroneously positioned Kaepernick and supporters in opposition to the American flag and military (Mangan, 2020). These comments resurrected this conversation and underscored the gap in understanding between social justice advocates and adversaries. This stance also proved immediately problematic with Brees's current and former teammates, supporters of kneeling, and Black people whose grandparents also fought for this country yet received starkly different homecomings (Prince, 2020).

Even before Brees's comments, American identities rested in unwavering opposition to one another. As the country became permeated with racial tensions, advocates of racial equity offered resolve in antiracist theory, demanding explicit identification of intentions. It was no longer acceptable to not be racist; individuals had to be actively antiracist to achieve genuine reform (Kendi, 2019). The resulting wedge drove detractors further apart as antiracists denounced those who failed to explicitly condemn racism. In Brees's case, his comments diverted the conversation from police brutality to antipatriotism and therefore did not align with the pleas for antiracist positioning. Fortunately, his post-comment commitment to antiracist reforms, years of service in communities of color, and support from teammates offered him a rare grace. Though the sports world begrudgingly moved past this incident, it inadvertently shed light on the psychological factors that silently fueled America's divide and showcased how the credence of the individual crystalizes.

Implicit and explicit racist systems and behaviors left Americans at odds, but critical race theory and social identity threat elucidate why. Critical race theory argues that white people are privileged to certain freedoms that perpetuate the injustices of nonwhites (Gill, 2016). Social identity threat theory argues that challenging an individual's identity strengthens their position as they further distinguish themselves from their contenders (Turner, 1982; Tajfel & Turner, 1986). At this intersection lie Brees's comments and the resulting responses. His football career irrefutably allotted him abnormal entrenchment in the Black community. Critical race theory showcases that regardless of these experiences, as a white man, Brees had privileges, experiences, and beliefs that would never fully align with those of Black people. Under social identity threat, those who identified as Black and those who identified as allies of Black people exuded outrage as they publicly distanced themselves. Distancing substantiated the credence of the individual for Brees and others.

It is likely that through this experience, Brees's credence of the individual who he believed himself to be was at odds with itself facing external attack.

Additionally, the credence of the individual for Black athletes and Black allies may have individually been at odds. If individuals were to position themselves as reformers and antiracists, then they would have to reprove comments and behaviors that undermined anything in contrast. Thus, folks refuted Brees's behavior, even if only momentarily, and he apologized for his remarks, committing to continue work that would uplift the Black community. Both instances fortified the credence of the individual. Ascending the hierarchy of culture, events like this eventually led to the assimilation of self with individuals who shared similar values.

CREDENCE OF THE COLLECTIVE

As beliefs shaping individual identities define the credence of the individual, beliefs shaping group identities define the credence of the collective. Here, psychologist Abraham Maslow's hierarchy of needs influences collective consciousness and, ultimately, a group's selfhood. Maslow cited belonging as one of the most basic human needs, finding that after physiological and safety requirements are met, the need for love and belonging motivates behavior. Utilizing Maslow's hierarchy to service the hierarchy of culture, aspirations related to belonging, such as friendship, acceptance, and affiliation (Maslow, 1943), give rise to a collective consciousness, the shared fundamental beliefs, customs, norms, and values of a set of people (Bell, 2013). Thus, the motivation to belong creates a collective consciousness from which individual beliefs become shared beliefs and transform the credence of the individual into the credence of the collective. As sports often facilitate activity through teams, athletes have spent the bulk of their lives immersed in a collective consciousness. The year 2020 exacerbated this immersion, fully elucidating the credence of the collective.

While athletes unified in protest of social injustice, Black athletes, in particular, established subgroups across leagues, sanctifying space for emotional support and strategic reform. The Players Coalition, an interleague athlete-led organization cofounded by Anquan Boldin and Malcolm Jenkins in 2017, had proven that an athlete's position retained tremendous power. In criminal justice reform, police and community relations, education, and economic advancement, Players Coalition has used their influence to hold elected officials accountable, drive legislative reform, and secure resources and funding for impacted individuals (Players Coalition, 2020). Though most groups partnered with Players Coalition to maximize their reach and resources, the formation of league-specific groups unified athletes under a highly concentrated collective consciousness focused on race, gender, and sport-specific issues.

Trailblazing a path, the Black Players for Change (BPC) was one of the first intraleague entities formed in the summer of 2020. While Americans still quarantined and marched for justice, sports leagues began resuming. The National Basketball Association (NBA) and Major League Soccer (MLS) were the first to restart their seasons, confining their athletes to isolation in "the bubble" (Battaglio, 2020) at the Disney World Orlando campus to avoid potential COVID-19 exposure. Both leagues would go fanless but vowed to keep their virtual audiences focused on social justice issues. The NBA embedded the phrase "black lives matter" onto their courts and incorporated social justice programming into their broadcasts. The players wore social justice phrases in place of their names on their jerseys and inserted social justice anecdotes into their media interviews.

During their opening ceremonies, the Black players in the MLS organized a show of total solidarity, grabbing national headlines. Unifying as a group that aims to end systemic racism in and out of soccer (Tenorio & Stejskal, 2020), the BPC wore black socks, pants, shirts, and gloves and raised their fists in a manner reminiscent of the Black empowerment protest of athlete activists Tommie Smith and John Carlos during the 1968 Summer Olympics. Several groups followed suit and formed additional intraleague entities, including the Black Women Players Collective (BWPC) of the National Women's Soccer League (NWSL), the Black Lacrosse Alliance (BLA) in the Premiere Lacrosse League (PLL), the Players Alliance in Major League Baseball (MLB), and Coaches for Racial Justice (CRJ) in the NBA. The formation of these groups helped athletes bloom elements of their identity previously sequestered in predominantly non-Black spaces. Seeking unity in tumultuous times, these collectives mirrored a society wrought with division. When asked why they came together, Earl Edwards, executive board member of the BPC, recognized Black MLS players were all going through and wanting the same thing (Tenorio & Stejskal, 2020): "We felt a time where we could come together as a group, create a voice for each other and take a step in the direction where we can implement some things to try to create some real, lasting change moving forward. We understood the power of coming together as a group would be the best way to be heard and try to implement some of those things we think can make a change."

Echoing these sentiments, executive board member of the BLA Jules Henningberg stated,

> Lacrosse is a predominantly white sport; that's something no one can really deny. But at the end of the day, there are Black boys and Black girls out there playing, and they don't see anyone like us playing at the highest level. If we could come together and be a beacon of hope and light for these young players, it could inspire them to keep going through everything of what it's like to be a

Black lacrosse player. We wanted to create change and push this game forward.
We knew the best way to do that was to start the Black Lacrosse Alliance.

Though these examples showcase how the credence of the collective
applies to the homogeneous spaces of these intraleague collectives, events
in 2020 also exhibited application to athletes as a total unit. Athletes united
under the credence of the collective beyond their sport, at professional and
collegiate levels. At the professional level, unity actualized following an
incident in the National Association for Stock Car Auto Racing (NASCAR).
When Bubba Wallace, NASCAR's only full-time Black driver (Li & Long,
2020), found a noose hanging in his racing garage, athletes representing all
major sports leagues immediately rallied behind him, condemning racism in
sports (Long, 2020). The noose was later proven to have been present since at
least the year prior (Martinelli, 2020), but that did not change the impact this
event had on coalescing athletes. Furthermore, for Black athletes, this event
substantiated the need for inclusivity, driving Michael Jordan, a previously
socially conservative athlete, to purchase a NASCAR team and sign Bubba
(Li & Long, 2020).

In collegiate sports, football players from the Pacific Athletic Conference
(Pac-12) penned an opinion editorial demanding profit sharing, increased
safety procedures, and tangible racial justice reforms before they returned to
play (Anonymous Football Players of the Pac-12, 2020). Though COVID-19
delayed their season and the Pac-12 has yet to meet the student athletes'
demands, unification occurred due to shared beliefs. In a wealth of examples,
athlete activists defined their identities based on their own beliefs and formu-
lated group identities based on shared beliefs. But further analysis of these
examples and others depicts a volleying flux between the credence of the
individual and the credence of the collective.

INTERNAL AND COLLECTIVE FLUX

According to the Institute for Diversity and Ethics in Sport (2019), of the
major sports leagues, Black athletes represent the majority in only the NFL,
NBA, and the Women's National Basketball Association (WNBA). While
this lack of representation led Black athletes in other leagues to create inclusive spaces, the establishment of these spaces initiated a flux where athletes
continuously attempted to balance the identity of self and the identity of the
group. This flux between the credence of the individual and the credence of
the collective produced emotions and actions that positioned the identities of
self and the group either in support of or at odds with one another. Important
to note, the credence of the individual and the credence of the collective

represent multiple facets for each athlete. Athletes identify with various groups, including but not limited to those based on interests, gender, race, and league, in addition to identifying holistically as an athlete. Thus, on some level, these identities will always be in flux.

As previously stated, the NBA was one of the first sports leagues to return to play under the premise that their season would remain in the bubble, and they would keep social justice issues prominent in their programming. But, less than two weeks into the NBA playoffs, an imbalance between the credence of the individual and the credence of the collective threatened the remainder of the season. On August 23, a white Kenosha police officer shot Jacob Blake in the back seven times, again sparking national outrage. Unique to the summer's previous victims, Blake survived the encounter, though he remains paralyzed from the waist down (Guardian, 2020). But, that night, as Americans awaited his prognosis, Black and non-Black athletes across the sports world unanimously refused to play.

Beginning with the Milwaukee Bucks, the NBA team closest to Kenosha, Wisconsin, the Bucks followed the lead of shooting guard George Hill and collectively announced they would not play that night's game in honor of Blake (Gregory, 2020). Other leagues and sports professionals followed suit. In an unprecedented move, sports announcer Kenny Smith, a former NBA athlete, walked off a live television set midshow in support of athletes and Black lives (Guardian, 2020). For the second time in history, but the first in the name of social justice, the NFL, NBA, WNBA, MLS, NWSL, MLB, and tennis halted games and practices.

The shooting of Jacob Blake caused current and former athletes to process their individual and collective identities. At the individual level, Black athletes and Black allies no longer wanted to tolerate racism. But, as professionals, they had contractual obligations to their leagues and networks. At odds with one another, the credence of the individual and the credence of the collective forced athletes into flux as they processed intolerance and obligations. Emotions produced by the credence of the individual led to actions taken by the credence of the collective. In parallel, actions taken by the credence of the collective led to emotions that influenced the credence of the individual. Otherwise stated, because athletes as individuals felt strong emotions, they decided as a group that their emotion would lead them to the action of not playing. But not playing as a unit led to emotions that impacted the individual. Once the credence of the individual and the credence of the collective were balanced at a comfortable level, athletes eventually resumed their seasons.

Examples earlier in the summer also support this theory. When NFL stars Josh Norman and Demario Davis visited five cities in five days to join fans in protest to hear their needs (Mercer, 2020), and when WNBA star Natasha

Cloud announced she would step away from the season to focus on social justice work (Shapiro, 2020), emotions and actions fueled an internal and collective flux from which athletes sought balance. Even with LeBron James announcing the start of a voting initiative titled More Than a Vote, the desire for equilibrium forced athletes to reckon with themselves and decide what they wanted to do about it.

CULTURAL CULMINATION

Once decisions were made, athletes reached the fourth tier of the hierarchy of culture, where their emotions and actions cemented their positions on issues and their legacies in society. Throughout most of the hierarchy, culture is in flux, but at cultural culmination, perceptions and legacies cement an athlete's position in culture. Here, the residue of decision is aspirationally tangible reform. As previously stated, athlete activism must include a commitment to policy reform (March, 't Hart, & Tindall, 2010). This commitment to policy reform existed unparalleled in 2020.

By November 2020, systemic reform and tangible contributions defined the legacy of athlete activism. Though prior to 2020, Players Coalition had secured a seven-year $90 million commitment from the NFL, resulting in over $2 billion in education funding, more than $9 million in total grants and contributions, and nine pieces of legislation passed (Players Coalition, 2020), in 2020 the BPC, BWPC, BLA, NBPA, WNBPA, and Players Alliance had all demanded change in and through their sport and established account-ability systems for reforms across their leagues. Specific to voting, LeBron James's More Than a Vote initiative turned several professional sports arenas into polling sites and ballot drop-off locations (Zucker, 2020), recruited forty thousand poll workers (Peter & Zigglet, 2020), and assisted in contributing over $27 million to over forty thousand recently returned citizens in an effort to restore their right to vote (Rodriguez, 2020). These efforts etched the names of individual athlete activists in history books. As evidenced through the hiring of Malcolm Jenkins as the first current professional athlete to serve as a contributor for CNN (Boylan, 2020), the merger of sport and politics was now not only accepted but expected.

CONCLUSION

Although arguably clichéd, the word *unprecedented* encapsulates all of 2020. Specific to sport, an arrayed occurrence of unusual events changed the previous position of athlete activists. The loss of Kobe Bryant, inception of a global pandemic, crystallization of Michael Jordan's legacy, and murder of Ahmaud Arbery, Breonna Taylor, and George Floyd all contributed to alchemizing athlete activists from dormant to dynamic. Thus, a once non-normative behavior was now commonplace. Analyzing these events through the lens of sport unearthed a hierarchy of culture from which to better understand sport as a microcosm of society. Defined by language, credence of the individual, credence of the collective, individual and collective flux, and cultural culmination, this hierarchy instrumentally conceptualized sport and a society intolerant of racism. Following a nine-minute and twenty-nine-second detonation, sport and societal culture transmuted in ways that will be studied for years to come.

RECOMMENDATIONS

Though athlete activism surged in 2020, and scholars such as Harry Edwards have dedicated their careers to this work, there still exists a lack of academic research on the subject. The recommendation from this research encapsulates the need to study further the varying facets comprising athlete activism. First, an analysis of social media could demonstrate how athlete activism has been changed by athletes, their employers, and the general public. Additionally, this review could explore the impact of language on both athlete activism and the events of 2020 writ large. Another critical factor to examine relative to the credence of the collective and internal and collective flux is groupthink. Though consensus reached resulted in positive actions toward system change, future research might explore the possibility and probabilities of negative works or how this space uniquely rejects groupthink. Lastly, further research could examine how external factors such as disruption, storytelling, adaptability, money, and powering through adversity influence athlete activism and the hierarchy of culture.

REFERENCES

Agyemang, K. J. (2011, March). Black male athlete activism and the link to Michael Jordan: Transformational leadership and social cognitive theory analysis. *International Review for the Sociology of Sport, 47*(4), 433–445. doi:10.1177/1012690211399509.
Altman, A. (2020, June 4). Why the killing of George Floyd sparked an American uprising. *Time*. https://time.com/5847967/george-floyd-protests-trump/.

Anonymous Football Players of the Pac-12. (2020, August 2). #WeAreUnited. The Players' Tribune. https://www.theplayerstribune.com/articles/pac-12-players-covid-19-statement-football-season.

Babiak, K., & Wolfe, R. (2009, November). Determinants of corporate social responsibility in professional sport: Internal and external factors. *Journal of Sport Management, 23*(6), 717–742. doi:10.1123/jsm.23.6.717.

Battaglio, S. (2020, November 3). How athletes have forced ESPN and other networks to change their game plan on mixing politics and sports. *Los Angeles Times.* https://www.latimes.com/entertainment-arts/business/story/2020-11-03/espn-networks-politics-sports-black-lives-matter-lebron-james.

BBC. (2020, July 16). The last 30 minutes of George Floyd's life. BBC News. https://www.bbc.com/news/world-us-canada-52861726.

Bell, K. (2013, April 16). Collective consciousness. Open Education Sociology Dictionary. https://sociologydictionary.org/collective-consciousness/.

Boylan, B. (2020, June 15). Saints news: Malcolm Jenkins hired as a CNN contributor on race and social justice. *Sports Illustrated.* https://www.si.com/nfl/saints/news/cnn-hires-malcolm-jenkins#:~:text=The%20two%2Dtime%20Super%20Bowl,to%20join%20the%20news%20network.

Buckley, C. (2020, February 6). Chinese doctor, silenced after warning of outbreak, dies from coronavirus. *New York Times.* https://www.nytimes.com/2020/02/06/world/asia/chinese-doctor-Li-Wenliang-coronavirus.html.

Chau, D. (2020, April 27). The mythos of Michael Jordan continues. *Atlantic.* https://www.theatlantic.com/culture/archive/2020/04/michael-jordan-the-last-dance-nba-savior/610687/.

Coombs, D. S., & Cassilo, D. (2017, July). Athletes and/or activists: LeBron James and Black Lives Matter. *Journal of Sport and Social Issues, 41*(5), 425–444. doi:10.1177/0193723517719665.

Davis, S. (2020, February 14). Kobe Bryant's tragic death sent shockwaves around the world and put a spotlight on how to grieve a public icon. *Business Insider.* https://www.businessinsider.com/how-kobe-bryant-death-rocked-sports-questions-celebrity-grieving-2020-2.

Ethnologue. (2020, November). How many languages are there in the world? Ethnologue Guide. https://www.ethnologue.com/guides/how-many-languages.

ESPN. (2020). Autopsies show Kobe, all in crash died instantly. ESPN.com. https://www.espn.com/nba/story/_/id/29180785/kobe-bryant-helicopter-pilot-had-no-drugs-alcohol-system-autopsy-shows.

ESPN. (2020, March 31). Michael Jordan series on ESPN moved up to April. ESPN.com. https://www.espn.com/nba/story/_/id/28974799/michael-jordan-series-espn-moved-april.

Faussett, R. (2020, June 29). What we know about the shooting death of Ahmaud Arbery. *New York* Times. https://www.nytimes.com/article/ahmaud-arbery-shooting-georgia.html.

Gatto, T. (2020, July 9). MLS is back tournament opens with players taking knee, Black power salutes. *Sporting News.* https://www.sportingnews.com/us/soccer/

news/mls-is-back-players-taking-knee-black-power-salute/1xuxvp176huoi1645pr lqsl90b\.

Gill, E. L. (2016, February). "Hands up, don't shoot" or shut up and play ball? Fan-generated media views of the Ferguson Five. *Journal of Human Behavior in the Social Environment, 26*(3–4), 400–412. doi:10.1080/10911359.2016.1139990.

Gregory, S. (2020, August 27). Why Jacob Blake's shooting sparked an unprecedented sports boycott. *Time.* https://time.com/5883892/ boycott-nba-mlb-wnba-jacob-blake/.

Guardian. (2020, August 27). Kenny Smith walks off NBA on TNT set in solidarity with bucks over Blake shooting. *Guardian.* https://www.theguardian.com/ sport/2020/aug/26/kenny-smith-nba-on-tnt-walk-off-basketball-tv.

Heyward, C. (2019, August). *Improving the effectiveness of athlete activism: An innovation model* (Doctoral dissertation). University of Southern California.

Kang, C., Alba, D., & Satariano, A. (2020, May 20). Surging traffic is slowing down our internet. *New York Times.* https://www.nytimes.com/2020/03/26/business/ coronavirus-internet-traffic-speed.html.

Kaufman, P. (2008). Boos, bans, and other backlash: The consequences of being an activist athlete. *Humanity & Society, 32*(3), 215–237. doi:10.1177/016059760803200302.

Kaufman, P., & Wolff, E. A. (2010). Playing and protesting: Sport as a vehicle for social change. *Journal of Sport & Social Issues, 34*(2), 154–175. doi:10.1177/0193723509360218.

Kendi, I. (2019). *How to be an antiracist.* London: Bodley Head.

Kramsch, C., & Widdowson, H. G. (1998). *Language and culture.* Oxford: Oxford University Press.

Levenson, E. (2020, September 24). A timeline of Breonna Taylor's case since police broke down her door and shot her. CNN. https://www.cnn.com/2020/09/23/us/ breonna-taylor-timeline/index.html.

Li, D., & Long, D. (2020, September 22). Michael Jordan buys spot to form NASCAR team, hires Bubba Wallace. NBC News. https://www.nbcnews.com/news/nbcblk/ michael-jordan-buys-spot-form-nascar-team-hires-bubba-wallace-n1240701.

Long, D. (2020, June 22). Athletes from various sports show support for Bubba Wallace. NBC Sports. https://nascar.nbcsports.com/2020/06/22/bubba-wallace-lebron-james-tyrann-mathieu-max-homa-athletes-across-various-sports-show-support-for-bubba-wallace/.

Los Angeles Times. (2020, June 18). Prosecutors say officer had knee on George Floyd's neck for 7:46 rather than 8:46. *Los Angeles Times.* https://www.latimes.com/world-nation/story/2020-06-18/ derek-chauvin-had-knee-george-floyd-neck-746-rather-than-846.

Mangan, D. (2019, February 15). Colin Kaepernick reaches settlement in national anthem kneeling collusion case against NFL. CNBC. https://www.cnbc.com/2019/02/15/colin-kaepernick-reaches-settlement-in-collusion-case-against-nfl-lawyer-says.html.

Marsh, D., 't Hart, P., & Tindall, K. (2010). Celebrity politics: The politics of the late modernity? *Political Studies Review, 8*(3), 322–340.

Marston, S. (2017). The revival of athlete activism(s): Divergent Black politics in the 2016 presidential election engagements of LeBron James and Colin Kaepernick. *FairPlay, Revista de Filosofía, Ética y Derecho del Deporte,* (10), 45–68.

Martinelli, M. (2020, June 23). FBI: Noose found in Bubba Wallace's garage had been there since at least October 2019. For The Win. https://ftw.usatoday.com/2020/06/nascar-bubba-wallace-noose-fbi-federal-crime.

Maslow, A. H. (1943). A theory of human motivation. *Psychological Review, 50*(4), 370–396. https://doi.org/10.1037/h0054346.

Mercer, K. (2020, June 15). Christ-followers Demario Davis, Josh Norman talk police reform, racism. Sports Spectrum. https://sportsspectrum.com/sport/football/2020/06/15/christ-followers-demario-davis-josh-norman-police-racism/.

Mervosh, S. (2020, June 29). What we know about the shooting death of Ahmaud Arbery. *New York Times.* https://www.nytimes.com/article/ahmaud-arbery-shooting-georgia.html.

Mull, A. (2020, June 3). Brands have nothing real to say about racism. *Atlantic.* https://www.theatlantic.com/health/archive/2020/06/brands-racism-protests-amazon-nfl-nike/612613/.

NBC News. (2020, June 9). Map: The rallying cry heard 'round the world. NBC News. https://www.nbcnews.com/news/world/map-george-floyd-protests-countries-worldwide-n1228391.

Newman, L. (2020, March 12). Report: Thunder head doctor ran to officials moments before tipoff vs. jazz. OKC Thunder Wire. https://okcthunderwire.usatoday.com/2020/03/11/report-thunder-head-doctor-ran-to-officials-moments-before-tipoff-vs-jazz/.

NFL. (2020, June 5). Twitter. https://twitter.com/NFL/status/1269034074552721408?s=20.

Oxford University Press. (n.d.). Emotional intelligence. Oxford English Dictionary. https://www.oed.com/view/Entry/258346?redirectedFrom=emotional+intelligence#eid.

Pelak, C. F. (2005). Athletes as agents of change: An examination of shifting race relations within women's netball in post-apartheid South Africa. *Sociology of Sport Journal, 22*(1), 59–77. doi:10.1123/ssj.22.1.59.

Peter, J., & Zillgitt, J. (2020, November 2). LeBron James aims to make a difference in election. How's it going? *USA TODAY.* https://www.usatoday.com/story/sports/2020/11/02/election-2020-lebron-james-political-push-make-difference/6100545002/.

Prince, D. (2020, June 7). Column: When Drew Brees uses the American flag to virtue signal, he ignores Black contributions to the military—and the systemic reasons many don't know their family history. *Chicago Tribune.* https://www.chicagotribune.com/sports/ct-drew-brees-colin-kaepernick-george-floyd-20200607-xhevtxbe6zgrjhjhbyihshovby-story.html.

Rodriguez, K. (2020, November 3). LeBron James and Michael Jordan help pay around $27 million in fines to help felons vote. REVOLT. https://www.revolt.tv/2020/11/3/21548420/lebron-james-pay-around-27-million-in-fines-to-help-felons-vote.

Sanderson, J., Frederick, E., & Stocz, M. (2016, March). When athlete activism clashes with group values: Social identity threat management via social media. *Mass Communication and Society, 19*(3), 301–322. doi:10.1080/15205436.2015. 1128549.

Schmittel, A., & Sanderson, J. (2015). Talking about Trayvon in 140 characters: Exploring NFL players' tweets about the George Zimmerman verdict. *Journal of Sport and Social Issues, 39*(4), 332–345.

Shapiro, M. (2020, June 22). Natasha Cloud to skip WNBA season for social justice work. *Sports Illustrated.* https://www.si.com/wnba/2020/06/22/natasha-cloud-forego-wnba-season-social-justice-work.

Suneson, G. (2020, April 12). World War I is among the times entire sports leagues were canceled before COVID-19. *USA TODAY.* https://www.usatoday.com/story/money/2020/04/12/16-times-entire-sports-leagues-were-cancelled-before-coronavirus/111525066/.

Tenorio, P., & Stejskal, S. (2020, July 8). Roundtable: Leaders of MLS's Black players for change on charting a way forward. *The Athletic.* https://theathletic.com/1915561/2020/07/08/roundtable-leaders-of-mlss-black-players-for-change-on-charting-a-way-forward/.

The Institute for Diversity and Ethics in Sport. (2019). *The racial and gender report card.* Orlando, FL: University of Central Florida College of Business. https://www.tidesport.org/racial-gender-report-card.

Yahoo Sports. (2020, June 3). Drew Brees: 'I will never agree with anybody disrespecting the flag.' Yahoo. https://www.yahoo.com/lifestyle/drew-brees-never-agree-anybody-190237557.html.

Waller, S., Polite, F., & Spearman, L. (2012). Retrospective reflections on the Black American male athlete and the 1968 Olympics: An elite interview with Dr Harry Edwards. *Leisure Studies, 31*(3), 265–270.

Zucker, J. (2020, July 1). LeBron James' 'More than a vote' pushing NBA arenas as 'Mega' polling sites. *Bleacher Report.* https://bleacherreport.com/articles/2898497-lebron-james-more-than-a-vote-pushing-nba-arenas-as-mega-polling-sites.

Chapter 18

Running Beyond the Regulation of Sport

Grant Bennett and Micah Holmes

YARDRUNNING

I was coaching my travel baseball team in Florida when Nike reached out to me about being a yardrunner. My initial thinking was that the calls were fake. They were hitting my DMs on Instagram also, but I thought it was a spam account. It wasn't until I got an email from the campaign leads explaining the HBCU highlights campaign that I realized this was for real.

"What could Nike possibly want with me?" was question one. Like, bruh, *it's Nike*! Part of my ignoring the initial taps from them had something to do with my not believing my narrative worthy of recognition from a company with such high-level popular appeal. Again, *it's Nike*, home to some of the greatest athletes, influencers, artists, and storytellers in the world. How does a twenty-three-year-old kid from Fayetteville, North Carolina, who does not rap or play professional sports, get their attention?

In the lab, we learn that life narratives create psychological continuity. We study Black men, Black boys, and the psychology of modern media, an elaborate and far-reaching ecosystem that too frequently focuses on narratives that minimize the beauty of Black bodies and Black intellect. This system, even though I was on the other side of a course that deconstructed it, had me caught up in the tentacles of imposter syndrome in those initial conversations with the company reps. I mean, I didn't fit the mold that they, in many respects, have been responsible for creating with their advertisements throughout the years.

My first memory of Nike came as a kid wanting a pair of Air Force Ones. There's a Shoe Carnival near the apartment complexes where I grew up. When it was time to go get new shoes for school, my mom would load us in the minivan and take us to that Shoe Carnival. The cool thing about the store was that it featured a spinning wheel that listed different deals you would get if you landed on the right tab, kind of like that big wheel on *The Price Is Right*. We would often go early in the morning and spin the wheel until we got to the buy-one-get-one-free deal.

Going into the first grade, I *really* wanted a pair of those Air Force Ones. At the time, the rap artist Nelly had a hit single by the same name charting on the radio. Everybody and their momma had a pair of those shoes, except for me and my brothers. I begged my mom for those kicks. But, in the end, I walked out of Shoe Carnival with a new pair of K-Swiss instead.

My parents are products of 1980s-era hip-hop. Accordingly, Run DMC got major play in the house. Their single "My Adidas" would blast on Saturday mornings as we deep-cleaned the crib. My mom used to work as a sales representative for Adidas, so growing up we never had Nikes. That pair of K-Swiss was an exception. It wasn't until I got my own job at sixteen years old—I bussed tables and washed dishes at a local restaurant—that I was able to go out and buy my first pair of Nikes, some Js. I spent my first check on a pair of Jordan Bordeaux 6s.

Though denied until I turned sixteen, I loved Nike. It had a lot to do with the company's unique ability to market stories. From their early success with Michael Jordan, Nike remains, at least to me, the leader in promoting cool, attention-holding narratives. I, of course, was locked into Nike campaigns growing up.

The "My Better Is Better Than Your Better" drop that featured Morehouse alum Saul Williams's song "List of Demands" hit hard. And I used to tune in weekly for the LeBron and Kobe puppet snippets during the NBA playoffs that Nike did. And then there were the classic Michael Jordan and Spike Lee commercials that made an indelible mark on popular culture. Fast forward and the company chose to highlight me as part of an HBCU campaign, this a few years after the Colin Kaepernick spots where Nike challenged us to "believe in something, even if it means sacrificing everything."

It was a surreal addition to an already remarkable 2021. Being relocated to my small town post-graduation in the middle of a pandemic pushed me to a mental state that had me questioning the growth I'd enjoyed at Morehouse. With Margaret Beale Spencer's phenomenological variant of ecological systems theory, we understand resiliency, identity, and competence formation for youth, given their evolving understanding of self and "other." My time at Morehouse afforded me experiences in Africa, at Harvard, and even on Wall Street. But those experiences seemed diminished the longer I stayed in

Fayetteville. I love my city. I love everything about it, but being there, kept from the larger world I'd jetted across just months prior, had me a bit twisted.

This distance from doing inspired me to create the Two-Six Project, a non-profit that serves as an incubator for initiatives including, but not limited to, sports, self-development, scholarships, educational programs, and the like. Our mission is to develop leaders from marginalized communities through intentional programming and thought leadership. By integrating initiatives that impact from a justice-oriented core, we strive to influence the community and to cultivate culture. This engagement in my community has led to so much. Within a twelve-month span, the work was highlighted or otherwise leveraged by Google, *Forbes*, Adobe, HBO, and (Mom's) Adidas based on the Two-Six agenda.

When I asked the Nike team why they chose me, they explained they were looking for an HBCU baseball player who embodied the spirit of Morehouse College. It was less about followers and clout and more about relative impact. I fit the bill.

The initiative was sparked from the racial turmoil experienced after the killing of George Floyd and is the brainchild of Howard University graduates Arinze Emeagwali and Richard Palmer. The purpose of the campaign is to highlight the intellectual strength, spirit, and culture of historically Black colleges and universities, to show their impact.

During conversations with the squad that was positioning me for the push, I was asked to reflect on impactful moments that shaped my experience at Morehouse. The Kobe Bryant Morehouse Mamba event I organized my senior year was top of mind.

As an athlete, I know how to play through pain. The way I grew in sports, coaches and parents would often push you to play through whatever situation was thrown at you. But it was tough to play through this—one of my heroes, Kobe Bryant, had passed away. Even more devastating was that his daughter, Gianna, died with him and several others in the helicopter crash.

The week following his death, I helped to organize a Morehouse Mamba basketball tournament. It was put on to raise funds for the MambaOnThree Fund. We packed five hundred students inside of Archer gym and held a moment of silence for all those lost in the crash. During the tournament, I had some of my friends interview other students about Kobe and his legacy. The narratives helped to clear the emotional haze with stories of connection that demonstrated the psychological unity within ourselves and relative to social spaces that we were taught about in class. I began to write.

The most difficult part of working through that moment was checking my emotions. They were all over the place with constant media prompts making it almost impossible to take a psychological breath. It was blurring my ability to find an authentic and honest connection to my hero. Really, to lesser effect, this happens frequently with music, sports, and politics. We psychologically link to mainstream folks in these spaces, and others, because of how they help us to make sense of ourselves and the world. No doubt I felt a loss with Kobe's tragic passing, but, not to sound cold, I had to keep that tragedy in context.

In the book *The Origin of Others*, Toni Morrison describes her relationship to a woman whom she engaged while sitting by a riverside near her home. Morrison described the experience:

> When we part, it is with an understanding that she will be there the next day or very soon after and we will visit again. I imagine more conversations with her. I will invite her into my house for coffees, for tales, for laughter. She reminds me of someone, something. I imagine a friendship, casual, effortless, delightful. She is not there the next day. She is not there the next following days either. And I look for her every morning. Finally, I approach the neighbor to ask about her and am bewildered to learn that the neighbor does not know who or what I am talking about. No one, not even people who have lived in nearby villages for seventy years, has ever heard of her. I felt cheated, puzzled, but also amused, and I wonder if I have dreamed of her. In any case, I can tell myself, it was an encounter of no value other than anecdotal. Still. Little by little, annoyance then bitterness takes the place of my original bewilderment. I immediately sentimentalized and appropriated her. Fantasized her as my personal shaman. I owned her or wanted to (and I suspect she glimpsed it).

Morrison's thinking helps me make sense of my appreciation of Kobe Bryant and also of how young men like me understand our own psychological balance in the midst of the trauma of his passing so abruptly. Morrison shares that she places ownership on the fisher woman, naming who she was supposed to be for her, not giving the woman agency to be free, at least in her mind. For me, and for many others, I gather that Kobe Bryant and the narrative I had for him was not who he was so much as who I needed him to be for me to understand the good parts of who I am. This was even found in who I might aspire to be, because Bryant reflected characteristics that I understood as being important. I think this is doubly the case with my being an athlete. His sudden passing allowed me to take stock of my emotions and to articulate myself acutely.

This is the model that many feel in relationship to celebrity and to sport specifically. The modern athlete is a hero by which we can understand our own psychology. It is also a lens through which Black people are assumed to be understood and their narratives owned by another. This can be seen in how people embrace figures ranging from Muhammad Ali to LeBron James to Colin Kaepernick.

Sketching back to connect the circle, Arinze Emeagwali and Richard Palmer with their Yardrunner brilliance gifted me interesting mirrors and windows (nod to Emily Style) in repping for Nike. I was able to do the psychology of orchestrating my inner strengths by appreciating good and accomplished identities that are doing good for others. I was also able to note the hero archetype with measured appreciation of Kobe Bryant, a model whose example made a positive difference for me. Humbly, I'm curious what my Nike adverts will mean for others. Only good things, I hope.

WHEN REGULATION ISN'T ENOUGH

Often, the best wins come in overtime. This fits for me, because where I'm from regulation really isn't enough to begin with. In 2020, Cleveland, Ohio, was the poorest city in the United States with a 30.8 percent poverty rate. The Census Bureau defines poverty as a family of three making less than $21,000 per year, and right now in Cuyahoga County, almost 220,000 people are living at or below the poverty line. Worse, more than half the adults in poverty are working jobs even though those jobs don't pay a living wage. This demands that difficult decisions be made between things like food, utilities, clothing, and other basic needs while still figuring the day-to-day, frequently with kids in tow.

In Cleveland, no one feels the impact of an impoverished environment more than children. Again, in 2019, the city ranked as having the highest child poverty rate at 46.1 percent, just down from 50.5 percent in 2018. Looking at these numbers alone can easily give an indication of young people in my city as being pretty miserable. And please, believe, it's tough going without, but as in many other American cities, as corny as it might sound, sports give us hope. They gave me a special kind of hope and self-definition.

As a little guy, football was my best friend. It was a protector, educator, and provider. An oddly shaped brown orb with sixteen lace holes and eight cross stitches gave me purpose in life. It gave me some of the most loyal friends in the world and a reason to unselfishly go to great lengths for the brother beside me.

When you didn't have a bite to eat outside of school lunch, you had football. You're wearing the same clothes on the daily, but you had football. When you didn't have a ride to practice, someone's mother on the team made sure you made it. I even remember some of my childhood teammates living with my coaches because their parents couldn't afford to wash their uniforms after a muddy practice, let alone find them a pregame meal.

The world of sports is deeply ingrained in the culture of Cleveland. From the "whoof, whoofs" coming from the Browns' famous Dawg Pound to a

Cavaliers dream that pulled one million people to downtown to celebrate a championship that King James built in 2016. His 110-by-112-foot-image on the Sherwin Williams building at the corner of West Huron and Ontario Street inspired us for years with "WE ARE ALL WITNESSES" to the greatness that sports ignited.

LeBron James was an Ohio kid through and through. He rose from poverty, adapted to changing situations, and embodied the blue-collar culture of Cleveland, working relentlessly for success even though the odds were stacked against him. Whether you were a kid who lived in the trenches of East Cleveland or Glenville or a kid from the wealthier neighborhoods of Solon and Twinsburg, LeBron James gave you hope.

On February 10, 2004, my father gifted me a LeBron James jersey that I still cherish. When I wore it to school, I felt like I was wearing a superhero costume. LeBron was my hero. Sports had us kids viewing coaches, older players, and professional athletes as role models. And my core group of friends identified the likes of LeBron James, Rich Paul, Maverick Carter, and Randy Mims as inspiration. LeBron empowered his close friends and gave them a platform to create their own identity within the sports and entertainment world, and at Benedictine High School, my friends and I came together with a plan to be that inspiration for the next generation.

Benedictine High School is dubbed the Home of Champions. The proof is in graduates ranging from the likes of Anthony and Joe Russo, directors of Marvel's *Avengers: Infinity War* and *Avengers: End Game*, to Rich Paul, CEO of Klutch Sports Group, who has marked over $300 million in contract negotiations. Benedictine was a pivot point for some greats. With this in mind, I'd often find myself lost in thought on what my impact could and would be on my community and beyond. I'd envision myself as Rich Paul closing million-dollar deals and giving back to my community, or making it to the NFL and giving back to the city. The constant was giving back to the younger members of my community, the most vulnerable among us. I didn't think that I'd have the opportunity to do this work so soon, however. But here we are.

Overtime means something to me. It has multiple meanings, in fact. It could be what my mother has to do to afford those new Jordans I've been hassling her for. Overtime could be the moment when my teammates and I have to give our all, even when we have nothing left to give, to get the win. Reggie, Joe, and I made it our mission to work overtime for the kids behind us, to be the role models they need us to be, and we used our love of sports, our sport selves, to make this happen.

Overtime Sports Group was born in the hallways of Benedictine High School in 2016. It's the result of collective thinking and doing from three high school seniors who wanted to give back to youth in our community by being there for them. Prohibitive costs to participating in youth football was the first hurdle. It was denying many who are most in need of the opportunity to be lifted, mentored, and molded by great role models. We wanted to connect young athletes to their idols in college and the pros, so we recruited Division I and NFL talent to lead young athletes through drills and give words of wisdom throughout the camp that allowed the young people to see themselves in those they looked up to.

To date, we've hosted several youth football camps for kids in Cleveland, free of charge. We've expanded the camp from a single day to a three-day weekend and have secured partnerships with major companies to provide free food and drinks to keep the kids fueled throughout the camp. We've even given away gaming systems and other gifts to reward students for their hard work.

Exponential growth was seen in the first few years of our work, but there was no greater moment than seeing our very first camp come to life. It was the realization of three young men's initiative to make our community better through sports because of what the game gave to us. Of course, sports is much more than just a game. It's a context for so many of us through which we test identities and pull together a self that is too often told it is not enough.

I've had the opportunity to test these identities within sports spaces and elsewhere, but my sports self is particularly special because it has afforded me the confidence and access to other arenas within which to grow. As David Wall Rice says in his book *Balance* (2008), there is a "fidelity" to this identity because of what it has seen me through and what it allows me to see in terms of possibility for myself and communities like those that I come from. How I appreciate and lift up this identity is the very definition of an unadulterated presentation of self.

Identity is a powerful notion that, of course, I consider on the regular as I step more and more squarely into adulthood. From an Oprah Winfrey Scholar at Morehouse College to an NBA internship to my present role in the National Football League's Rotational Program, who I am as a Black man who centers sport beyond stereotypes is part of my ever-present work to be.

Not unrelated, I was recently watching the docudrama *Colin in Black and White*. In the episode that dealt with Colin Kaepernick and his baseball team winning a championship, Kaep was referred to by an adult onlooker as "one of the good ones." This suggested that his Blackness was better than the Blackness of the African American ball players on the other team. I could relate.

No matter the marginalized contexts I've come through from Cleveland to now, "others" often need to separate me from the "Blackness" of the communities I come from. It's as if there is cognitive dissonance at play in considering the successes I've realized. For me, that unadulterated presentation of self, that fidelity to who I am and how I've gotten to where I am, can't be separated from the kid I was growing up in Cleveland.

To be real though, I am one of the good ones, but so are we all. I'm obligated to work overtime to show as much.

Chapter 19

Love You, Man

Negotiating Racism, Isolation, and Vulnerability in Black Male Peer Relationships

Malachi Richardson

Like music, personality has come to be understood by popular theorists as a daily expression of traits rather than a static set of characteristics. In his artfully named work *Balance*, David Wall Rice seeks to capture the essence of lived identity in psychological and sociological theory. Rooted in the narrative writing of some of Black culture's most prolific hip-hop artists, identity orchestration posits the self as an intensely intricate "container for many identities or self-aspects." Identity orchestration is the process by which these self-aspects are driven into "balance" with each other and involves an attempt to "fit" one's identity to one's world in order to make sense of it. The genius of this idea is that the changing of one's world is directly related to changes in the formation and expression of identity. If this is true, the past 365 days, shadowed by the pervasive disease known as COVID-19, the unjustified killings of Black men and women, and a widely supported bid to erase Black suffrage must surely make for some heretofore unencountered expressions of Blackness in context.

However, in pushing this work forward, it is important to account for the significant interconnectedness of Black identity, for our relationships are as much a definition of our world and who we are as is our very name. With this in mind, the purpose of this work is to apply identity orchestration to lived experiences through the narratives of three Black men adapting their identities through this unique and nearly unrecognizable American context. The focus here is to push the theoretical underpinnings of identity orchestration to not only account for the process of identity development individually but to include the development of personality, reciprocally as it often happens outside of the pages of psychological study.

The process of expanding this function employs the building blocks of identity formation as outlined in the identity orchestration model. These are identity dilemma articulation, unadulterated presentation of self, burden of proof, and acute identity expression. From this foundation the narratives of three young professional Black men have been parsed for indications of these processes and the role that their relationships with other Black men enact in the process of identity orchestration this year. The examination of their narratives has created the following important considerations of identity orchestration in context.

IDENTITY IMAGINING

Identity dilemma articulation is the process by which one is able to discuss or identify the possible identities available to them. In much of popular writing, this process is approached in the circumscribed parable of the rapper, the drug dealer, or the baller. In reality, identity dilemma articulation exists as the imagination of young Black men, ripe with a vast number of possible selves.

Various narratives provided by the participants of this work suggest that identity dilemma articulation is actually dependent on relationships with other Black men. For instance, one participant, a physician, reported that the isolation imposed by the risks of COVID-19 are most harmful because "having a relationship with someone who looks like you and seeing how they walk through the world is . . . important." Accordingly, the most important function of our relationships with Black male peers is to have opportunities to see how others make their way. Identity dilemma articulation was also evident in the way that Black men have adapted to unfamiliar environments. The same participant notes, "I don't have anyone I can be my full authentic self around. Instead I try and build gardens in which I have people where we have specific common interests." He is not only aware of maintaining multiple identities but also acknowledges that he has "always been a bit of a chameleon" and consciously "fits [his] presentation to the group." His admission here is evidence of sustained identity dilemma articulation as a form of code-switching.

In addition to indications of identity dilemma articulation in its classical form, discussions with these Black men indicate that relationships in the context of fear and isolation have necessitated unique processes involving this aspect of identity formation. For instance, when asked about changes in his self-concept over the past year, one participant explained, "Over time I channel my most arrogant cocky friends in order to build confidence. They were loud and boisterous and leaders. I was able to model strength from what I saw in them. I was able to channel them and borrow it."

His admission is evidence of his ability to assume the identities of his friends as a way of simultaneously voicing possible selves (identity dilemma articulation) and affirming himself through an accounting of strengths and weaknesses (acute identity expression). In fact, it may be more appropriate to describe this process as acute identity expression *through* identity dilemma articulation. In much the same way that the character Hypolita, from the popular HBO series *Lovecraft Country*, learned to "name" herself, Black male relationships exist as spaces where we can explore, affirm, assume, and reject possible selves. This relational space of possibility has become a resource for Black men that allows them to reinforce themselves by modeling others in new ways.

RELATIONSHIPS OF REFUGE

Ask any Black person about 2020 and you'll likely hear the incredulity of someone who has never been more grateful to celebrate a new year. Unanimously, the Black men included in this writing described a gauntlet of recurring traumas that were familiar but undeniably overwhelming. As one might expect, the constant threat of death or victimization has heightened a sense of vulnerability for Black men and has placed a premium on the way they value their relationships with each other.

As one participant explained, "Because we're at home and thinking about these deaths [George Floyd, Ahmaud Aubrey], we think about these people [friends] more frequently." This heightened sense of importance has changed the form and function of their relationships in several ways.

First, when asked about what they are now willing to say in their conversations with friends that they were less likely to say just last year, all three men replied, "I love you." Across all three interviews, the subjects explained that there have been changes in the way they communicate. One participant remarked that he has become "less inclined to lie about [his] emotional well-being these days." Another remarked, "We talk about loss, rest, and fatigue differently. We're all having to sit in it. There's nothing to distract you from the current daily lived reality." The increased honesty of self-expression can also be understood as an increased willingness to enter a state of unadulterated presentation of self that directly contradicts existing stereotypes of how Black males communicate (burden of proof).

In addition to changes in the way Black men communicate with each other, there were also differences in the function of these relationships over the course of this year. Participants described relationships that served the function of providing a space outside of the grief, racism, and stereotypes that dominate the outside world. However, the nature of these refuges and their method of nourishment differed among speakers. One participant described relationships that had been taxed to the point of exhaustion by events around them:

> When we come to the killing of Black bodies I feel like in my friendships, so many of us are numb to that. Because we've seen it so much. It hurts in a deeper way. In some friendships I can't even engage that as a reality. I can't even process it. We couldn't give it space because we'd fall apart. Because when it came to conversation, we couldn't even discuss it. We'd used the same words, we cried the same tears. We'd done it so many times that we just didn't have anything else. We just didn't have any more bandwidth for it.

These fatigued relationships had to adapt to a different form of caring that allowed for them to escape from these realities. For this speaker, relationships that were once used as a place to dialogue on the very topics that were most pervasive this year became spaces to be temporarily relieved of the burden of experiencing or fighting against their impact. He explained, "The world wanted to take this up and it's like 'we been taking this up, we been through this.' We were there to be joy and just exist—avoiding a task in silence together."

The form of care and repair changed from active confrontation of issues to passive reassurance. In the same way a Black person may be relieved to see a Black bystander observing their interaction with a police officer or may be naturally inclined to sit near a Black stranger in a crowded café, friendship became a place where he could be reassured simply by their presence rather than the actual content of discussion. This change in the function of relationships, in turn, directly related to changes in his identity over the course of the year.

When asked about these changes, the same speaker replied, "I'm reflecting on this weird thing I do in therapy where I refer to myself as 'we' where I know that my friends are great and I am great through them. I felt that when I first got my homies I can do anything, I can go anywhere, I can try this, I can do that, and I know I have home." The current state of his relationship facilitates this understanding by allowing him to easily tap in to the nonverbal caring provided by his peers.

IRON SHARPENS IRON

While the relationships between some Black men took on a format of nonverbal reassurance, others became arenas where friends challenged and pushed each other toward more authentic presentations of themselves. One participant explained, "Our conversations have gotten much more serious. We always talked about politics and our personal lives but with everything that happened—we're talking about real shit." He proudly remarked, "We've challenged each other," and recalled that it was in one of his group chats that he first encountered the video of George Floyd's murder and witnessed a "political awakening" in some of his more conservative friends. The challenging within the context of this group is a sustained and reciprocal encouragement toward unadulterated presentation of self.

Through continual examination and engagement, the Black men in these relationships pushed through this unadulterated presentation to construct an acute identity expression. This is evident as the participant is asked to reflect on how his relationships and self-concept have changed over the past year: "It's been because I've had the realization that you can't really run from your feelings when you're with the people who allow you to be who you want to be." Another participant similarly noted that one aspect of the value of his relationships is that he has a space to be heard, validated, and *held accountable.* The challenging of ideas and identities is the process of holding each other accountable within these spaces. It is being held accountable to the most authentic aspects of your identity and being forced to shed those that are inorganic or imposed.

For example, one speaker explained that self-disclosure about an underwhelming sexual encounter led to a "flood of vulnerability" about similar experiences from many of his friends. He surmised that this experience led to the realization that "yeah, we performed but at some point there has to be an awareness of the performance." There has to be an awareness of the behaviors and identities that stem from outside, from popular notions about what it is to be Black and male in American society. The reorientation of this particular constellation of peers toward a more direct and authentic relationship with each other over the course of this year ultimately had important implications for the way he performed identity orchestration. When asked about how his relationships have shaped his identity, this speaker explained,

The pain of COVID, how it quickly went from being a white thing to a Black thing. I think of the protests, the politics, the turmoil in my own life. What I wrestle with this year is how am I going to relate to that pain. I've had to evolve an understanding of myself. What I've experienced this year has pushed me to not to turn from myself and say "NO NO NO—it matters if this thing makes me upset, it matters if this makes me sad, it matters that I missed shit." I've been pressed to wrestle with who I am, and what I've learned is not only is it okay to be me but I *have* to be me.

In this exposition of unadulterated presentation of self, the speaker, benefiting from continued "sharpening" by his peers, reaches a point at which acute identity expression becomes not only possible but necessary.

The distillation of an acute identity through this process appears to also have several implications for how Black men operate outside of their close relationships with their peers. One implication is the way in which Black men operate in spaces where they are not often welcome. For instance, our physician participant voiced frustration at feeling unable to express himself at work: "I work in a white space—it was really tough to go to work and see all this stuff and feel passionately about it because people are disinterested . . . 'man this shit is fucked up! You had to be like 'it's a shame.'" When asked about the implications of the events of this year on his identity, the same speaker remarked, "It has made me a little more hostile. Any time you end up bargaining with the devil, you lose. So now it's like 'I want to be seen with respect but not amiability. I want to do my job and I don't want to be your brother. Unless you're on the same agenda we don't really need to interact outside of the hospital.'" From this, it is apparent that the way in which he now moves through predominately white spaces includes a more pronounced and unadulterated presentation of self.

Other participants have expressed an increased scrutiny of the people with whom they form relationships outside of their existing friendships. One speaker remarked, "I prioritized people I wanted to see in order to prioritize my health. This smaller group of friends gives me life and energy. The people that I spend time with are the ones I ended up dedicating time to. It was a conscious choice I ended up making during the pandemic." Another explained, "My relationships with Black men—the expectation that we have is that we're all of substance. We're all trying to be decent people." It appears as though these men intend to maintain acute identity expression through maintaining only those relationships that can foster unadulterated presentation of self.

IN CLOSING

We've endured a lot this year. Black people have been exposed to complex and enduring traumas that have reached a crescendo in the late hours of 2020. However, as is always our strength, we have used each other to support, to escape, to challenge, to correct, to love, to inspire, and to defend in our collective adversity. As we grow in our relationships with each other, we also grow in our own identities.

Though 2021 appears to hold the promise of even greater challenges, it also holds the prospect of greater growth and support from those we love. In the words of one of our Black men, it is important, now more than ever, to remember "whenever we meet we can see each other beyond how the world sees us."

Chapter 20

Worldwide

Robert X. Shannon

Black folk in America are frequently understood in terms of survival rather than in terms of success. The abilities and attributes that Black people use to survive are not dissimilar to those abilities and attributes common to standard successes. Rice (2008) communicates that, through narratives of survival, "abilities and attributes can inform identities that are psychologically stabilizing and socially rewarding." Of course, within this text a significant stabilizing process is identity orchestration, the balance of multiple identities into a cohesive, healthy, whole self.

Here, I offer a sketch of how the process of identity orchestration has shaped my experiences as a thinker and international development practitioner and how I believe the construct might broadly inform international development and social transformation.

At base, it is impossible to understand Black identity development absent the context of racism (Jones 2003). Black Americans live within the systemic and omnipresent constructs of cultural, institutional, and individual racism. We are "descendants of a displaced race . . . who exist today cloaked in the legacy of dehumanization, oppression, and marginalization" (Rice 2008). This American racism is an extension of global white supremacy and colonialism.

Still, as awful as these realities are, the context of racism does not define the self or the worth of Black people. The tensions can, in fact, inform a particular nimbleness, adaptability, resilience, and defiance.

NINETEEN

At nineteen I didn't know that I would pursue a graduate degree and become an international development consultant. I was focused on trying to make it through undergrad. Honestly, I was just trying to make it in general. I wanted to be successful one day, but I didn't know exactly what that meant. In fact, I didn't yet know who I was beyond the stereotypes that were offered up for me to adopt.

These stories and examples of who I was supposed to be impacted me more than I realized at the time, and there is still a residual behavior or two that I have based on those low expectations of me. I've made decisions to alter my movements, police my behavior, and inconvenience myself to accommodate the discomfort of those whom Ralph Ellison called "sleepwalkers," white folks whose fears of me could potentially place me in harmful situations. With my lived experience, I've shown up in ways that non-Black people rarely have to. It's a taxing type of preoccupation, a dance that consumes more of my mental space than I care to admit. At nineteen, though, I developed a drive to know myself more fully, beyond what was set for me to be.

I know I'm not alone in this identity journey. We all have intersectional and multifaceted identities that are defined by the contexts and histories of the places where we operate, our relationships with others, and the meanings we put to these experiences. Considering these multiple pulls on the self, finding balance can be daunting. For those who are defined as marginal, a white gaze can confuse even more, having us consider a false choice between being ourselves and playing into respectability practices, dangerous to the self because of the high potential for suffocating identity authenticity.

This is a lot of psychological noise, but holding some contexts constant allows for clarity and focus in terms of identity understanding if not development. For me, the choice to attend Morehouse College is an example of reducing the noise that can cloud effective identity development. It was a space where my identity balance could be tempered by the school's history and the peers with whom I was enrolled. Morehouse offered my self a type of home, a place of comfort, safety, and security. This is typical of historically Black colleges and universities, worship spaces, and other culturally grounded hush harbors (French and Boykin 2022) where Black people can find psychic stability amid a mainstream that can be toxic.

Certainly, home should be a safe space for self-exploration, creative expression, and the pursuit of aspirations. Although Black folks have found ways to explore our identities and passions in spite of the confines of American contexts, and found ways to beautifully and masterfully reimagine these constraints as paths for innovation and ideation, some have also sought the freedoms that America has denied them outside the national context. Black scholars, writers, and artists have found greater space to express their creative and intellectual abilities beyond this country.

My choice to attend Morehouse as a young man was turning the knob of that door to another country. The college, now understood as a home of sorts, was actually a guide to home, to safe psychological spaces.

Morehouse pointed me to Africa. I was drawn to the continent, the place of my ancestors, in hopes that I would secure an even deeper understanding of who I was. While my career aspirations and future ambitions of self were not yet fully formed, at nineteen a seed was planted.

LEARNING REFLEXIVITY

I felt such pride when I took my first steps onto African soils. It felt like a dream realized. My family never made the trip to Africa, so it felt inaccessible. And yet here I was, standing in West Africa—Ghana. I was awestruck by the Blackness. Of course, I knew Ghana was Black, but there was something profound about experiencing Black faces, Black entrepreneurship, Black architecture, not just seeing it or reading about it from a remove. The vibrancy of Accra reminded me in some ways of Atlanta. I reflected on what my friends visiting Atlanta might have felt when I took them through the West Side for the first time, a full variety of ATL Blackness on display.

When first settling in to Ghana, I felt self-conscious and a bit misfit. I was trying not to get ripped off too badly by the taxis or at the market. It took some getting used to, but I also began to feel a sense of relief. I had space to breathe; my own Blackness no longer felt alarming or even noteworthy. That's not to say I didn't stick out. In Africa, just as we encounter cultural differences, so too do Africans encounter Black Americans as different, but they view our culture, behaviors, and language as *different* rather than *deviant*. At least this is how it's been explained to and experienced by me. The differences sit more lightly and with a new perspective. I began to think about double-consciousness (Du Bois 1903) and orchestrating fresh-eyed identities into a single healthy self.

I realized quickly that I carried with me so many dominant cultural assumptions and beliefs about this continent that had no relevance in my present experience. As I began to strip away stereotyped notions I had of people and places in this special context, I found myself also peeling away beliefs I had internalized about myself. I started to more fully comprehend how the stories we'd been told about Africa and our people helped to marginalize and malign both, thereby justifying exploitation, dehumanization, and colonization of them, and, by extension, of me. Ghana provided a space for me not only to learn a different version of its history but also to begin retelling my own history, reframing my own identity.

We need space and opportunity to explore our identities. For some, that space can be found in work, art, family, travel, and the like. The space I needed was having an academic and professional career outside of American racism. So many Black folks before me have similarly experienced this transformative space to breathe, to explore other ways of being. They include James Baldwin in Europe and Turkey, Ta-Nehisi Coates in France, Maya Angelou and W. E. B. Du Bois in Ghana, Malcolm X in Ghana and Mecca, and so many more.

With some of the weight of being Black in America lifted off us, we have the opportunity to more cleanly engage our identities. We are able to stretch ourselves beyond comfort zones, to become uncomfortable in constructive ways that are different from the discomfort of being outcast. We are also able to reflect on our experiences and our identities in the American context with greater perspective, like astronauts looking back at Earth from the porthole of the Space Shuttle, seeing our blue sphere in an entirely new, and hopefully special, way.

Time outside of the United States gives us the room to realize that so much of the identity we are seeking is not located elsewhere; despite our roots and our connection to Africa, the pilgrimage does not lead us to a "holy grail" of self. Instead, it gives us the freedom to find within ourselves this thing we have been looking for—not something new we must acquire; something we've always been in possession of but, because of the haze of race in America, has been difficult to locate. We learn about the histories and places that are a part of us and, in doing so, grow to know ourselves better. We don't have to assume another identity—as Africans or diasporics—to become whole; rather we need this weight lifted to allow us to breathe, to find who we have been at our core all along.

As we are given space to explore our complex inner lives, our selves, and our identities, we can also begin to better understand and to reimagine our role in relation to others and to the World House (King 1967). As I continued spending time in Ghana, first as a student and later as a development practitioner working with nonprofits and government, not only was I able to explore my own identity, but I also became more aware of the baggage I brought with me into this context as an American.

Being Black, I'd never felt like a full citizen in the United States, since our national identity seemed so intrinsically rooted in whiteness. In Ghana, my Americanness became almost inescapable. Because of this, in many ways I experienced privilege connected to my national identity. At the same time, I realized that this Americanness also brought with it the baggage of the history of American-African relations, and I began to think more critically about what this meant in terms of my responsibility as a young Black American studying and working internationally.

Although, at times, I felt a kinship to the Ghanaians with whom I worked, feeling my presence more acceptable to communities that are rightfully critical of "white saviors" parachuting in, I also began to see hesitancy and distrust. This was not necessarily because of what I looked like or anything that I had done but because of others' past experiences with Americans.

As someone raised in communities distrustful of hegemony, of outsiders and outside solutions, I understood. Just as the history of Black folks in America has shaped my own identity, it was clear to me that the history of colonialism and exploitation had ongoing implications for the communities in which I worked and my relationships to them. Although I share roots with some of the people I aimed to serve, these roots were mired in a history—mine, theirs, and ours together—that required deeper thought and reflection.

There is extensive literature documenting the legacy of colonialism in the types of aid programs that are funded, the locations where they are funded, and how these programs are carried out (see, for example, Schmitt 2020). What has been less thoroughly studied is the legacy of colonialism and the impact of *who* does development work. This irrespective of calls for greater racial diversity within the INGO community (Bruce-Raeburn 2019). This is where my identity as a Black man engaging in development work gives me a unique perspective and skill set. An expanding body of scholarship draws attention to the importance of reflexivity on the part of development practitioners, suggesting that self-reflection and an assessment of positionality are integral to identifying inequalities between those who do development work and those whom this work is intended to benefit (Kagal & Latchford 2020; Strumm 2020; Yao & Vital 2018).

Reflexivity and the Black experience of double-consciousness does not come naturally. It has to be thoughtfully developed, as there isn't a singular experience of double-consciousness. As Dayal (1996) writes, "It would be foolish to suggest that all diasporics are automatically in possession of double consciousness . . . neither the existential accident nor the choice of diaspora confers upon an individual or group that transcendental sophistication of double consciousness. . . . The cosmopolitan doesn't share the same cultural location as the refugee or exile."

Blackness is not a monolith, and Black identity can become static as one's adaptation to a particular setting constrains the fluidity necessary to ongoing identity development (Rice 2008). However, while Blackness does not inherently give one a leg up in terms of working ethically in international settings, I would argue that one can effectively and ethically use the Black experience in the embrace of reflexivity, this in turn enhancing one's contributions in international work.

My Black experience has pushed and enabled me to explore a career path overseas, to work in communities, places, and with languages unfamiliar to me. The challenge of going beyond myself, being forced into continuous adaptation, reflection, and identity construction, has made me psychologically healthier and more whole. In turn, I believe that this nimbleness, adaptability, and reflexivity position me as a Black development practitioner to be well suited to do the difficult and creative work of reimagining development. Self-reflection alone is a prerequisite for, but insufficient to, achieving broader goals of development work; as Smith (2013) writes, "Individual transformation must occur concurrently with social and political transformation. That is, the undoing of privilege occurs not by individuals confessing their privileges or trying to think themselves into a new subject position, but through the creation of collective structures that dismantle the systems that enable these privileges."

Here is where I think the strength of working through the Black experience as development practitioners lies, and why I believe that the calls for increasing the racial diversity of development organizations are necessary, not only to benefit individuals seeking to work in the field but also to benefit the work that we do.

THE NEED

As development practitioners, the burden rests on us to prove our intentions to the communities within which we work, communities that for too long have been exploited and thought of in reductionist ways. We must think critically about the intentions of the organizations we work with, bringing knowledge-gain from the distrust we have learned as people oppressed, to ensure that the work we support is supportive and antioppressive in rhetoric and in action.

We need organizations to be driven by racial and social justice–focused mission statements, staffed by diverse employees, and assessed with markers of success sourced from the communities of attention. We also need to recognize the value we get from our work, to acknowledge that this is not a selfless endeavor but one that allows for a more authentic self. We need to use our own insight into what it means to be voiceless, what struggle is, to push us to be more intentional about avoiding extinguishing the voices of others. In doing so, we use our experiences with marginalization, the skill of reflexivity, and the ability to adapt and balance in new and changing contexts to be more thoughtful about our work and more sensitive to those we aim to serve.

We also need scholarship to intentionally and explicitly explore the connections among race, reflexivity, and development work.

TOWARD HOME

There are so many parallels between the Black experience in America and the experience of citizens of so-called developing countries around the world. With hegemony, Black people are understood as deficient, at best, as compared to a white norm. And the Global South is pathological compared to the West. Those born into politically constructed poverty around the globe are viewed as less whole, less healthy, and less human in order to justify the colonial and neocolonial forces that have acted on and shaped their circumstances. As Rice (2008) writes, "With the illustration of [Black people] as 'disconnected' there is almost always the situating of [them] in a context of dire straits, far, far away from education"; similarly, those in the Global South are frequently portrayed, even by those educated and experienced in the field, who should know better, as homogenous, rural, poor, and uneducated.

We so often fail to acknowledge the variability of circumstances within these countries or the rich histories of literature, art, commerce, and science that have meaningful modern implications. We use terms that reify the Global South as somehow less than Western countries: *developing* as opposed to *developed*, manipulating the word to infantilize so-called developing countries while simultaneously ignoring the sociocultural and relative infancy of the United States.

In appropriately reconceptualizing Blackness and the Global South as healthy and whole, rather than diseased and in need of saving, we shift from focusing on the "treatments" that we have been prescribing for generations to "collaborations" that have the capacity to serve everyone. This is hard, complex work. "There is no simple antioppression formula that we can follow, we are in a constant state of trial and error and radical experimentation," Smith (2013) writes.

Becoming more reflexive about the context, the motivations, and the identities of the individuals serving marginalized communities opens the door to more creatively and collectively reimagining what the future can be, "adding to our collective imagining of a 'beyond'" (Smith 2013).

If our World House is not yet safe or comfortable for too many of us, we are charged to do the work of collectively imagining a new concept of home, reckoning with our individual and collective identities.

I've worked through the process of self-construction, used my experiences to orchestrate self-balance, and I believe this process has given me tools that can help me to serve others better, to work with others to reimagine "home." The poet Warsan Shire puts it well: "At the end of the day, it isn't where I came from. Maybe home is somewhere I'm going and have never been before."

REFERENCES

Bruce-Raeburn, A. (2019). Opinion: International development has a race problem. *Devex.* Retrieved from https://www.devex.com/news/opinion-international-development-has-a-race-problem-94840

Dayal, S. (1996). Diaspora and double consciousness. *The Journal of the Midwest Modern Language Association, 29*(1), 46–62.

Kagal, N., & Latchford, L. (2020). Towards an intersectional praxis in international development: What can the sector learn from Black feminists located in the global North? *Gender & Development, 28*(1), 11–30.

Rice, D. W. (2008). *Balance: Advancing identity theory by engaging the Black male adolescent.* Lanham, MD: Lexington Books.

Schmitt, C. (Ed.). (2020). *From colonialism to international aid: External actors and social protection in the Global South.* Cham, Switzerland: Palgrave Macmillan.

Smith, A. (2013). *Unsettling the privilege of self-reflexivity.* New York: Routledge.

Strumm, B. (2020). Using critical reflection to question self and power in international development. *Gender & Development, 28*(1), 175–92.

Yao, C. W., & Vital, L. M. (2018). Reflexivity in international contexts: Implications for U.S. doctoral students international research preparation. *International Journal of Doctoral Studies, 13*, 193–210.

Chapter 21

Crack's Residue

Donovan X. Ramsey

I hardly ever saw Michelle, who lived just a few doors down the block from my family. I don't actually remember ever meeting her, but I was definitely afraid of her. My mom would drag our house phone from room to room by its long white cord and talk at length with her friends. On more than one occasion, I overheard her complaining about Michelle from Down the Street.

Michelle had too many strange people going in and out of her house, I heard. It was all just "so sad" my mom would say with a slow shake of her head. She would move on to other topics, but my imagination stayed fixed on Michelle and what might be going on just a few feet away.

I was sitting on our front porch with my older sister one Sunday afternoon when a van pulled up and parked right in front of Michelle's place. Out of it came an older woman and a little girl, each resembling our mysterious neighbor in her own way.

Because my sister knew everything, I asked her who the strangers were. "Duh! That's Michelle's family," she said, and the girl was Michelle's daughter.

"Why don't she live with her mom?" I asked.

My sister shrugged her shoulders and answered, "I don't know. Probably because Michelle is a crackhead."

I learned then that there was a real person behind every "crackhead." Like me, they had moms. They could even be moms. The revelation left me gob-smacked. I would return to it whenever I heard mention of Michelle from Down the Street.

Crackhead was a go-to insult when I was growing up—so-and-so was "acting like a crackhead," "yo mama" was a "crackhead." The word was everywhere in the culture, as were stories of crack addicts behaving badly.

I suppose we made *crackhead* a slur because we were scared. That's what children do, I think, when they're in search of power over things that frighten them; they reduce them to words, bite-size things that can be spat out at a moment's notice.

Crack baby entered the lexicon alongside *crackhead*. In 1985, a young neonatologist named Ira Chasnoff published one of the earliest studies on the effects of cocaine use in pregnancy in the *New England Journal of Medicine*. Based on preliminary results from a study of just twenty-three women, he concluded that infants exposed to cocaine had "significant depression of interactive behavior and a poor organizational response to environmental stimuli." He wrote, "These preliminary observations suggest that cocaine influences the outcome of pregnancy as well as the neurologic behavior of the newborn."

Chasnoff's research, however limited, immediately found its way into the national dialogue around crack in the late 1980s. Conservative politicians and pundits, already a few years into the crack epidemic, were eager for ammunition in their narrative war on drugs, Democrat-controlled big cities, and the poor people of color who called them home. From Chasnoff's study and some others, they conjured the "crack baby."

Although its many elements were always present in the American imagination, the idea of the crack baby crawled into the collective consciousness during this period. Crack babies were, as the stories went, infants born afflicted due to their exposure to cocaine in the womb. They were the "tiniest victims" of the crack epidemic—deformed, brain dead, and expected to overwhelm taxpayer-funded public services. Exactly how many crack babies were born was, it seems, secondary to the spectacle of their existence.

Within just a few short years, the national media was in a full-blown panic over crack babies. The stories—run by reputable outlets including Time, the New York Times, Newsweek, the Washington Post, Rolling Stone, and countless television programs—almost all began the same way, describing scenes of underdeveloped infants struggling for life in incubators.

"At a hospital in Boston lies a baby girl who was born before her time—three months early, weighing less than 3 lbs.," begins *Time*'s "Crack Kids." "Her tiny body is entangled in a maze of wires and tubes that monitor her vital signs and bring her food and medicine. Every so often she shakes uncontrollably for a few moments—a legacy of the nerve-system damage that occurred when she suffered a shortfall of blood and oxygen just before birth."

Some of the pieces seem to have been written to evoke pity: "Crack Comes to the Nursery," "Crack Kids: Innocent Victims," "Crack Babies Born to Life of Suffering," "Crack's Toll among Babies: A Joyless View, Even of Toys," "Childhood's End: What Life Is Like for Crack Babies." Others suggested blame and burden: "For Pregnant Addict, Crack Comes First," "Crack's Tiniest, Costliest Victims," "A Time Bomb in Cocaine Babies," "Disaster in Making: Crack Babies Start to Grow Up," "The Cost of Not Preventing Crack Babies."

"Maternity wards around the country ring with the high-pitched 'cat cries' of crack babies," one author wrote for *Time*. Another piece in the *New York Times* quoted a psychologist as saying that, in infants, "crack was interfering with the central core of what it is to be human." In a 1988 interview with NBC News, George Miller, a Democratic congressman representing California's seventh district concluded, "These children, who are the most expensive babies ever born in America, are going to overwhelm every social service delivery system that they come in contact with throughout the rest of their lives."

Washington Post columnist Charles Krauthammer wrote in a 1989 column, "The inner-city crack epidemic is now giving birth to the newest horror: a bio-underclass, a generation of physically damaged cocaine babies whose biological inferiority is stamped at birth." Later in the column, Krauthammer quoted family policy expert Douglas Besharov as saying, "This is not stuff that Head Start can fix. This is permanent brain damage. Whether it is 5 percent or 15 percent of the Black community, it is there."

Of crack babies, Krauthammer decided, "Theirs will be a life of certain suffering, of probable deviance, of permanent inferiority. At best, a menial life of severe deprivation . . . the dead babies may be the lucky ones."

Crackhead, crack baby, superpredators—these terms came to dominate the American imagination in the 1980s and 1990s. And because so much news coverage of the crack epidemic, and the debate around it, was racialized, these characters became stand-ins for the nation's urban centers and, ultimately, Black America. Crack cast a shadow over the entire community—especially its young people.

I don't think my peers understood that at the time. I certainly didn't. For my generation, born in the 1980s and coming of age in the 1990s, crack's shadow was just something we navigated. It threatened to envelop us, but we did our best to outrun it. We avoided the police who profiled us as drug dealers and gangbangers. We resisted the low expectations of teachers who regarded us as potential crack babies incapable of learning.

For many, navigating crack's shadow meant distance—distance from crack, from addicts, from dealers, from the streets. "The crackheads, they're all 25 and up. They go walking around looking dirty and trifling, trying to sell $50 worth of food stamps for a real $20 bill. Kids aren't into that," one teenager told the Washington Post in a 1994 story about crack's end. "Gold is played out," she added as a commentary on the drug dealer aesthetic.

We live now in a post-crack era. Rates of crack use in most cities hit their peak around 1989, plateaued, and started to decline soon after. Researchers are reluctant to declare an end to any epidemic, but by 1996 first-time crack users were few and far between.

There are, for sure, individuals still using the substance in America today, but they're a small cohort of mostly veteran users with fewer and fewer people opting for the drug each year. Researchers believe those who came of age during the epidemic are to thank for crack's end—for our choices in youth and our invention of the "crackhead."

According to a 2006 study published by the Journal of Sociology and Social Welfare, "Since the early 1990s, inner-city youths have been purposefully avoiding crack and heroin, having seen the devastation these drugs brought into the lives of older community members."

"They considered 'crackhead' a dirty word and even took to abusing crackheads," noted another report issued by the US Department of Justice. "Such a change in attitude among youths heralded the beginning of the decline phase of the crack epidemic."

To that end, the "crackhead" served its purpose. It warned young people like me away from hard drugs. It scared us sufficiently, but at what cost? What did we lose in the process of distancing ourselves from, however distressing, real elements of our community?

In the field of psychology, identity dilemma articulation is a form of identity orchestration closely aligned with W. E. B. Du Bois's concept of double-consciousness. As an expression of identity balance, identity dilemma articulation is a dilemma created by the realization of a divided identity.

Perhaps our attitudes about the crack epidemic—the ways we talk about the history of it or avoid it altogether—illustrate such a split. They're evidence of the extent to which that experience has been excised from community identity.

Indeed, those who survived the crack epidemic, Black and Brown people in particular, hardly ever talk about it. If we do, it's discussed wearily like a trauma long accepted, in hushed voices and with thousand-yard stares. And the ways we talk about the crack epidemic, or don't in some cases, reveals our deep misunderstanding.

There is perhaps no better evidence of our misunderstanding of the epidemic than the enduring myth of the "crack baby." Despite all the coverage crack babies received in the late 1980s and the policies their tragic stories spurred, the crack baby turned out to be nothing more than a media creation generated from scant science.

Thirty years after Ira Chasnoff published his landmark study on the effects of cocaine use in pregnancy, the crack baby myth was finally exploded. Hallam Hurt, a neurologist then chair of neonatology at Philadelphia's Albert Einstein Medical Center, began researching the effects of prenatal cocaine exposure on developmental outcomes in 1988. When she finally concluded her research in 2015, the results were astounding: there were no significant differences in the development of children exposed to cocaine in utero versus those who were not.

Hurt's study was of 224 babies born at Einstein split into two groups: half whose mothers had used cocaine during their pregnancy and the other half who weren't exposed to the drug at all. All of the babies selected were born full term, to control for prematurity. All were from low-income families, and nearly all were Black. They were evaluated periodically beginning at six months old and then every six or twelve months on through their adulthood. "We were really preparing for the worst," said Hurt.

Participants returned to Einstein periodically over the next twenty-three years to have every aspect of their development measured. Their IQs were measured in preschool. As adolescents, their brains were scanned using an MRI machine. Hurt and researchers found time and time again that cocaine-exposed children developed on par with the others in the study.

For example, at four years old, the average IQ of the children exposed to cocaine was 79.0 while the average for the nonexposed children was 81.9. At the age of six, nearly a quarter of the children in each group scored below average for math, letter, and word recognition. These results were well below national averages, signifying to researchers that both groups were being impacted by something far more powerful than crack. "Poverty is a more powerful influence on the outcome of inner-city children than gestational exposure to cocaine," Hurt said in a lecture on her findings.

There was more: a survey of the children at seven years old revealed that 81 percent had seen someone arrested, 74 percent had heard gunshots, 35 percent had seen someone shot, and 19 percent had seen a dead body. Hurt and her researchers deduced that those types of environmental factors were impacting the children's development, with the children who reported high exposure to violence more likely to show signs of depression and anxiety and to have lower self-esteem.

"We have a lot of information about the children and in particular the home," Hurt said. "And it turns out that the children that were scoring at or above average had more nurturing and cognitively stimulating home environments regardless of cocaine exposure. It didn't make a difference."

Of course, Hurt and other physicians make a point to caution against cocaine use during pregnancy. Its effects are similar to those of tobacco. It can raise the blood pressure of expectant mothers to dangerous levels and even cause a pregnant woman's placenta to tear away from her uterine wall. For those reasons, it's associated with premature birth. And it's probably a handful of premature babies—their small size, shallow breathing, lack of interaction, and tremors that inspired Ira Chasnoff's early conclusions about cocaine-exposed babies.

The myth of the crack baby was widely accepted as gospel, perhaps because it mapped so well onto existing ideas of Black biological inferiority and cultural pathology and stoked anxieties regarding violent crime and the cost of America's social safety net. Indeed, in the form of the crack baby, America was delivered a perfect symbol for its animosity toward black America—a ticking time bomb of violence and expense created because Black mothers cared too little about themselves and their offspring.

But even after crack's decline, the crack baby myth stuck. Such myths—moreover, the shame they produced—are the epidemic's residue. These traces of the crack epidemic exist primarily in the American imagination, and it's quite possible that they'll never be erased. Yet, they need not be.

I think often of my old neighbor Michelle from Down the Street and wonder what became of her. I like to imagine that she left the neighborhood for treatment. She got clean and moved into a big house with her daughter, who can't remember a time when they weren't attached at the hip.

Years of covering the criminal legal system tell me that outcome is unlikely, though. It's more probable that she was criminalized for her addiction and gobbled up by the system. If Michelle is alive today and clean, she probably lives with the residue of the epidemic—a criminal record, chronic illness, trauma, guilt, and shame.

For her sake and that of so many others, it's past time that we reconcile the crack epidemic with the rest of Black history and identity. We must take its measure, make meaning of it, and incorporate that meaning into the greater story of who we are.

It's time we begin the difficult work of excavating the real stories of the individuals, families, and communities who were swept up in the crack epidemic. A part of that work is putting ideas like "crackhead," "crack baby," and "superpredator" to rest.

They were always constructs after all, distortions of flesh-and-blood people. The objects of our fears shouldn't have been those people—our people, us—but instead the forces that created them.

Chapter 22

A Contemporary Spelman College Social Identity as Motivated by the 2012 Violence Against Women Course Petition

Brielle McDaniel

This work problematizes the Spelman College tagline, "A choice to change the world" (Spelman 2012), by situating the social identity of "scholar-activist" within larger discourses of identity, consciousness, and agency. By considering student attitudes, ideas, and perceptions regarding the performance of identity articulated by women in hip-hop, Spelman students habitually leverage their consciousness and agency so as best to combat matrices of domination embedded in culture. The college is bound by a commitment to the empowerment of women and therefore supports initiatives such as the Violence Against Women Fall 2012 course petition to ban misogynist music within the gates of the institution. This display of intellectualism joined by action articulates a consistent and verifiable social identity among the students who attend Spelman College. The goal of this piece, then, is to provide a useful model for identity change that meets sources of knowledge with collective agency in order to transform systematic gender oppression, especially in media. The aim is to illustrate the process of identity verification characteristic of identity control theory (Burke 1991) as evidenced by Spelman College's commitment to scholar-activism. As identity control theory supports, identity verification is achievable on all bases of identity and in this example carries transferable knowledge useful in practices geared toward the transformation of society overall.

THE PETITION

Dear Office of Student Life and Engagement:

"All I want for my birthday is a big-booty hoe."

These are the types of lyrics we are surrounded by while perusing local vendors each Market Friday here at Spelman College. As Spelman women, agents of change, global citizens entrusted to bring about free-thinking dialogue wherever we may go, is it acceptable for us to be subject to demeaning, misogynistic, homophobic, and erotically explicit lyrics in spaces we occupy? Additionally, what about the visitors who enter our campus and encounter this music as their representation of Spelman?

As Market Friday is an arena for our own community and creative expression, having all-male DJs constantly reinforce the notion that we exist only in relationship to the male gaze directly contradicts the values of Spelman. (See earlier dress code letter.)

Rather than play the infectiously offensive synthetic reels of Rick Ross, Young Jock, Lil Wayne, Two Chainz, why don't we introduce more women-friendly musical diversity into our soundtracks?

We, as socially aware Spelman women, propose to create our own misogyny-free playlists in order to make the musical selection more democratic and representative.

Like the Nelly protests in the past, Spelman women have historically been conscious of the standard for what we as students allow to permeate our campus.

We echo the sentiment that students should have a good time socializing and appreciate the efforts and activities the office organizes. However, it would be of great help if we may be able to determine what having a good time means.

Respectfully,

Dr. Spence's Violence Against Women Class,

Fall 2012

STATEMENT OF THE PROBLEM

Spelman College, a historically Black, private, liberal arts women's college of approximately 2,100 students is located in Atlanta, Georgia, and carries a rich heritage of innovative social change. Whether it is the 1960s student-led movements for racial equality and civil rights—with student involvement in initiatives such as An Appeal for Human Rights (1960)—or the First National Conference on Black Women's Health Issues in 1983 (Silliman et al. 2004:1), the recurrent instances of mobilizing into action taken up within the Spelman context evidence a space that fosters the consciousness of Black women.

In their choice to attend Spelman College, women share in an elaborate history of change, geared especially toward uplifting the lives of Black women. Therefore, it seems appropriate, as debates remain cyclical at Spelman surrounding women's solidarity and resistance to expressions of systematic gender violence in popular cultural mediums such as hip-hop music, to investigate the tenets of identity, consciousness, and agency at the college. Within this uniquely defined space for women, the institution impresses on its students a charge to deconstruct cultural norms that violently permeate the lives of women. Spelman is an exclusive space where social justice ideology is maintained not only in the curriculum but also through the activities in which students engage—such as the required twenty-two hours of community service between the first and second year (Spelman 2012). It is even perpetuated in the various institutional brandings where Spelman packages its identity—albeit reducing such a distinctive experience to a commodity on the market of exchange—where Spelman defines itself as "a choice to change the world" (Spelman 2012). Both consciousness and agency present themselves as critical constructs upon which the Spelman College social identity necessarily depends.

Situated at the nexus of social consciousness and collective agency, "a choice to change the world" is based on institutional brand promises that promote the production of a student body of "free and forward-thinking women" (Spelman 2012). The scholar-activist posture upon which institutional identity depends, and that the Spelman women positively reinforce, develops through practice, not theory alone. The habits of "change-agents" through which the college derives its cultural capital are fostered through a commitment to active engagement of learning materials (Bourdieu in Lemert 2010:436). Through a critical engagement of the global phenomenon of violence against women embedded in neoliberal, racist, transnational patriarchal structures of dominance, Spelman College women enter the process of liberation attendant to educational praxis (hooks 1994), by cultivating a sociological imagination (Mills 1959) through which they are able to make meaning by situating themselves within larger discourses whose focus is the transformation of the social location of women of color.

The Fall 2012 Violence Against Women course petition to ban misogynist music on Spelman's campus animates the mobilization that Angela Davis (1998) and Patricia Hill Collins (1998) describe when challenging the commoditization of women's bodies and voices. The processes of narrative creation and meaning making allow women the opportunity to exert oppositional force, wherein the Violence Against Women course petition offers a site for empirical investigation of the Spelman College social identity, distinguished by its commitment to consciousness and agency. The petition challenges the imposition of patriarchy in the college through the display of Spelman women reclaiming their public spaces and privileging students' voices.

While the petition echoes a conception of power, on par with Foucault (1978), wherein social actors employ an active role in defining meaning, it also acknowledges the limitation of power (Smith 1990), which is to operate within the context of hegemonic norms, impeding the ability of marginalized groups to experience transformation without generating greater shifts in public consciousness that become reflected in the cultural resources used to communicate meaning. The petition further demonstrates the collective effort of Violence Against Women course members to combat linguistic and sexual violence against women in popular culture, particularly hip-hop. Such action conveys not only a response to social injustice but also the process of mobilizing around a cause in order to catalyze change.

The petition came about through the concerns of a few students, who met after class to view the 2 Chainz "Birthday Song" music video just before the artist was set to headline the Morehouse and Spelman 2012 Homecoming Hip-Hop concert. Classmates joined in solidarity to protest the portrayal of women in the media as well the narratives allowed to permeate and dictate the spaces of an institution dedicated to the empowerment of women.

Although it grew in support, the Violence Against Women petition was initially met with intense backlash via Twitter and other social media networks. The use of technology amplified the discourse surrounding the petition among Atlanta University Center students, many of whom had never seen the petition. While the petition demands the administration enforce its Market Friday policy, which censors violent and misogynist music (Spelman 2012), a series of misconceptions surrounding its contents circulated the campuses. Tales of individual DJs being discriminated against, and the false notion that the platform sought to criticize the musical tastes of individual students, contributed to the backlash, which was paramount to an inconsistent social identity, evidenced by students' choice to oppose limiting displays of misogyny, ultimately perpetuating violence against women.

While social media networks compromised the intent of the petition by allowing unfounded information to spread quickly, campuswide discussions sought to address the concerns of those who had questions or who stood in opposition. It proceeded that simple exposure to the petition and its contents offered a significant solution to the initial backlash. Many students agreed with the position of the college not to support violence against women and not to collude in the spread of such messages.

While it is clear that all movements are accompanied by backlash, the hostility toward the petition reveals a lack of critical engagement among many Spelman students who failed to make the connection between their individual racial and gendered identities and the systematic oppression of women of color demonstrated in misogynist music. By challenging the music selections endorsed by the college, the petition challenges dominant notions of patriarchy informing the relationship of other Atlanta University Center institutions to Spelman, rearticulating this space as one designated specifically for women.

Thus the petition critiques experiences of male privilege and female repression. Although much of the backlash and resistance to the petition came in the form of violent and threatening messages via social networks, it is demonstrative of the violent and repressive nature of patriarchal ideology, which the petition seeks to redress through consciousness raising. The goal of the petition, to define women's spaces and to combat systematic oppression, requires the student body to actively choose the messages that fill their spaces. The necessary plan of action follows that students reengage with larger movements to redefine representations of Black female bodies within popular culture by protesting misogynist music, boycotting pornographic imagery, and other forms of resistance, as well as through continued consciousness-raising efforts such as forums, discussions, and videos to negotiate healthy and uplifting images of Black women in the media.

As this social movement forever develops on the college campus and through national efforts, thinking here seeks to verify the Spelman College social identity by highlighting the consciousness and agency of students. This is captured in the form of thoughts, attitudes, and perceptions of the student body as to the linguistic representations articulated by women in hip-hop lyricism. Through a thorough engagement of the way in which women at Spelman think and perform race and gender, we are better able to focus efforts at increasing solidarity in order to combat the violent and marginal representations of women in popular culture. The ultimate goal is to provide a useful model for identity change—backed by theory and observation—that meets sources of knowledge with collective agency in shaping the representations of women in media. This is imperative, as the consumption and production of media imagery has the ability to affect both the way others perceive Black women and the way Black women perceive themselves.

The social identity of the college is reinforced and can be validated through its demonstrated embrace of critically engaging systems of oppression. Scholar-activists who change the world are analyzed in this ethnomethodological study that captures the essence of the Spelman College identity.

Thus, I consider student attitudes, ideas, and perceptions regarding the performance of identity articulated by women in hip-hop to demonstrate the negotiation of consciousness and agency in performing consistent, verifiable identities by Spelman students. At Spelman College, women claim a space where their self-definitions promote both awareness and response to assaults made against human rights. Although the Violence Against Women petition critiques all hip-hop music, this thinking focuses on women's self-definition and further utilizes the lack of female artists within the medium to demonstrate the importance of collective agency as a means to better represent women's interests. The work of Spelman women moving toward positive change does not exist only within the vacuum of the college. Once consciousness is awakened, women must exert control over the resources used to communicate information on Black women. By claiming their voices, Black women move to become producers and not just consumers of knowledge.

Through a triangulation of theories and constructs, I explore ways in which the Spelman College student might think on and beyond the Fall 2012 Violence Against Women course petition to ban misogynist music on campus—a fundamental assumption being that Spelman College's commitment to scholar-activism is a foundation of the Spelman social identity.

THINKING THROUGH LITERATURE

A self-making narrative is something of a balancing act. It must, on the one hand, create a conviction of autonomy, that one has a will of one's own, a certain freedom of choice, a degree of possibility. But it must also relate the self to a world of others—to friends and family, to institutions, to the past, to reference groups. But the commitment to others that is implicit in relating oneself to others of course limits our autonomy. We seem virtually unable to live without both, autonomy and commitment, and our lives strive to balance the two. (Bruner 2003:78)

The argument here draws from bodies of sociology, social psychology, and comparative women's studies to conceptualize the role of consciousness and agency in the formation and performance of identity, with particular attention to the constructs of race and gender that uniquely define the proposed investigation site, Spelman College.

IDENTITY

An individual's self-concept, or identity, is informed by membership in a social group, wherein the individual maintains a social identity and the social group itself is the result of social processes reflective of larger social structures. The social group, which consists of individuals who perceive themselves as members of the same social category, acknowledges the process of socially constructing groups where characteristics such as race, class, and gender are differentially categorized to serve sociohistorical political agendas. Both the formation and performance of identity necessarily depend on the sites where information sharing occurs, informing the values, beliefs, attitudes, and behaviors of individual social actors.

THE SELF

The works of William James (1890), George Herbert Mead (1929), Charles Horton Cooley (1902), and Erving Goffman (1955) aid in understanding the co-relationship of subjectivity and objectivity in the construction and performance of identity. This performance is a sustained dynamic of acting and being enacted upon by society through all interactions, formal and informal. Each author posits the belief that the self emerges through interactions with others; as Cooley (1902) asserts in his "Looking-Glass Self," consciousness of self is developed by the judgments of others. Given this sentiment coupled with Goffman's (1955) theory of interaction ritual, the comprehension of the ways in which we interact with others can be understood as face-work, through which individuals seek to save face or create only positive perceptions of self for others to avoid negative judgment.

Both James and Mead focus on the various aspects of the self—examining the "I" as the subjective and active element of self and the "me" as the objective self. In "The Self and Its Selves," James (1890) discusses his theories of the empirical, or social self, also known as "me," which seeks recognition from others, and the sense of personal identity, or the pure ego referred to as "I." It is James's theory that the constituents of the self are the material, social, spiritual, and pure ego, in which the construct is a thinking and feeling subject and object. Mead, however, argues that individual consciousness, which James conceptualizes, is the result of placement within the social world, as the self does not develop in isolation from others but rather is created by society. This signifies the focus on social identity in this research design. In his "The Self, the I, and the Me," Mead (1929) suggests the "me" is the conformed self, much like James's concept of the "I," which is influenced by others' symbols, and conditions the "I," which Mead theorizes is composed of our own natural impulses.

Like James and Mead, Cooley (1902) focuses on the reflexive self in his "Looking-Glass Self," but rather than theorize the constituents of the self as the proceeding two, he expands on Mead's theory of societal influence on the self. Cooley argues an individual's perception of self is based on what they think others perceive of them. Given this theory, knowledge of self is dependent on the constant influence of others, and without such influences an individual is incapable of knowing themselves.

In accordance with Cooley's theory of knowledge of self, based on the perceptions of others, Goffman explains the way in which individuals engage in rituals to maintain self-image. In his "On Face-Work," Goffman (1955) explains, through interaction ritual, individuals seek to create and to maintain face, or positive self-image. As the perceptions of others construct our identities and sense of self, it is important to maintain face, as losing face results in humiliation and is an unacceptable offence toward the group. Individuals are active agents who interpret the ways in which they are acted on and then react in the form of impression management.

These theories of self illustrate the ways in which the construction of self is a reflection of social life.

PERCEPTIONS

A consideration of perception management offers an interesting perspective on the ways in which individuals manage resources in the creation and expression of identity. Brewer (2007) states, "Scholars in this area [cultural consumption] argue that the products we consume are used to construct a sense of self as well as to communicate that self to others. In the most basic sense, the goods we consume are used as tools that allow us to enact our identities" (p. 12). This connects to Belk (1988), who explains music as a tool oftentimes used to control perceptions of identity where, for example, the male rapper performs his role through the possession of goods associated with hip-hop culture—money, cars, and women—that allow for others' successful interpretation of the identity performance.

By definition, the categorization of social identities engages the process of "othering." To elaborate, race, for example, is biologically insignificant but politically momentous when, again for example, voting rights are reserved only for those who fall within the parameters of the racial majority. In the process of social comparisons between the self and other group members, there exists the acknowledgment of group differences (i.e., the intergroup comparison principle) (Brewer 2007). The social category itself is seen as acting on the individual's concept of self, whereby the individual gauges their identity in accordance with the meanings of the particular social category.

SOCIAL IDENTITY AND INTERGROUP RELATIONS

Tajfel (1982) defines social identity as an individual's "knowledge that he belongs to certain social groups together with some emotional and value significance to him of this group membership" (272). Sociology's conflict theory, which assumes preexisting social structures reinforce systems of inequality between the higher social classes, is the basis of social identity. Social identity theory asserts the influence of group membership on social identity, recognizing that members of social groups see themselves as sharing similar attitudes, beliefs, and behaviors (Hogg 2006). The preexisting social structures, or social categories that reinforce systems of inequality and shape the congruent attitudes and beliefs of ingroup members, are often referred to by feminist scholars as interlocking oppressions such as race, class, gender, nationality, religion, and sexual orientation. Hogg and Abrams (1988) explain that the meaning of each social category is derived through a process of comparison with other groups.

This theory has received mixed support from social psychologists who claim the social identity theory too greatly overlooks the role of individualism in identity formation (Turner and Oakes 1986). However, two principles for understanding intergroup relations guide this sociological approach to identity formation. The first relates to social categorization of similar and dissimilar group members, and the second deals with the positivity principle, which explains an individual's positive regard for the group of which one is a member because of its reflection on individual identity.

Ginetta Candelario's *Black Behind the Ears* (2007) utilizes a sample of thirteen hair books presented to Dominican hairstylists in New York City, for the purpose of eliciting narratives about Black, white, and Hispanic standards of beauty. The study employs the method of photo elicitation in which the researcher shows respondents past Polaroid images of themselves and records their introspective narratives, which reveal perceptions of self. Similarly, Candelario's study uses the photos in hairstyle books to explore Dominican associations with white versus Black standards of beauty. Participants also responded to a questionnaire that further explored the respondent's concept of beauty and found that Dominicans more closely associate ideal standards of beauty with those of whites. The images of Black models were described as dirty, big nosed, and large mouthed (Candelario 2007:229). This study illustrates the "positivity principle" of Tajfel's social identity theory (1982), which assumes a positive evaluation of groups to which an individual belongs because individuals tend to have a positive self-image and reflect on similar individuals positively, as a reflection of themselves. Accordingly, the narratives provided by Black female rappers should reflect both a positive social and individual identity.

NARRATIVE

Narrative theories of personality explain that as individuals approach late adolescence, they create internalized narratives of self that serve as a means for recognizing the self as an author able to make sense of the social world through evaluation and categorization (Singer 1995). Narrative theory understands the life story as a construction of identity informed by social, historical, and political contexts. Identity construction, then, raises questions about function and agency (Lizardo and Skiles 2009). In connecting concepts, identity construction is an approach to understanding identity as complex and informed by personality and life story and may be explored through discourse analysis. Discourse analysis focuses not only on method but also on the nature of language and its relationship to the central issues of social science (Wood and Kroger 2000). Discourse analysis explains the combined approaches to discourse that incorporate data collection and analysis with theoretical assumptions. Storytelling is always bound by the social and historical context in which the story is produced. Hence, narratives reflect not only the orator but also the society that yields the conditions ultimately shaping the individual's life experiences. Here, identity is conceptually understood as the vehicle through which life stories are transported and transposed.

CONSCIOUSNESS

American sociologist C. Wright Mills (1959), in his "The Sociological Imagination," theorizes the spirit of the mind as a quality of intellect that recognizes the social and historical meaning of the individual to society. Described as the most fruitful form of self-consciousness (in Lemert 1993:356), this form of human reason carries a certain intimate reality of the self in connection with larger social realities, also referred to as positionality (in Lemert 1993:358). This positionality afforded by the sociological imagination allows for widespread definitions of human reality and enables the ability to understand personal problems as reflective of larger social problems. Through the sociological imagination, one also possesses the ability to regard the present as a minute point in history (in Lemert 1993:356).

INTELLECTUAL POWER

Like Mills (1959), Hofstadter (1963) also grapples with the development of human reason within the historical frame of American fundamentalism and antipostmodernism between the 1950s and 1960s. His 1965 study *Anti-intellectualism in American Life* concludes intellectual power is one of the fundamental manifestations of human dignity and the legitimate end goal of life (p. 46). Using both primary and secondary analysis of political, religious, business, and educational texts, Hofstadter asserts that US "anti-intellectualism" is deeply embedded in eighteenth-century religious institutions, giving the act of knowing a quality of righteousness closest to the divine (p. 28). Hofstadter writes, "Anti-intellectualism is founded on a set of fictional and abstract antagonisms . . . pitted against emotion, character, practicality, and democracy" (pp. 45–46). Intellectualism must be understood as a force that fluctuates and draws power from varying sources, for which the antithetical relationship to anti-intellectualism reflects a set of ideas and attitudes toward a "life of the mind" (p. 5). Intelligence is then understood for its practical ability to meet clearly set goals, while intellect on the other hand represents a critical, creative, and contemplative side of mind (p. 25). Social attitudes and political behavior, therefore, create the atmosphere in which thinking takes place.

The works of Du Bois (1903), C. W. Mills (1959), and Hofstadter (1963) critique the historical formation of American intellect—or a lack thereof—and position modes of ideation within the context of American anti-intellectualism as a form of political domination. Politics must then be understood beyond a system of governance, by which a set of ideas enforce control, toward a spirit of civic engagement and conscious decision making. It is a quality or sense of involvement in the processes of exercising and experiencing power or powerlessness. The development of a sociological imagination therefore requires the deeply critical (sociohistorical and methodological) engagement of ideas and their formation through time.

Ironically, in the current age of information, ideas seem even more confined to social groups, despite potential for universal connectivity. Race, class, gender, and other marginal characteristics circumscribe social spaces and tend to stifle the development of the sociological imagination. As Nicholas Carr (2008) explains in his article "Is Google Making Us Stupid?," "media are not passive channels of information. They supply the stuff of thought, but they also shape the process of thought" (p. 57). The ability to gauge one's positionality enables the critical consciousness through which individuals speak back to the constraints of power and develop an oppositional voice. So, politics of the sociological imagination involve the critical work of developing and transforming ideas—activism. This requires the ability to identify those resources that repress power by fostering anti-intellectualism.

Central to the discussion of the politics of the sociological imagination rests the concept of power—and by extension liberation. Often expressed as a quality of authority or an ability to control, power extends itself to the capacity to achieve objectives and therefore calls into question whose objectives and what purposes dominant ideologies serve. The systematic control of American conscientiousness signals a decree of anti-intellectualism for the purpose of antiliberation. The "massification" of society as C. Wright Mills (1959) posits, disturbs the "free ebb and flow of discussion" characteristic of the "Great American Public" (p. 298) where participants deemed equal develop opinions. Instead, the dictates of mass media relate to individuals what they should think by normalizing the experiences of a "majority" to the lives of minorities. The mass production, or perhaps the "massification," of media has indeed contributed to the tendency to maintain a set of thoughts and ideas consistent with popular culture, where the public functions as a mass and no longer forms critically conscious opinions, instead opting to think in a reductionist fashion. By engaging the very ideologies that inform relationships to the social world, each author not only questions the institutions that systematically reinforce power dynamics in the form of cultural hegemony but also challenges individual and collective agency in the form of public discourse that transforms the framing of ideas.

KNOWLEDGE IN HIERARCHICAL POWER STRUCTURES

Both Dorothy Smith (1974) and Simone de Beauvoir (1949) examine the ways in which identity and awareness of self are shaped by hegemonic constructions such as gender and race roles. Smith's (1974) "Knowing a Society from Within: A Woman's Standpoint" conceptualizes standpoint as the objective knowledge of one's position in society, such as society's orientation toward male privilege. Similar to the work of Du Bois (1903), De Beauvoir's (1949) "Woman as Other" explains double-consciousness as women's understanding of self through objectification, negotiating identity in accordance with the perceived male gaze (Steinem 1990). This double-consciousness is sustained by media exploitation and marketing strategies that influence the ways women gauge accepted roles and thus the ways they present themselves according to these hegemonic standards.

AGENCY

At the heart of intellectual work, Du Bois (1924) states, is the search for truth through reason and justice (p. 29). Hofstadter (1963) personifies intellect as the "spirit of the mind" by which the imagination engages in play and piety for creative and humanistic learning (pp. 29, 33). Such a form of liberal, progressive, and radical thought (p. 38), intellectualism is often the scapegoat for a tradition of "Know-Nothingism" that views intellect as a form of power and privilege (pp. 34, 36). In what Hofstadter (1963) refers to as "continental isolation, village society, the Protestant denominations, and a flourishing industrial capitalism" (p. 42), he suggests, "it had been our hate as a nation not to have ideologies but to be one" (p. 43). However, in the "revolt against modernity," Hofstadter explains social phenomena such as the "Great Inquisition" (1950s) as less about communists and more about revenge against "liberals, New Dealers, reformers, internationalists, intellectuals, and a Republican administration that failed to reverse liberal policies" (p. 41) by which communism was the weapon of fear deployed through "advertising, radio, the mass magazines, and the advance of popular education" (p. 123). The closed access to means of production in the mass media invokes what is referred to as the technologies of the intellect, understood as the relationship between technology and the ability to form ideas. The national deployment of a rhetoric rooted in fear of the new, under the guise of anti-intellectualism, creates stagnancy in the ability to construct thoughts and results in the question, "What would thinking cause?" (Hofstadter 1963:55).

In his 1924 commencement address to Fisk University, Du Bois challenges the nature of "Negro" education in institutions controlled by white planters. He declares the academy responsible for the development of human reason and dissents against the undemocratic rule that governed Fisk's campus in 1924, influenced heavily by the interests of white financiers. In this analysis, Du Bois asserts freedom of spirit, self-knowledge, and recognition of the truth, the spirit with which the academy must be equipped. Of freedom of spirit, he explains a freedom from the power of repression, understood as an imposed silence and censorship (Foucault 1978:4, 17) and suggests in its response, the staging of protest, by talking back to power structures with an oppositional voice. Illustrative of such protest, he offers the example of Harvard alumni protesting the ban of "Negroes" and Jews to the university and likens the public voice of protest to that described by C. Wright Mills's (1956) concept of the public.

Of this, Du Bois stresses the importance of dialogue and discussion to achieve publicity or a public visibility by which the forms of repression demonstrated at Fisk are made public information. Following publicity, Du Bois seeks the mobilization of the alumni into an organization and, finally, demands elective representation of the group on the decision-making boards (p. 82). To this end, Du Bois sees fit the revival of the university newspaper *The Fisk Herald* as a means to communicate intellectual reason (p. 84). On self-knowledge, Du Bois explains the development of personhood, particularly among Blacks who endured the inhumane conditions of Jim Crow. Self-knowledge, he explains, enables the individual to understand themself as possessing power (p. 69). Truth he expresses as a process and search, much like Hofstadter's (1963) conceptualization of truth as a quest for new uncertainties (p. 30). Hofstadter likens his concept of truth to human reason, where truth and those "uncertainties," which are held as factual, develop within the dynamics of power.

The university, as Du Bois suggests, is responsible for the cultivation of human reason as an institution of education—for which education is understood as the process of seeking truth through knowledge, as a form of freedom (p. 83). Education is seen as the learning property of the community, and society is duty-bound to support the endeavors of knowledge production (p. 81), yet as C. Wright Mills (1959) explains, the quest for educational enlightenment, and by extension, liberation, cannot be achieved without the actualization of the sociological imagination.

POWER IN ACTION

From the conflict paradigm of sociology arises critical theory, which encourages social change through its critique of knowledge and power relations in contemporary societies (Wallace and Wolf 2006:102). From this framework, French sociologist Pierre Bourdieu (1990)—and American anthropologist Oscar Lewis (1966)—theorize the cultural reproduction of power relations through an analysis of social stratification and the practice of false consciousness that, through symbolic violence, inversely affects cultural capital and thus social mobility; Billingsley (1973), Ramos-Zayas (2006), and Trueba (2002) are all grappling with the transformations of post–twentieth century American society through a rearticulation of the values that inform cultural and social capital, facilitated by an engagement in oppositional scholarly dialogue with predominant knowledge structures (Hill-Collins 2008) in order to restructure power relations.

Each scholar analyzes not only the social construction of knowledge but also the ability to exert agency within and between social spaces, ultimately restructuring the social conditions (race-class-gender-citizenship dynamics) that produce advantage. In the tradition of empiricism, these phenomenological and ethnomethodological studies problematize the human experience. By use of qualitative research methods such as participant observation and field notes, each captures the subjective nature of identity performance within autonomous and objective fields (Bourdieu 1990) conferring various forms of symbolic capital. Thus, all action depends on the social location, or standpoint (Smith 1990), of the actor whose knowledge and experiences are shaped by the interplay of various subject positions and whose potential for agency, in the form of talking back to power structures—as seen in the works of Billingsley (1973), Ramos-Zayas (2006), and Trueba (2007)—demonstrates the cultivated sociological imagination (Mills 1959), which challenges the production of knowledge within hierarchical power structures (Hill-Collins 1998:17).

PRAXIS AS ACTUALIZATION

The works of Patricia Hill-Collins and William Gay (both in O'Toole, Schiffman, and Kiter Edwards 2007), as well as Johnnetta Betsch Cole and Beverly Guy-Sheftall (2003), support the protest of both covert and overt forms of institutional violence. As William Gay explains in "The Reality of Linguistic Violence Against Women" (2007), language is an institution from which covert manifestations of power are reinforced (p. 468). Deborah Cameron states, "Sexist language teaches us what those who use it and disseminate it think women's places ought to be: second-class citizens, neither seen nor heard, eternal sex-objects and personifications of evil" (in O'Toole, Schiffman, and Kiter Edwards 2007:470). The language alone signifies deeper issues of cultural violence. However, sexist language is given potency by sexism, which carries with it the possibility of violent force. Gay (in O'Toole, Schiffman, and Kiter Edwards 2007) further explains, "When we realize the important connection between language and consciousness, we can also see how changing our language can lead to not only changed thought but also changed action" (p. 472). The linguistic violence demonstrated in hip-hop music, especially, derives its power from the attitudes it reflects, words that actively erode marginalized communities from within, through an embedded abuse of the self-image (Betsch Cole and Guy-Sheftall 2003:205, 209, 214).

Devaluation and violence are twin enemies of Black women in the media, where women's bodies are portrayed as half-naked, promiscuous, man-hungry, and lacking in self-esteem, which contributes to the internalization of sexism (Betsch Cole and Guy-Sheftall 2003:199). The domination, control, and objectification of Black women's bodies, Patricia Hill-Collins argues (in O'Toole, Schiffman, and Kiter Edwards 2007), derives from the sexual objectification of Black bodies by white men during the nineteenth century, upon which racist and sexist politics reinforced oppression (p. 395). The reduction of Black women to animals through the pornographic imagery of misogynistic hip-hop and other forms of popular culture reinforces the legacy of slavery assigned to Black women whose bodies are cheaply bought and sold as the breeding ground for male sexual exploits (Betsch Cole and Guy-Sheftall 2003:200).

Feminist theorist bell hooks (1994) explains education as the practice of freedom, as it develops intellect for engagement in praxis, that is applying action to knowledge by practicing ideas, producing change in the world through activism. Du Bois (1924), Mills (1959), Hofstadter (1963), and Hill-Collins and Gay (both in O'Toole, Schiffman, and Kiter Edwards 2007), as well as Betsch Cole and Guy-Sheftall are all grappling with the role of human reason in human affairs by theorizing politics of knowledge and power. Each explains the spirit of the mind as a quality of ideas that develop within the context of power systems and therefore sees knowledge as a product of power from which the means of education derive their structure. The function of the sociological imagination is therefore the development of intellect and transformative (oppositional) voice outside the confines of power. Each scholar not only analyzes the American construction of knowledge through technologies of the intellect but also further deconstructs notions of power as legitimized through practices of communication. Education is therefore understood as a means by which to achieve self-actualization, challenging notions of domination and marginalization by understanding one's placement in the social world.

The actualization of the sociological imagination not only locates biographical and historical sites as impactful social forces in private and public life; it cultivates a critical consciousness by which individuals learn, question, reflect, and engage in the process of meaning making. The sociological imagination, therefore, extends itself beyond awareness of sociohistorical positionality, toward the political activism attendant to power and liberation.

HABITUS

Pierre Bourdieu seeks to reconcile the relationship between constructions imposed by social structures and people's practiced and practical action according to their perception of the social world. He bases his empiricism on the understanding that the structures constitutive of the social world also construct consciousness and therefore curtail agency. In *The Logic of Practice*, he (Bourdieu 1990) explains:

> The conditionings associated with a particular class of conditions of existence produce habitus, systems of durable, transposable dispositions, structured structures predisposed to function as structuring structures, that is, as principles which generate and organise practices and representations that can be objectively adapted to their outcomes without presupposing a conscious aiming at ends or express mastery of the operations necessary in order to attain them. Objectively "regulated" and "regular" without being in any way the product of obedience to rules, they can be collectively orchestrated without being the product of the organising action of a conductor. (p. 53)

The habitus that Bourdieu characterizes here explains the way in which social relations become concrete in spatialized form (LeFebvre 1991), or rather the way in which fields exhibit structured spaces of dominant and subordinate positions based on the amounts and types of capital structuring the space (Bourdieu 1990). The habitus is always oriented toward practical function, from which presumably common-sense behaviors reinforce the social, historical, and political agendas that produced the field. The habitus can also be explained as a practical conclusion to past experiences. Here, the practical is understood as the "already realized ends, procedures to follow, paths to take" that construct the social world. The society therefore constitutes the subject, to which human thought and action are the objects, or tools, of practice that legitimate the habitus (Bourdieu 1990:53).

Most critical to this theory of practice, which explains knowledge and agency as mere performances of historical power relations, is the concept of capital. As in economics, capital refers to wealth. Social capital refers to positive social outcomes, such as useful information, personal relationships, and the capacity to organize groups, that allow people to draw on resources from other members of the networks to which they belong. Cultural capital, on the other hand, refers to the "way in which tastes, and perceptions of what is beautiful or valuable, differ between different classes—and how the elite constantly distances itself from popular taste" (Bourdieu 1990:113). However, the social and cultural capital that constitute social location within the field are reproduced through behavioral patterns that often conceal the true power structures and interests working in the field and do not offer a model for liberation.

The theorists regarded throughout this writing offer useful tools of analysis to explain power relations, constructions of knowledge, and by extension agency. Here, the dimensions of political mobilization and social transformation are contextualized as critical to the negotiation of identity, while self-actualization facilitates upward mobility by challenging existing power structures.

HIP-HOP AND FEMINISM

Joan Morgan's (2011) theory of hip-hop feminism asserts women's rights in the hip-hop generation. This wave of feminism was wrought by the civil rights and women's movements for those born between 1965 and 1984, who struggled between "the contradictions of loving an art that is reluctant to include you; loving men who at times, refuse to portray you in your totality; and rejecting sexual objectification while actively and proudly embracing your sexuality. Although hip-hop feminism has gone through phases, it has always, at some level, dealt with these incongruities" (Morgan 2011:2). The goal of hip-hop feminism is not to debate the misogyny that inarguably exists in hip-hop. Instead, the goal is to explore the progressive identities of Black women who are able to freely express themselves, without the backlash and cries of "respectability" politics. Present work applies hip-hop feminism to the lives of women belonging to generation Y.

The push here was a synthesized literature review that explains identity as an agentive process by which to engage subjective and objective positionality and to capacitate meaning making. The dynamics of race and gender that uniquely characterize the space at Spelman College offer sites through which to deconstruct hierarchical power structures and enter the process of self-definition. Thus, doers of identity control actualize intellectual and activist potential and in so doing construct verifiable identities to which meanings and perceptions affirm the practices of liberation from repression and create the conditions for meaningful social change.

The antimisogyny petition (2012) at Spelman College therefore offers a useful example of identity verification, where the student body of scholar-activists generated a change in music consumption practices in order to uphold the institutional standard of women's empowerment and additionally reclaimed their right to control the messages that enter their spaces. This analysis offers two important contributions to the literature: first, I introduce identity verification as an agentive process that enables meaning making, and second, I offer a contemporary discourse of the articulated social identity by Black women in hip-hop lyricism.

HERE AND NOW AND IDENTITY ORCHESTRATION

In conceptualizing the role of critical consciousness and agency in the formation and performance of identity, the theory of identity orchestration—specifically, identity dilemma articulation, unadulterated presentation of self, and burden of proof assumption—proves useful. Following is a pass at communicating how self-aspects and their overlap contribute to varying levels of self-complexity. Moreover, there is the positioning of the ways in which Black people habitually leverage consciousness and agency in order to combat matrices of domination. The assumption is that the role of resistance to expressions of racial violence are essential in orchestrating a balanced identity.

AGAIN, CRITICAL CONSCIOUSNESS

Identity orchestration establishes the universal context of racism (Jones 2003) as a factor in figuring the psychological negotiation of Black identification (Rice 2008). This epistemological/ontological orientation highlights the tension between structure and agency that Black individuals negotiate in their orchestration of racialized self-concepts into a balanced identity. Again, while social structures shape individuals, individuals also shape social structures. The dialectic between structure and agency underscores the influence of each construct on the other. While social actors employ an active role in defining meaning, hegemonic norms impede the ability of marginalized groups to experience transformation without generating greater shifts in public consciousness that become reflected in the cultural resources used to communicate meaning (Foucault 1978; Smith 1974).

Critical consciousness (Freire 2000) describes the ability to recognize systems of oppression and to take action against them. This type of awareness can be thought of as a complex process wherein changes in knowledge and perspectives lead to shifts in behavior. As such, critical consciousness requires awareness of the self that extends to historical, cultural, and political contexts. This understanding of the self in connection with larger social realities is known as positionality (Lemert 1993); within the universal context of racism, positionality allows the individual to understand personal problems as reflective of larger social problems—and also enables the individual to engage with presupposed notions of reality. Identity is conceptually understood as the vehicle through which life stories are transported and transposed; it is also the site that serves as a litmus test for notions of reality that repress the individual as either verifiable or merely reinforcing hierarchical power structures intended to maintain the status quo.

Identity orchestration requires the individual to not only reflect on realities but also to intervene. It is this intervening that allows for transformation as the individual manages perceptions of self within the context of universal oppressions such as racism and sexism. As a result of challenging oppressive conditions at the micro level, the individual generates a new understanding of themselves and other group members and contributes to the reauthoring of narratives surrounding the group(s) to which they belong. The goal of critical consciousness is not only to develop a critical awareness of the assumptions that shape interpretations of reality inequity but also to exercise choices that either sustain or alter that reality.

AGENCY

Essential to the theory of identity orchestration is the presupposition that agency is an important part of identity development (Winston in Rice 2008). Central to the concept of agency is that of social structures and the dialectic between the two; social structures (such as race, gender, and social class) shape individuals, just as individuals shape these structures. While agency refers to the actions taken by people to express individual power, it is imperative to recognize structural constraints that limit decision making and behavior, especially in the context of pervasive structures such as racism and sexism. The cultural reproduction of power relations that reinforce social stratification hinge on false consciousness and symbolic violence (Bourdieu 1984). The goal of agency, then, is to engage in oppositional dialogue with predominant knowledge structures in order to rearticulate norms and values and to restructure power relations that maintain the status quo (Hill-Collins 2008).

As a function of identity orchestration, agency describes the exertion of power within social spaces that reproduces advantage and disadvantage. The process of orchestration involves talking back to power structures and challenging the knowledge produced within them (Hill-Collins 2008). Accordingly, agency is understood to be the utilization of consciousness and power to engage in the work of protest so that the individual can achieve homeostasis, or balance. Therefore, coordinating orchestration requires the individual to not only be active and engaged in their personal identity but also to feel a sense of connection and commitment to their social identity. The individual expression of agency contributes to the power and action of the collective.

SELF-COMPLEXITY

The theoretical framework of intersectionality posits multiple social categories (e.g., race, gender, socioeconomic status) that intersect at the micro level of individual experience to reflect interlocking systems of privilege and oppression at the macro, social-structural level (e.g., racism, sexism, heterosexism). The core tenet of intersectionality is the notion that social identities are not independent but instead are multiple and interdependent. The perspective asserts that race and gender constitute each other such that one identity alone cannot explain oppression without the intersection of the other identity. Double-consciousness (Du Bois 1903), then, extends beyond the negotiation of Black cultural and American norms to include the ways in which Black women also negotiate patriarchy and the male gaze (Steinem 1990). The negotiation of multiple bifurcated identities has been coined "double jeopardy" and describes the dual discrimination of racism and sexism experienced by Black women (Beale 1970). Research suggests Black women place equal importance on their race and gender identities, and the unified identity of Black-woman is rated as more important than either of the single identities (Settles 2006). In addition to examining racial identity, racialized gender identity plays an important role in how Black women define themselves, as race and gender are both interconnecting and important components of the self.

ORCHESTRATION

Narrative theory understands the life story as a construction of identity informed by social, historical, and political contexts. Accordingly, identity orchestration raises questions about function and agency of individuals (Lizardo and Skiles 2009).

The following section expands the application of the identity orchestration framework to include Black women in order to further demonstrate the model's utility in understanding multiple negotiated identities and necessarily incorporates gender and racialized gender performance into the dialogue.

In October 2020, hip-hop phenom Megan Thee Stallion penned an op-ed in the *New York Times* discussing calls to "protect Black women." In this piece, she provides a complex analysis, integrating both her race and gender identities into an orchestrated balance, as demonstrated in three expressions of identity orchestration.

IDENTITY DILEMMA ARTICULATION

Identity dilemma articulation describes a form of identity orchestration wherein an individual recognizes a conflict among their identities. The misalignment between the individual's culture and structural norms produces a dilemma (Rice 2008). Here, the narrative provided by a Black woman extends the race self-complexity illustrated by double-consciousness (Du Bois 1903) to further examine the psychological processes wherein an individual negotiates multiple bifurcated identities simultaneously—specifically racism and sexism.

> From the moment we begin to navigate the intricacies of adolescence, we feel the weight of contradictory expectations and misguided preconceptions. Many

of us begin to put too much value to how we are seen by others. That's if we are seen at all. . . . The issue is even more intense for Black women, who struggle against stereotypes and are seen as angry or threatening when we try to stand up for ourselves and our sisters. There's not much room for passionate advocacy if you are a Black woman. . . . Beyond threats to our health and lives, we confront so much judgment and so many conflicting messages on a daily basis. (Thee Stallion 2020)

Megan describes the complex process of recognizing a dichotomy between the articulated personal identity and the imposed social identity. The individual operates as both self and other—both Black and woman in a context that marginalizes both identities. For example, Black women are often stereotyped as "mammy" figures as well as sexually promiscuous and aggressive (Brown-Collins 1993). Contrastingly, white women are often portrayed as hardworking and "feminine" (Cox 1993). Black men are also stereotyped as being violent and suspicious (Hunter & Davis 1992). Stereotypes about Black women are uniquely bound by both race and gender, where stereotypes associated with Blackness and womanhood compound—the Black woman is stereotyped as aggressive along racial lines and as nurturing along gender lines, though the notion of being nurturing is juxtaposed with being aggressive and suggests misalignment between both sets of stereotypes.

This recognition elucidates the dialectic between the personal and the social. Identity dilemma articulation, then, describes the bridging between the individual and society. Balancing the identity into a coherent whole, or bridging the two divergent selves, requires the ability to critically engage the social structure and adopt that which serves the individual and reject that which misaligns with the understanding of self. This is a radical act that requires the individual to reject as truth that which has been imposed by society. The individual employs critical consciousness in order to legitimize or to challenge the dynamics of power and status that inform racism and sexism.

UNADULTERATED PRESENTATION OF SELF

Unadulterated presentation of self is a form of identity orchestration that focuses on the agency of individuals as they present the self as uncompromised by social-structural systems of racism—and in this case sexism as well. This form of orchestration demonstrates the individual proving to self the validity of identifying as Black and woman. "The remarks about how I choose to present myself have often been judgmental and cruel, with many assuming that I'm dressing and performing for the male gaze. When women choose to capitalize on our sexuality, to reclaim our *own* power, like I have, we are vilified and disrespected" (Thee Stallion 2020).

Individuals not only refract the social structure but also reconstruct it. As Megan explains, it is an exercise of power to present the self as desired, despite the mainstream critiques that seek to invalidate her identity expression. Despite racism and sexism, which inform assumptions about how she should show up in the world, Megan describes an act of resistance. She is able to "choose" to "reclaim [her] own power" and demonstrates the complexities of critical consciousness and critical agency. This reclamation demonstrates an essential form of speaking back to power structures that often overlook and silence Black women (Fryberg & Townsend 2008). An unadulterated presentation of self describes the process by which individuals extend control to shape their performance and to control how others view them. This can also be described as impression management, where the behaviors expressed by the individual seek to create a desired impression (Goffman 1955).

BURDEN OF PROOF

Burden of proof assumption deals with the ways in which individuals confirm or disconfirm stereotypes.

> If we dress in fitted clothing, our curves become a topic of conversation not only on social media, but also in the workplace. The fact that Serena Williams, the greatest athlete in any sport ever, had to defend herself for wearing a bodysuit at the 2018 French Open is proof positive of how misguided the obsession with Black women's bodies is. . . . I would know. I've received quite a bit of attention for appearance as well as my talent. I choose my own clothing. Let me repeat: I choose what I wear, not because I am trying to appeal to men, but because I am showing pride in my appearance, and a positive body image is central to who I am as a woman and a performer. (Thee Stallion 2020)

Here, Megan addresses the policing of Black women's bodies and the attendant stereotyping of Black women as sexually promiscuous. The examples of herself and Serena Williams illustrate the ways in which stereotypes infringe on Black women, even overshadowing their accomplishments. Though hegemonic norms constrain Black women through the imposition of stereotypes, both Megan and Williams take an active role in redefining the meaning surrounding their identities, which are not limited to the physical. In choosing to present unadulterated versions of themselves *and* in participating in the disruption of stereotypes by speaking openly about the repression, both women seek to generate shifts in public consciousness.

The process of identity orchestration challenges notions of domination and marginalization by not only locating biographical and historical sites as impactful social forces in private and public life but also cultivating a critical consciousness by which individuals learn, question, reflect, and engage in the process of meaning making. Identity orchestration extends itself beyond awareness of sociohistorical positionality toward balance of an identity that is oppositional and defiant in the face of oppressive contexts such as racism and sexism.

Identity orchestration describes an agentive process that invokes a complex interplay of identity, knowledge, power, and protest wherein individuals reflect on positionality and engage in meaning making. The universal context of racism described in *Balance* (Rice 2008) offers a site through which to deconstruct hierarchical power structures and to understand the process of self-definition employed by Black people.

Thus, doers of identity control and actualize intellectual and activist potentiality and in so doing construct verifiable identities to which meanings and perceptions affirm the practices of liberation from repression and create the conditions for meaningful social change.

REFERENCES

Beale, F. (1971). *Double jeopardy: To be black and female*. Radical Education Project.

Bourdieu, P. (1984). *Distinction: A social critique of the judgment of taste*. Cambridge, MA: Harvard University Press.

Bruner, Jerome. (2003). "The narrative creation of self." In *Making stories: Law, literature, life*. Cambridge, MA: Harvard University Press.

Cole, J. B., & Guy-Sheftall, B. (2003). *Gender talk: The struggle for women's equality in African American communities*. New York: Ballantine Books.

Collins, P. (1998). *Fighting words: Black women and the search for justice*. Minneapolis: University of Minnesota Press.

Cooley, Charles Horton. (1902). "The looking-glass self." In *Social theory: The multicultural and classic readings*, edited by C. Lemert (189). Boulder, CO: Westview Press.

Du Bois, W. E. B. (1903). *The souls of black folk*. Oxford: Oxford University Press.

Du Bois, W. E. B. (1924). *The education of Black people: Ten critiques, 1906–1960*. Amherst: University of Massachusetts Press.

Foucault, Michel. (1978). *The history of sexuality*. New York: Pantheon Books.

Freire, Paulo. (2000). *Pedagogy of the oppressed*. New York: Continuum.

Fryberg, S. A., & Townsend, S. S. M. (2008). The psychology of invisibility. In G. Adams, M. Biernat, N. R. Branscombe, C. S. Crandall, & L. S. Wrightsman (Eds.), Commemorating Brown: The social psychology of racism and discrimination (173–93). New York: American Psychological Association.

Goffman, Erving. (1955). "On face-work." In *Social theory: The multicultural and classic readings*, edited by C. Lemert (338–42). Boulder, CO: Westview Press.

Hill-Collins, Patricia. (2008). *Black feminist thought: Knowledge, consciousness, and the politics of empowerment.* East Sussex, UK: Psychology Press.

hooks, bell. (1994). *Teaching to transgress: Education as the practice of freedom.* New York: Routledge.

Lemert, C. C. (1993). *Social theory: The multicultural and classic readings.* Boulder, CO: Westview Press.

Lizardo, Omar, & Skiles, Sara. (2009). "Highbrow omnivorousness on the small screen? Cultural industry systems and patterns of cultural choice in Europe." *Poetics, 37*(1), 23.

Rice, David Wall. (2008). *Balance: Advancing Identity Theory by Engaging the Black Male Adolescent.* Lanham, MD: Lexington Books.

Settles, I. H. (2006). Use of an intersectional framework to understand Black women's racial and gender identities. *Sex Roles, 54*(9–10), 589–601.

Smith, Dorothy. (1974). "Knowing a society from within: A woman's standpoint." In *Social theory: The multicultural and classic readings*, edited by C. Lemert (167–72). Boulder, CO: Westview Press.

Steinem, Gloria. (1990). "Sex, lies, and advertising." In *Women, culture, and society: A reader*, edited by B. Balliet and P. McDaniel (173–83). Dubuque, IA: Kendall/Hunt.

Thee Stallion, Megan. (2020). "Megan Thee Stallion: Why I speak up for Black women." *New York Times*, October 13, 2020. https://www.nytimes.com/2020/10/13/opinion/megan-thee-stallion-black-women.html.

Afterword

Balance at Fourteen

Biko Harris Rice

I'm a fourteen-year-old kid who loves to play basketball—and to talk about it, mainly through my podcast, *Opinionated Basketball*, with my friend Charles. I also love listening to music. You might hear me bumping Kanye or Jay-Z one day, Lil Durk or Tyler, The Creator, the next. I have an awesome family. Both of my parents are college professors, and I have a little brother who's in the first grade; he is an intelligent and hilarious person.

Over the past year, I started focusing on basketball more, quitting soccer right when COVID hit and then progressively getting better at the sport. I'm currently in the eighth grade, having transferred to an independent school at the beginning of my seventh-grade year.

The new school is drastically different from the one I grew up in and left. My brother is still there and so are my closest friends. My new school was very welcoming when I started in person, after COVID precautions lifted a bit. In considering my decision to leave my old school, I thought and still think it a good decision. I do feel a certain way in leaving friends who are still there; however, if I went back in time to that moment when I chose to switch schools, I would do it again.

I know I'm fortunate to be able to go to such a good school, where I can still be myself and not have to worry about anything socially. I've made friends with great people, through basketball mostly. Our basketball team was solid last year and is even better this year (because I am starting). I have way better relationships with the teachers at my present school than at the one prior. And even though the work has gotten more challenging, it's easier to complete now that I have teachers who show they care about my long-term academic success.

My favorite classes are Latin and science. I also really like civics and band. Overall, school is great. The students are cool, basketball is fun, classes are good, and the teachers are very helpful.

If I'm not at home or at school, you can find me at practice with my AAU team, in a basketball game, or practicing in my backyard. Basketball is *the* best sport, and so much of my life is centered around it. After my school season last year, I realized that I desperately needed to get better. I joined a team that two of my friends, Dylan and Vincent, were on, and ever since I have gotten better and more confident on the court. We've had a game every Saturday it seems like, and they are a great way for me to stay in shape and to develop my mind.

Again, I also love talking about basketball on my podcast with my guy, Charles. I'm able to express any opinion that I have regarding the game. We usually record once a week. We started the podcast about a year and a half ago, and both of us have expanded our knowledge of the game through each other's perspectives. Charles is someone I'm very close with, and even though we live in two different states, we talk, text, and play video games frequently. I've known Charles since I was a baby.

I'm proud of the friendships that I've made with good people. As I stated earlier, I'm cool with all of the guys on my school team, but I also live around a lot of guys that go to my old school, and who I play outside with whenever we get the chance. I am also close with my AAU teammates, who I see multiple times a week. We're a bunch of very silly people and never have any problems with each other, which is crazy to me considering we are very competitive.

With my parents playing different kinds of music all the time, it's always been a focal point in my life. I listen to music a lot, mainly rap. It can get me hyped up for something, and it can help me finish my homework or just relax. I am able to connect with the people that I listen to because they are examples of talented (mostly) Black people that have made a great living with a talent they love. I respect many of the artists for that, even though some of the topics they share might not be the most kid-friendly.

None of the things that I do would be possible without my parents and my brother. They have shaped me as a person and provide unconditional support. My mom is selfless and the nicest person I know. She is always doing work but somehow finds time to do things with me and my brother. She is the reason why I am on my AAU team, and she coordinates almost everything that I do. My mother is the very definition of an excellent human being.

My dad is the coolest person I know. People say that I am just like him, which is a great compliment in my opinion. He always has a clean pair of shoes on, with his socks pulled up like he's an NFL player, and a jacket or two or three on, depending on what the weather is like. He is a hard worker too, although he spends a lot of time in his den either watching TV or sleeping to make up for writing and thinking until very early in the morning. My dad is the person I can talk to about anything, and most of the advice that he gives me ends up being very helpful.

My brother is a mix of me and my dad. He is the happiest person I know and is always there for me when I need him. He is very intelligent, like I stated in the beginning, but he, of course, gets on my nerves from time to time. We have a great relationship regardless, and he is a great brother.

Basketball, school, music, friends, and family—not necessarily in that order—are very important things in my life. My dad explains them as identities that I orchestrate. Whatever the case, they are each their own thing but are connected because of their significance to me. They give me a balance, as I can always have one or more of them to lean on when I need them the most. Each activity or thing *or identity* has uniquely made up the self I am today, and I understand that I am blessed because of them.

Index

Abdul-Rauf, Mahmoud, 203
Abebe, Nitsuh, 21
Abrams, D., 265
Academic Politicalization (Gordon, E. T.), 118n20
academic success, 155–57, 163–68, 169, 171, 281; Black churches echoing, 160–62; causal variables for, 158–59
Accenture (firm), 94, 96
achievement. *See* success
activism, 3, 23, 108, 255, 257, 259, 272; by Black athletes, 202–3, 206–10
activity-based educational setting, 158
acute identity expression, 16, 89, 149–51, 192; by Black men, 235, 237–38; in diss tracks, 43–44; by Rakim, 18, 24; unadulterated presentation of self compared to, 42–43
adaptive identity, 8, 9–11, 87, 170–71; of Black men, 233–34
Adidas, 226
admissions, higher education, 137–40, 141, 143
adolescence, Black, 16, 19–20; college personal statements and, 138–39, 144–45
aesthetics, Black athlete, 201–3
affirmative action, 143, 146–47

Africa, 58, 60, 114, 243–44. *See also specific countries*
Africare (NGO), 96
agency, 10, 69, 114, 127, 173, 266–68; collective, 255, 257, 259–60, 266; of Ice Cube, 18–19; identity orchestration and, 274–78; in racialized societies, 61–62
Air Force Ones (Nike shoes), 228
Air Jordans 11 (Nike shoes), 112, 116n5
Akron, Ohio, 193–94
Algorithms of Oppression (Noble), 82
Ali, Muhammad, 202–3, 206
"All Black Everything" (Peterson TEDx Talk), 117
Allison, Sophia Nahli, 80–81
All Three Coasts Hip-Hop Festival, 4–5
American culture, 7–8, 56, 148, 206, 209
American dream, 23, 85
American Idol (television show), 31, 33
AmeriKKKa's Most Wanted, 15, 19, 20
Andersen Consulting, 92–94
André 3000, 40
And Still I Rise (documentary), 102
Angelou, Maya, 102–3, 107, 244
anticipated exhaustion, empathy and, 181–83

visibility, 18, 24–25, 112, 149, 269; hip-hop and, 16, 17, 42–43; in "Otis" music video, 22–23
Vossler, J. J., 146
vulnerability, 20, 43–44; of Black men, 235, 237

Waddell, Celeste, 99
Wade, Dwayne, 192
Wade Gayles, Gloria, 93
Waka Flocka, 42
Wale (rapper), 33
Wall, Arthur A., III, xx
Wall, Arthur Albert ("Buddy"), xvii–xxi
Wall, Arthur Allen, xx
Wall, Brenda, xx, 115, 118n17
Wall, Evelyn Jones, xx–xxi
Wall, Stokely, xxi, 121–24
Wallace, Bubba, 216
Washington, DC, xvii
Washington Post, 251
Watch the Throne, 14, 15–16, 21–23
West, Donda, 21
West, Kanye (Ye), 14, 20–24
West Africa, 114–15, 245
West Coast hip-hop, 15, 40
white men, 93, 123–24, 212–13, 269
whiteness, 67, 102, 244; beauty standards and, 81–82
white people, 101–2; appropriation by, 111, 112; journalism by, 106–7, 189–90, 250, 252–53; as teachers, 122–24
white privilege, xix, 143, 213
white supremacy, xviii, 112, 125, 130, 201, 241

white women, 106, 133, 276
Williams, Saul, 203, 226
Williams, Serena, 277–78
Williamson, A., 31
Willoughby, T., 168
Winston, Cynthia E., 14, 28n6, 60, 69, 82
The Wire (television show), 27n2
Wisconsin, 217
WNBA. *See* Women's National Basketball League
"Woman as Other" (de Beauvoir), 266
Women's National Basketball League (WNBA), 203, 216, 217–18
World War II, 212, xxin3
Wormsley, Alisha, 77
writing, 4, 33, 89, 106, 108, 111, 116; by Angelou, 102–3; high-stakes, 137–39, 145, 149, 151. *See also* personal statements, college

X, Malcolm (El-Hajj Malik El-Shabazz), 85, 103, 202
"Xplosion," 37
Xxxtentacion, 42

Yahoo Music, 39
yardrunning, Nike initiative, 225, 227, 229
Ye. *See* West, Kanye
"You Don't Want Drama," 43
Young Money Radio, 35

Zimmerman, B. J., 30
Zimmerman, George, 111, 116n2, 116n3

About the Contributors

DAVID WALL RICE

David Wall Rice is professor of psychology at Morehouse College and principal investigator of the Identity, Art, and Democracy Lab. David graduated from Morehouse with a bachelor of arts degree in psychology and earned a doctorate in personality psychology from Howard University. With a master's degree in journalism from Columbia University, David frequently applies his research to cultural criticism and social impact programming. He has served on the editorial advisory boards for both the *Journal of Negro Education* and the *Journal of Popular Culture*; he has provided commentary for C-SPAN, NPR, CBS News, CNN, and MSNBC; and his writing and opinion have appeared in the *Washington Post*, the *Los Angeles Times*, the *New York Times Magazine*, *Vibe* magazine, and *Ebony* among other media outlets. His writing is also represented in the Cornell Hip-Hop Collection as part of the Adler Hip-Hop Archive.

GRANT BENNETT

Grant Bennett is graduate associate in the Identity, Art, and Democracy Lab. Grant is a 2020 graduate of Morehouse College with a bachelor of arts in psychology. He currently works as analytics and operations specialist in the Human Resource Associate Rotational program at Google. His work explores data analytics as a means to improve equity and retention for marginalized communities. His background as a former college baseball athlete, entrepreneur, producer, and researcher have led him to engage in meaningful work with various brands and organizations. As a researcher he has engaged in projects at Harvard Business School, UC Berkeley, Stanford Graduate School of Business, UNC Charlotte, and Vanderbilt University. Outside of research, Grant has worked on projects for Adobe, Adidas, *Forbes*, HBO, and the

Clinton Global Initiative. He was recently named the 2021 Nike Yardrunner for Morehouse College. In addition, he serves as the founder and executive director of the Two-Six Project. The organization is a 501c3 tax-exempt organization created to assist marginalized students through intentional programming from his hometown.

C. MALIK BOYKIN

C. Malik Boykin is assistant professor in the department of Cognitive, Linguistic, and Psychological Sciences (CLPS) at Brown University. Malik received his doctorate in social and personality psychology from UC Berkeley, his MA in social-organizational psychology from Teachers College, Columbia University, and his BS in psychology from the University of Maryland University College—after first attending Howard University. He was a presidential postdoctoral fellow for two years at Brown in the department of CLPS before his current faculty appointment. His research focuses on intergroup relations, hierarchy, prejudice, mentorship, and racial identity. Several of these themes inform his research on attitudes toward HBCUs and bias in decision-making algorithms. He has affiliate appointments with both the Center for the Study of Race and Ethnicity in America and the Data Science Initiative. He has previously secured funding from the Ford Fellowship Foundation, the Greater Good Science Center, and the Society for Multivariate Experimental Psychology to conduct his research. Dr. Boykin is a member of the Society for Personality and Social Psychology, the Society for Industrial and Organizational Psychology, and the Omega Psi Phi fraternity.

JACQUE-COREY CORMIER

Jacque-Corey Cormier is currently clinical assistant professor of health policy and behavioral sciences in the School of Public Health at Georgia State University. Dr. Cormier was born a metro-Atlanta Georgian, cultivated into a Morehouse man, and earned his graduate degrees from Georgia Southern University (MS in experimental psychology) and Georgia State University (PhD in community psychology). He is a researcher and educator who recognizes community mobilization, critical consciousness, and inclusive group participation as salient to health-related research and social change processes. Dr. Cormier has engaged marginalized, underserved communities through his research management consulting, program evaluation training, and applied, experiential courses that he produced for graduate and undergraduate students to collaborate with various agencies and organizations utilizing practical, degree-related skills. His values drive him toward service, equitable solutions, and critical action as exemplified by his kinfolks and other role models. Dr. Cormier has served his array of communities through substantial roles such as vice president of the American Association of University Professors' GSU chapter, a member on multiple GSU committees, one of 21st Century Leaders' (21CL; youth-serving nonprofit) inaugural junior board chairpersons, 21CL summer institute director, career planning mentor, and public health advocate. In 2019, 21CL recognized him as an exceptional program alumnus leading the way in educational endeavors as a 30 for 30 Alumni awardee. He has recently appeared on NPR's *Close Look* with Rose Scott, 2021 Dragon Con panels, and Atlanta local news to discuss topics related to public health, leadership development, and diversity efforts. Dr. Cormier plans to continue serving as an agent for positive, sustainable change wherever there is a transformation needed for systems, institutions, and individuals.

GREGORY DAVIS

Gregory Davis is Richard Taylor Law Teaching Fellow at UCLA School of Law and teaches critical race theory. His research lies in affirmative action, discrimination, empirical legal studies, and critical race theory. He previously worked as a quantitative researcher at Facebook, where he worked on product development and user research. Davis received his BA magna cum laude from Morehouse College in 2010, his JD/MA in law and Afro-American studies from UCLA in 2014, and his MA in psychology and PhD in African American studies from Harvard University in 2016 and 2020, respectively. At UCLA, Davis was the editor in chief of the Dukeminier Awards Journal of Sexual Orientation and Gender Identity Law and a Graduate Opportunity Fellow. Davis's publications have appeared in the National Black Law Journal and the Dukeminier Awards Journal, among others.

ASHA L. FRENCH

Asha French is a writer from Louisville, Kentucky. She earned her BA in communications at Howard University, her MFA in creative writing at Indiana University, and her PhD in English at Emory University. She is currently a postdoctoral research associate at Brown University. Her essay collection, *Mama Outsider*, was a finalist for the Kore Press Memoir Award in 2017, and she is currently at work on a book about the author Toni Cade

Bambara, which will be published by the University of Arizona Press. Her work has been published in *Pluck!*, *Ebony*, *Poetrymemoirstory*, *Warpland*, *Autostraddle*, *Mutha*, and the *New York Times*, and she has work forthcoming in *Kweli Journal* and the journal *Feminist Studies*. She is a member of the Affrilachian Poets.

ASHA GRANT

Asha Grant (she/hers) is educator, digital content producer, writer, community librarian, and independent bookshop owner deeply invested in amplifying the voices of Black women, femmes, and gender expansive people. Asha received her Bachelors of Arts degree in English from Spelman College, minoring in African diaspora studies and comparative women's studies. She received her Masters of Arts in English education with a concentration on Black female education and literacy from Teachers College, Columbia University. She has been featured in publications including the Los Angeles Times, Oprah Magazine, and Shondaland.com. Asha is director and founder of the LA chapter of the Free Black Women's Library. Asha is also the founder and owner of The Salt Eaters Bookshop, a literary sanctuary in Inglewood prioritizing books, comics, and zines by and about Black women, femmes, and gender expansive people. Asha currently resides in her hometown of Los Angeles. When she is not sourcing vintage copies of Sula, she is delighting in a seasonal pint of Jeni's ice cream.

MIKKI KATHLEEN HARRIS

Mikki K. Harris uses a journalistic approach to understanding the cultural context of community, both past and present, through the use of innovative visual storytelling. She is a multimedia journalist whose work over the past twenty years has focused on community-based power as examined through the tools of journalism and cultural studies. She uses storytelling to shift perspective in dynamic ways that both preserve and carry culture. She uses oral history, documentary photojournalism and video, as well as writing to document and shape stories of impact. Her article and photos in National Geographic provide a look into this work. A graduate of Spelman College with a bachelor's degree in economics and a master's degree in journalism from Boston University, Mikki is a photojournalist by training. She has served as a Visual Journalism Fellow at the Poynter Institute, has photographed six of the past eight US presidents, and has worked as a photojournalist for the *Atlanta Journal-Constitution*, *USA Today*, and the *Newark Star-Ledger*. Two of her images illustrating life in Harlem were exhibited at the Studio Museum in Harlem, New York, in 2005, and her images of the National Urban League are a part of Google's *Arts and Culture* digital exhibit. Two student investigative reporting magazines that Mikki taught the visuals for and edited won the Robert F. Kennedy Journalism Award. Mikki became a certified drone pilot in 2019 and cofounded the Atlanta Drone Lab while working in her current role as a senior assistant professor of journalism at Morehouse College.

WILLIAM MARCEL HAYES

William Hayes is currently chief executive officer of Boys' Latin of Philadelphia, an all-male college preparatory school educating young men in grades six through twelve. He is a 2007 graduate of Morehouse College and a founding member of the Identity Stasis Lab. He received a master's in prevention science from Harvard Graduate School of Education and a doctorate in education leadership and policy from Vanderbilt University. He began his teaching and school leadership career in Boston before becoming a principal in Cleveland Public Schools. He went on to be the founding principal of two charter schools in Camden, New Jersey, before transitioning into his current role in West Philadelphia.

CHELSEA HEYWARD

Chelsea Heyward's work focuses on improving the effectiveness of athlete activism, emphasizing innovation, social capital, and, most critically, engaging in action beyond awareness. Through LaChica Sports and Entertainment, Players Coalition, and SHIELD 1 Foundation, Heyward's years of practitioner experience in athlete impact have supported professional and collegiate athletes across twelve professional sports leagues and over a dozen colleges and universities. Heyward is also a sport and US culture professor in the graduate program of sport management at CSULB and a sport, culture, and power professor in the JMester program at Morehouse College. She holds a doctorate in education from the University of Southern California.

MICAH HOLMES

Upon graduation, 2020 Morehouse graduate and Oprah Winfrey Scholar Micah Holmes began serving as a coordinator at the National Football League (NFL) in their highly selective Junior Rotational program. In 2016, while still in high school, Holmes cofounded Overtime Sports Group, a sports marketing company focused on enhancing the voices, marketing opportunities, community relations, professional development, and public relations for their roster of athlete clients. This brainchild was initially born out of a desire to help send less privileged children to youth camps. Within the organization, he carved out a role exclusively focused on youth outreach and development of their summer youth camp. Since its inception, his organization has conducted three free youth football camps for more than two hundred Cleveland youth.

JASON M. JONES

Jason M. Jones graduated from Morehouse College in 2010 with a bachelor of arts in psychology and was a member of the Identity Stasis Research Lab—now the Identity, Art and Democracy Lab—from 2007 to 2010. Jason went on to earn a master's of science in psychology and later a doctor of philosophy in personality psychology from Howard University. After completing his doctorate, he worked in the health care industry, in organizational development at Ascension, to help improve associate experiences and increase diversity and inclusion practices among physicians. Jason is currently a postdoctoral research associate at Winston-Salem State University, exploring the conceptualizations and psychosocial and sociocultural factors of intimate partner violence among Black college students. In addition, his current research focuses on the personality development and well-being of Black former NFL players and athletes by exploring their storied lives and personalized goals.

CARLTON "CAL" LEWIS

Carlton "Cal" Lewis is returning citizen, author, activist, public speaker, and future lawyer. He holds an MBA and is a graduate of Morehouse College. He writes both nonfiction and fiction. Raised and currently living in Atlanta, Georgia, his writings reflect the realities of a city and a life he knows well. Currently, Cal is a law school student at Atlanta's John Marshall Law School, and upon graduation he plans to practice as a criminal defense attorney. When Cal is not at work on his next book or studying hard in law school, he can usually be found blogging and interacting with readers on his website, CALwrites.com.

BRIELLE MCDANIEL

Brielle McDaniel is alumna of Spelman College where she studied sociology and public health. Brielle also attended Teachers College, Columbia University where she received a Masters Degree in sociology and education policy. Brielle currently works for the New York City department of education as the director of research, analytics, and policy where her work focuses on expanding equity and access for students entering middle and high school. Outside of her professional endeavors, Brielle nurtures a passion for volunteering, and developing opportunities for Black students and other students of color. Brielle's credo maintains that we can run fast alone, but we run farther together.

KRISTIN MOODY

Kristin Moody is empathy researcher and educator who uses the science of empathy to build authentic connections across diverse people. She is inspired by the biological instinct humans have to empathize with one another and the potential empathy has to address the most pressing threats to civilization. She first learned about the power of empathy as a high school teacher, where she saw the impact relationship building made on student and teacher outcomes. Kristin went on to formally study empathy and integrate that understanding into support for individuals and organizations seeking improved culture, equity, and access to authenticity. She now teaches, researches, and explores empathy frameworks to help diverse people connect in ways that promote, celebrate, and leverage authenticity. Kristin received her BA in English and secondary education from CUNY Hunter College, MS in education and leadership from Pepperdine University, and EdD in organizational leadership and change from the University of Southern California. Her research on the role of empathy in urban high school student outcomes won Dissertation of the Year for USC in 2018. She completed additional study in the neuroscience of learning from the Annenberg Foundation and positive psychology from UPenn, and she holds a professional coaching certificate from the International Coaching Federation. She is a private coach and consultant and teaches empathetic leadership at Morehouse College and empathy building at the American University of Ras Al Khaimah.

DONOVAN X. RAMSEY

Donovan X. Ramsey is journalist, author, and an indispensable voice on issues of racial identity, politics, and patterns of power in America. His commentary on racial politics during the Obama era has been featured in the *New York Times*, and his reporting and commentary on the criminal justice system have appeared in outlets including the *Atlantic*, *GQ*, *Gawker*, *BuzzFeed*, *Vice*, and *Ebony*, among others. Ramsey covers Black LA for the *Los Angeles Times*. He served before as the commentary editor at the Marshall Project, a Pulitzer Prize–winning nonprofit news organization that seeks to create and sustain a sense of national urgency about the US criminal justice system. Before the Marshall Project, he worked as an editor and writer at a number of outlets, including Complex, NewsOne, and NBC's theGrio.com. Ramsey holds a master's degree from the Columbia University Graduate School of Journalism and a bachelor's degree in psychology from Morehouse College. He lives in Los Angeles and is currently completing his first book, a history of the crack cocaine epidemic for One World, an imprint of Penguin Random House.

MALACHI RICHARDSON

Malachi Richardson is clinical psychologist at the Child Guidance Clinic, where he provides therapy and psychological assessment services for the Superior Court of Washington, DC. He has particular expertise in forensic assessment, psychopathology, adolescent development, and trauma exposure. A graduate of Morehouse College and the University of Virginia's Curry School of Education, Dr. Richardson is particularly passionate about providing services to underserved communities and working with justice system–involved youth. He has provided assessment and therapeutic services for adolescent populations in various forensic institutions including the Superior Court of Washington DC and Blue Ridge Detention Center in Charlottesville, Virginia. In addition to his clinical experience, Dr. Richardson draws on his research experience in the areas of mentoring, identity development, and violence exposure to create a detailed and well-informed understanding of the presenting issues for his adolescent clients. Across the scope of his work, Dr. Richardson is committed to providing services that consider the cultural and contextual factors that influence conceptualization, treatment, and outcomes for justice system–involved youth.

ROBERT X. SHANNON

Born in Wilmington, North Carolina, but with roots in Southwest Atlanta, Robert Shannon is Morehouse graduate who participated in the Morehouse Pan-African Global Experience study abroad program in Accra, Ghana, during his junior year of college. This experience helped shape his future career trajectory; he stayed on at Morehouse after graduation, leading student trips and community development work in Ghana, and then enrolled in the Master of Development Practice program at Emory University, an applied international development program aimed at critiquing and improving on traditional models of development. Robert worked with CARE International in Atlanta and Sri Lanka and with the Carter Center in Ghana and Liberia; he currently works with an international consulting firm supporting research and evaluation for government and nongovernmental clients. Robert also prioritizes mentorship and supporting the development of young scholars, working with a STEM-focused high school enrichment program and conducting guest lectures at Morehouse and Emory. Robert's research interests include gender and masculinity, mental health, youth leadership development, and community vitality.

BRENDA WALL

Brenda Wall is licensed psychologist and ordained minister based in Dallas, Texas and in Atlanta, Georgia. She has focused her professional career on the empowerment of marginalized communities and in developing understanding across cultural divides. Dr. Wall has held academic appointments as professor, college vice president, and university department chair. Her media imprint has been demonstrated through work as a weekly television show host and a self-titled daily radio call in show. Dr. Wall has maintained a private clinical practice for over three decades and has leveraged her academic training from Vassar College, Boston University and George Washington University toward practical, solution oriented work. Dr. Wall presently serves as counselor for the Lovett School in Atlanta.

CYNTHIA WINSTON-PROCTOR

Cynthia Winston-Proctor is narrative personality psychologist. She is professor of psychology at Howard University as well as a founder of both the Identity and Success Research Laboratory and the Narrative Personality

Psychology Health Collaborative. Dr. Winston-Proctor's research draws on multiple disciplines of psychology, such as personality, developmental, cognitive, educational, cultural, and neuropsychology, to explore the role of narrative processing and autobiographical reasoning in the development of narrative identity and success across the life course. She also studies the psychological science of broadening participation in computer science and mathematics. During her early career, she received the National Science Foundation's Early Career Award, the foundation's most prestigious award for early career scientists. She has published her research in a variety of academic journals. Dr. Winston-Proctor coauthored two books published by Taylor & Francis focused on behavioral cybersecurity, applications of personality psychology, and computer science. Building on her interdisciplinary research and consulting practice, she has created Life Synergy, a new narrative personality education model to promote healthy living. Dr. Winston-Proctor has also held appointments as a Howard Hughes Medical Institute Research Professor at Brown University, director of internship and fellowship programs at the Congressional Black Caucus Foundation, director of the National Science Foundation Alliance for Graduate Education and the professoriate at Howard University, a visiting scholar at the University of Michigan, and a visiting scholar at the Chicago School of Professional Psychology. Dr. Winston-Proctor earned her bachelor of science degree in psychology from Howard University and her PhD in psychology and education from the University of Michigan.